Explainable AI for Healthcare

This book explores the transformative potential of Explainable AI (XAI) in enhancing healthcare delivery and XAI's role in fostering transparency, trust, and accountability in AI-driven medical decision-making. Covering technical foundations, practical applications, and ethical considerations, it offers valuable insights into how XAI can improve clinical decision-making, patient outcomes, and healthcare operations. Through real-world case studies, the book illustrates the practical benefits of XAI in diverse healthcare scenarios. It also addresses the challenges and solutions related to deploying XAI, making it an essential resource for professionals and researchers.

- Detailed exploration of the methodologies, algorithms, and regulatory considerations underpinning XAI in smart healthcare systems
- Diverse case studies demonstrating practical applications and benefits of XAI across various healthcare domains, enhancing understanding through tangible examples
- Exploration of innovative XAI applications in diagnosis, treatment, patient monitoring, and care delivery, showcasing its potential to revolutionize healthcare practices and improve outcomes
- Discussion on how XAI promotes patient engagement by providing clear explanations of AI-driven diagnoses or treatment plans, enhancing patient understanding and participation in their healthcare
- Breakdown of XAI techniques, algorithms, and interpretability strategies, helping medical professionals understand and trust AI-driven decision-making processes.

Explainable AI for Healthcare

Real Life Applications and Use Cases for Practitioners

Aman Kataria and Sita Rani

CRC Press
Taylor & Francis Group
Boca Raton London New York

CRC Press is an imprint of the
Taylor & Francis Group, an **informa** business

A CHAPMAN & HALL BOOK

Front cover image: thinkhubstudio/Shutterstock

First edition published 2026
by CRC Press
2385 NW Executive Center Drive, Suite 320, Boca Raton FL 33431

and by CRC Press
4 Park Square, Milton Park, Abingdon, Oxon, OX14 4RN

CRC Press is an imprint of Taylor & Francis Group, LLC

ISBN: 978-1-032-91112-0 (hbk)
ISBN: 978-1-032-90676-8 (pbk)
ISBN: 978-1-003-56142-2 (ebk)

DOI: 10.1201/9781003561422

Typeset in Times
by KnowledgeWorks Global Ltd.

Contents

Preface

The rapid integration of artificial intelligence (AI) in healthcare has opened new frontiers for diagnosis, treatment, and patient care. However, as these intelligent systems grow more complex, the need for transparency and interpretability becomes critical. *Explainable AI for Healthcare: Real Life Applications and Use Cases for Practitioners* addresses this vital challenge by offering practical insights into how explainable AI (XAI) techniques can be effectively implemented across real-world healthcare scenarios.

This book is crafted for healthcare professionals, data scientists, and researchers seeking to bridge the gap between AI-driven solutions and clinical trust. By presenting diverse use cases—ranging from diagnostic imaging to predictive analytics—it highlights the importance of interpretability in fostering adoption, improving outcomes, and ensuring ethical standards.

Each chapter offers a balanced mix of technical depth and domain relevance, making it accessible yet comprehensive. We hope this book empowers practitioners to harness the power of AI responsibly, with clarity and confidence, in the service of better healthcare for all.

Aman Kataria
Sita Rani

About the Authors

Aman Kataria, PhD, is a Faculty member in the domain of Electronics and Communication at the University Centre for Research and Development, Chandigarh University, Gharuan, Mohali, Punjab, India. He worked previously as an Assistant Professor at Amity Institute of Defence Technology, Amity University, Noida, Uttar Pradesh, India. He received the B.Tech. degree in Electronics and Communication engineering from the state government engineering institute, Malout Institute of Management and Information Technology (MIMIT), Malout, in 2010, and the Master's and PhD degrees in Electronics and Instrumentation Control Engineering from the Thapar Institute of Engineering and Technology, Patiala, Punjab, India, in 2013 and 2020, respectively. He worked as a Lecturer at the Electronics and Communication Department, National Institute of Technology, Hamirpur. He worked as a Project Associate with the CSIR-Central Scientific Instruments Organization from August 2020 to December 2022. At CSIO, he worked on Texas Instruments DLP5530Q1EVM, in which he had the experience of projecting customized images on the screen of DMD, which assisted in the projection of vital information on the screen of Head-up Display (HUD), to be deployed in fighter aircraft of the Indian Air Force. He has contributed to various research activities while publishing papers in various SCIE and Scopus-indexed journals and conference proceedings. He has also published four international patents. His research interests include machine learning, artificial intelligence, image processing, cyber-physical systems, the Internet of Things, and soft computing.

Sita Rani, PhD, works in the Department of Computer Science and Engineering at Guru Nanak Dev Engineering College, Ludhiana. She earned her PhD in Computer Science and Engineering from I.K. Gujral Punjab Technical University, Kapurthala, Punjab, in 2018. She completed Postdoc from the Big Data Mining and Machine Learning Lab, South Ural State University, Russia, from May 2022 to August 2023. She has also completed Postgraduate Certificate Program in Data Science and Machine Learning from the Indian Institute of Technology, Roorkee in 2023. She has more than 20 years of academic, administrative, and research experience. She is an active member of ISTE, IEEE, and IAEngg. She has been recognized in the **Top 2% Scientists** list published by Stanford University for the year **2024**. She is the recipient of the ISTE Section Best Teacher Award-2020, and International Young Scientist Award-2021. She has contributed to various research activities while publishing articles in the renowned SCI and Scopus journals and conference proceedings. She has published several national and international patents and authored, edited, and coedited 11 books. Dr. Rani has delivered many expert talks in A.I.C.T.E. sponsored Faculty Development Programs and keynote talks in many National and International Conferences. She has also organized many International Conferences during her 20 years of experience. She is a member of the Editorial Board and a reviewer of many international journals of repute. She has also served as vice-president of SME and MSME (UT Council), Women Indian Chamber of Commerce and Industry (WICCI) since November 2021 to February 2025. Her research interests include data science, artificial intelligence, machine learning, blockchain technology, smart healthcare, and sustainable development.

1 Introduction to Explainable AI in Smart Healthcare Systems

1.1 INTRODUCTION

The term "explainable AI" (XAI) describes strategies and tactics that help humans comprehend, interpret, and see AI models. Ensuring trust, equity, and accountability is essential as AI systems grow more complex, particularly in vital industries like healthcare, finance, and law (Dwivedi et al., 2023). By emphasizing important aspects, logic, and possible biases, XAI seeks to shed light on how models arrive at decisions. Model-agnostic strategies (like SHapley Additive exPlanations [SHAP] and Local Interpretable Model-agnostic Explanations [LIME]), interpretable models (like decision trees and rule-based systems), and visualization techniques are examples of common approaches. The need for explainability in AI-driven decisions is emphasized by regulatory frameworks such as the EU's General Data Protection Regulation (GDPR) and US's Health Insurance Portability and Accountability Act (HIPAA). XAI guarantees adherence to moral and legal requirements, improves user trust, and aids in model debugging (Xu et al., 2019).

XAI is applied in many industries to improve trust and transparency. It clarifies AI-driven diagnosis and treatment suggestions in the medical field. XAI is used in finance for risk assessment, credit scoring, and fraud detection. XAI is used by autonomous systems, such as self-driving cars, to explain their decisions and increase safety. Applications for law and compliance guarantee the interpretability of AI-driven legal judgments. XAI is used by HR to guarantee hiring equity. It is useful for threat detection and analysis in cybersecurity. By making AI-driven recommendations more understandable, XAI enhances user confidence in marketing and retail. These applications support sector-wide operational, ethical, and legal transparency requirements (Saranya & Subhashini, 2023).

1.1.1 DEFINITION AND IMPORTANCE OF XAI

The term "XAI" describes strategies and tactics that enable human comprehension, interpretation, and transparency of AI models. It seeks to make clear how AI systems decide in order to maintain accountability, fairness, and trust. Particularly in crucial fields like healthcare, finance, and law, XAI assists users in understanding model predictions, identifying biases, and adhering to ethical and legal requirements. Interpretable models, post-hoc explanations (like SHAP and LIME), and visualization tools are some of the methods. XAI promotes responsible AI deployment and

DOI: 10.1201/9781003561422-1

improves human-AI collaboration by making AI decisions more understandable and rational (Das & Rad, 2020; Saini et al., 2022).

XAI is essential for building trust, fairness, and accountability in AI systems. It increases adoption and transparency by assisting users in understanding AI decisions. By identifying and reducing biases, XAI guarantees morally righteous and equitable results. AI explainability is required by regulatory frameworks such as GDPR, so compliance is essential. By making AI-driven predictions more understandable, XAI lowers risks in high-stakes industries like healthcare and finance. Additionally, it helps developers debug models, increasing their accuracy and dependability. XAI guarantees that AI systems complement human decision-making rather than replace it by improving human-AI collaboration. This results in safer, more accountable, and more efficient AI applications across a range of industries.

1.1.2 Key Concepts and Terminology

XAI's core ideas and technologies improve AI accountability, transparency, and trust. AI decisions are made clearer by ideas like interpretability, fairness, and local/global explanations. AI applications across industries can be made ethical, dependable, and compliant with regulations by using technologies like SHAP, LIME, decision trees, and visualization tools, which also assist users in understanding model behavior and identifying biases (Longo et al., 2020; Nagahisarchoghaei et al., 2023).

Key Concepts

- **Interpretability vs. Explainability**: Interpretability refers to the extent to which a human can understand an AI model, while explainability provides justifications for its decisions.
- **Global vs. Local Explanations**: Global explanations describe overall model behavior, while local explanations clarify individual predictions.
- **Post-hoc vs. Intrinsic Explainability**: Post-hoc techniques explain black-box models, while intrinsic methods use inherently interpretable models.
- **Fairness, Accountability, and Transparency (FAT)**: Ensures AI models are ethical and unbiased.

Technologies and Methods

- **SHAP (Shapley Additive Explanations)**: Assigns importance values to features.
- **LIME (Local Interpretable Model-agnostic Explanations)**: Generates interpretable local approximations of complex models.
- **Decision Trees and Rule-Based Models**: Naturally interpretable AI models.
- **Counterfactual Explanations**: Shows how changes in input affect predictions.
- **Feature Importance and Visualization Tools**: Techniques like saliency maps and partial dependence plots (PDPs) aid explainability.

1.1.3 ROLE OF XAI IN DECISION-MAKING

In decision-making, XAI is essential because it improves accountability, transparency, and trust in AI-driven systems. It guarantees that predictions and suggestions made by AI are comprehensible, acceptable, and useful (Kaur & Saini, 2023; Sahoh & Choksuriwong, 2023; Saini & Preeti, 2024).

Key Roles of XAI in Decision-Making
- **Improving Trust and Adoption**: Users are more likely to rely on AI when they understand its reasoning.
- **Enhancing Accuracy and Debugging**: Helps identify errors and improve model performance.
- **Ensuring Fairness and Bias Detection**: Detects and mitigates biases for ethical AI decisions.
- **Regulatory Compliance**: Meets legal requirements for explainability in sensitive areas like healthcare and finance.
- **Supporting Human-AI Collaboration**: Provides interpretable insights that assist experts in making informed decisions.

By making AI decisions transparent and interpretable, XAI helps organizations to implement AI responsibly while improving outcomes across industries.

1.2 SMART HEALTHCARE SYSTEMS: A BRIEF INTRODUCTION

Smart healthcare systems integrate advanced technologies like AI, IoT, and big data to optimize healthcare delivery, improve patient outcomes, and reduce costs (Figure 1.1). Predictive analytics, early diagnosis, and tailored treatment recommendations are all made possible by AI in these systems. While IoT devices, like wearables and sensors, offer real-time patient vitals monitoring, allowing for continuous care outside of traditional settings, machine learning (ML) models examine large medical datasets to identify trends and forecast health conditions. Electronic health records (EHRs) facilitate smooth provider collaboration by storing and exchanging patient data (Khang et al., 2022; Minopoulos et al., 2022).

1.2.1 EVOLUTION OF HEALTHCARE WITH AI

The evolution of healthcare with AI has been transformative, driving innovations in diagnosis, treatment, and patient care (Xie et al., 2025). The role of AI in smart healthcare paradigm is summarized in Table 1.1

Here's a brief overview of the key stages.

1.2.1.1 Early Developments (1950s–1990s)

AI research began in healthcare with early systems like rule-based expert systems (e.g., MYCIN), which were designed to assist in diagnosing infections and recommending treatments. These systems relied on pre-programmed knowledge and logic.

Transforming Healthcare with Smart Technology and Data Integration

Internet of Medical Things

Network of connected devices sharing health data.

Electronic Health Records

Digital versions of patient charts for real-time, secure data access.

Artificial Intelligence

AI technologies for predictive analytics and personalized medicine.

Telemedicine

Remote healthcare services using telecommunications technology.

Wearable Health Devices

Devices monitoring health metrics for patient empowerment.

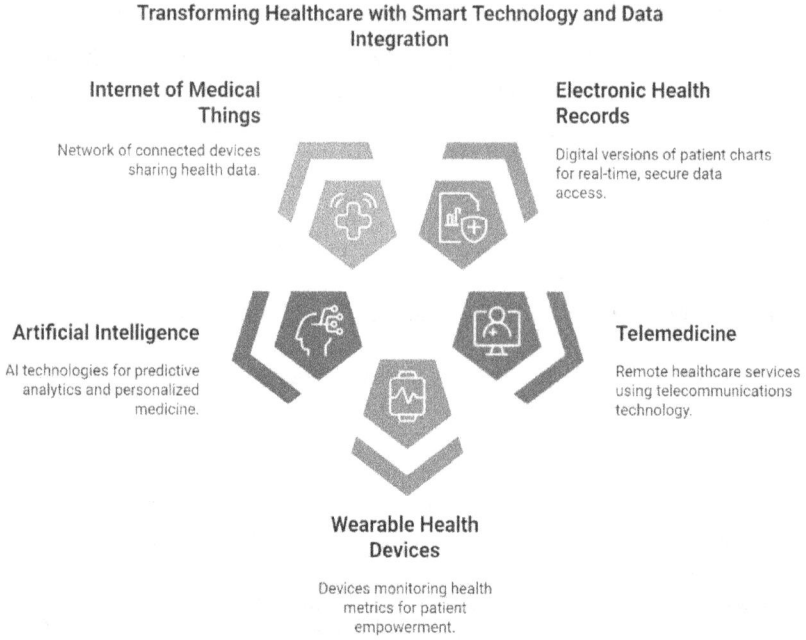

FIGURE 1.1   Smart healthcare systems.

TABLE 1.1
AI in Smart Healthcare Systems

Area	Role of AI
Diagnosis and Detection	AI analyzes medical images, detects anomalies (e.g., tumors), and predicts diseases like cancer, diabetes, or heart conditions.
Personalized Treatment	AI uses patient data (genomic, historical, etc.) to tailor individualized treatment plans for optimal outcomes.
Predictive Analytics	AI models predict patient conditions, disease progression, and potential health risks, enabling early intervention.
Clinical Decision Support	AI assists healthcare providers by suggesting the most appropriate treatments and medical interventions based on patient data and best practices.
Remote Monitoring	AI processes data from wearables and IoT devices to monitor patient vitals in real-time, enabling continuous, remote care and alerting healthcare providers to changes.
Drug Discovery	AI accelerates drug development by analyzing biological data, predicting molecular behavior, and identifying potential drug candidates.
Operational Efficiency	AI automates administrative tasks (e.g., scheduling, claims processing) to reduce overhead and improve hospital efficiency.
Telemedicine and Virtual Care	AI-powered virtual assistants assist in remote consultations, triage, and symptom checking, improving access to healthcare.
Patient Engagement	AI-driven apps and wearables empower patients to manage their health, track progress, and receive personalized recommendations.

1.2.1.2 Data-Driven Revolution (2000s–2010s)

With the rise of EHRs and digital data, AI moved toward data-driven approaches. Machine learning models began analyzing large datasets for pattern recognition, disease prediction, and clinical decision support. AI-powered tools like IBM Watson emerged, showcasing the potential for AI in oncology and other specialties.

1.2.1.3 AI-Enhanced Personalization (2010s–Present)

AI now helps in the field of personalized medicine, tailoring treatments based on individual patient data. Machine learning algorithms assist in diagnosing conditions like cancer, heart disease, and neurological disorders, improving accuracy and speed. AI-powered predictive analytics also helps in anticipating patient needs, reducing hospital readmissions, and improving care outcomes.

1.2.2 KEY COMPONENTS OF SMART HEALTHCARE SYSTEMS

Key components of smart healthcare systems include (Bawa et al., 2024; Kumar et al., 2024; Rani et al., 2024):

- **IoT and Wearable Devices**: Continuous health monitoring through sensors and smart devices.
- **Artificial Intelligence (AI) and Machine Learning (ML)**: Data analysis for diagnostics, treatment recommendations, and predictive analytics.
- **Electronic Health Records (EHRs)**: Digital storage and sharing of patient data for seamless access.
- **Cloud Computing**: Scalable storage and real-time data access for healthcare providers.
- **Telemedicine and Remote Monitoring**: Virtual consultations and home-based patient monitoring.
- **Big Data Analytics**: Processing large datasets to identify trends and improve decision-making.
- **Blockchain Technology**: Secure, tamper-proof patient records and data sharing.
- **Robotics and Automation**: AI-assisted surgeries, robotic rehabilitation, and hospital automation.
- **5G and Edge Computing**: Faster, real-time communication between devices and healthcare systems.
- **Cybersecurity Measures**: Protecting sensitive patient data from breaches and cyber threats.

1.2.3 CHALLENGES IN TRADITIONAL AI-DRIVEN HEALTHCARE

Traditional AI-driven healthcare faced several challenges, including:

- **Black-Box Nature**: AI models, especially deep learning, lacked transparency, making it difficult for doctors to trust or validate predictions.

- **Bias and Fairness Issues**: AI systems often exhibited biases due to imbalanced training data, leading to disparities in diagnoses and treatment recommendations.
- **Regulatory and Compliance Barriers**: Lack of interpretability hindered AI adoption in healthcare due to strict regulations (e.g., HIPAA, GDPR).
- **Limited Clinical Adoption**: Physicians were hesitant to rely on AI without understanding how decisions were made, reducing real-world application.
- **Data Privacy and Security Risks**: AI required vast amounts of patient data, raising concerns about security, breaches, and unauthorized access.
- **Generalization Challenges**: Traditional AI struggled with variability in medical data (e.g., different demographics, imaging standards), limiting its reliability.
- **Lack of Human-AI Collaboration**: The opaque nature of AI decisions made it difficult for doctors to integrate AI insights into clinical workflows.
- **Legal and Ethical Concerns**: Unclear AI-driven decision-making complicated accountability in malpractice cases and ethical dilemmas.

1.3 SIGNIFICANCE OF EXPLAINABILITY IN HEALTHCARE

Explainability in healthcare guarantees accountability, openness, and trust in AI-driven choices. It improves diagnosis, treatment planning, and patient outcomes by assisting clinicians in comprehending AI recommendations. It becomes simpler to identify errors, detect bias, and comply with regulations, which lowers risks and improves equity. XAI ensures patient safety, data security, and legal clarity in AI-assisted healthcare applications while promoting human-AI collaboration that improves clinical adoption and ethical decision-making (Sadeghi et al., 2024; Saraswat et al., 2022).

1.3.1 BUILDING TRUST WITH CLINICIANS AND PATIENTS

In the healthcare industry, explainability is essential to fostering patient and clinician trust in AI-driven treatment choices. To confidently incorporate AI models into their practice, clinicians must comprehend how these models produce diagnoses or treatment recommendations. By encouraging collaboration, transparent AI helps medical professionals to validate findings, identify possible biases, and improve clinical judgments. Explainability guarantees that patients understand the reasoning behind diagnoses or treatment options, boosting their trust in AI-assisted care. Enhancing patient involvement, following medical advice, and overall healthcare results all depend on this trust. Additionally, XAI reduces the risks associated with black-box models by supporting ethical considerations, legal accountability, and regulatory compliance. Healthcare is safer and more dependable thanks to XAI, which bridges the gap between AI and human expertise.

1.3.2 REGULATORY AND ETHICAL CONSIDERATIONS

Explainability is crucial for ethical AI implementation and regulatory compliance in the healthcare industry. Laws like GDPR and HIPAA guarantee patient data privacy and accountability by requiring transparency in AI-driven decisions. By making AI decisions auditable and interpretable, XAI assists healthcare providers in meeting these standards. In terms of ethics, XAI reduces prejudices, encourages equity, and avoids discriminatory results in diagnosis and therapy. By allowing physicians to verify AI suggestions, it lowers the possibility of mistakes and malpractice. Transparent AI also upholds patient autonomy by allowing informed decision-making and consent. Moreover, explainability fosters trust among stakeholders, ensuring that AI applications align with medical ethics and societal expectations. By integrating XAI, healthcare systems can achieve responsible, safe, and equitable AI-driven decision-making. Additionally, transparent AI respects patient autonomy by enabling informed consent and decision-making. Furthermore, explainability increases stakeholder trust and guarantees that AI applications conform to social norms and medical ethics. Healthcare systems can attain responsible, secure, and fair AI-driven decision-making by incorporating XAI.

1.3.3 ADDRESSING BIAS AND UNCERTAINTY

Addressing bias and uncertainty in AI-driven decision-making in the healthcare industry requires explainability. Certain patient groups may be disproportionately affected by biased results from AI models trained on unbalanced datasets. XAI makes decision-making processes transparent and interpretable, which aids in identifying and reducing these biases. AI-generated recommendations can be carefully examined by clinicians, guaranteeing equity and enhancing diagnostic precision. Furthermore, complicated medical conditions and disparities in patient data frequently lead to uncertainty when making healthcare decisions. Clinicians can evaluate AI confidence levels, comprehend model reasoning, and make well-informed decisions thanks to XAI. Explainability improves patient safety, trust, and fair treatment by lowering bias and elucidating ambiguities. It guarantees that AI enhances human expertise rather than replaces it, resulting in more dependable and moral healthcare solutions.

1.4 METHODS AND TECHNIQUES FOR EXPLAINABILITY IN AI

In AI, explainability depends on a number of techniques that can be divided into model-specific and model-agnostic strategies. Interpretability is inherent in model-specific approaches like rule-based models and decision trees. For complex models like deep learning, model-agnostic techniques such as SHAP, LIME, and counterfactual explanations offer post-hoc interpretability. Transparency in neural networks is improved by saliency maps, feature importance analysis, and attention mechanisms. Furthermore, surrogate models use easier-to-understand models to approximate black-box behavior. In AI-driven healthcare, hybrid approaches that combine several strategies increase usability and trust while making sure that decision-making procedures are open, moral, and understandable to all parties involved (Holzinger et al., 2020; Mittal et al., 2024).

1.4.1 Post-Hoc Explainability Methods

Post-hoc explainability methods provide insights into AI model decisions after training, enhancing interpretability without altering model architecture. Common techniques include (Gaspar et al., 2024; Rao et al., 2022):

- **SHAP (SHapley Additive exPlanations)**: A cooperative game theory-based post-hoc explainability technique called SHAP gives AI model predictions feature importance. By taking into account each feature's marginal contribution across all possible feature combinations, it computes Shapley values, which equitably divide the model's output among input features. SHAP offers both local interpretability (feature contributions for specific predictions) and global interpretability (feature impact across the dataset).

  Consistency, accuracy, and equity in feature attribution are among SHAP's main benefits. It is extensively utilized in healthcare AI to comprehend risk assessment, treatment recommendations, and diagnostic models. To improve interpretability, SHAP provides a range of visualization techniques, including dependence plots and summary plots. For complex models, it can be computationally costly. In spite of this, SHAP is still a potent instrument for enhancing openness, confidence, and legal adherence in AI-driven decision-making, especially in vital domains like finance, healthcare, and autonomous systems.

- **LIME (Local Interpretable Model-Agnostic Explanations)**: A post-hoc explainability technique called LIME approximates complex AI models with more understandable, simpler models to aid in their interpretation. It generates slightly altered samples, modifies the input data, and then observes the model's predictions. To explain individual predictions, these samples are then fitted to a locally weighted interpretable model, like a decision tree or linear regression.

  LIME is especially helpful in high-stakes industries where transparency is essential, like healthcare and finance. Text, images, and tabular data are just a few of the data types to which it can be applied. LIME's primary benefit is its capacity to offer local interpretability without necessitating changes to the initial AI model. Its explanations, however, might differ based on the perturbation process, which could cause instability. Despite this, LIME is still a popular tool for increasing accountability and trust in AI-driven decision-making by facilitating stakeholder access to complex models.

- **Saliency Maps**: Saliency maps are post-hoc explainability techniques that show which parts of an input have the greatest influence on the decision made by an AI model. Saliency maps, which compute the gradient of the prediction with respect to the input, are frequently used in deep learning, especially in image classification and medical imaging, to highlight pixels or features that affect the model's output. To improve interpretability, techniques such as SmoothGrad, Integrated Gradients, and Grad-CAM (Gradient-weighted Class Activation Mapping) refine saliency maps. These methods make AI more transparent and reliable by assisting in determining which aspects of a picture, text, or data affect model predictions.

Saliency maps are extensively utilized in autonomous systems for object detection, natural language processing for text interpretation, and healthcare AI for disease diagnosis from medical scans. Despite their effectiveness, they occasionally draw attention to unimportant details, necessitating careful examination. Saliency maps are still essential for comprehending the behavior of deep learning models in high-stakes scenarios, despite their drawbacks.

- **Counterfactual Explanations**: By demonstrating how slight modifications to input characteristics can change an AI model's judgment, counterfactual explanations offer interpretability. In order to help users understand why a particular prediction was made and what needs to change for a different outcome, they provide answers to "What if?" questions.

  In a loan approval model, for instance, a counterfactual explanation might suggest that a $5,000 increase in income would lead to loan approval. This approach improves user trust, equity, and transparency, particularly in AI applications for healthcare, finance, and law. Although useful, creating realistic counterfactuals can be computationally demanding and requires striking a balance between interpretability and viability.

- **Partial Dependence Plots (PDPs)**: Model-agnostic explainability methods called PDPs show how one or more input features relate to a model's predictions. PDPs average out the effects of other features and show how altering a particular feature affects the expected result. These plots are helpful for comprehending the behavior of global models, especially in intricate AI models like deep learning and random forests. In applications like risk assessment, healthcare, and finance, PDPs assist in identifying trends, nonlinear relationships, and feature importance.

  Although PDPs offer intuitive insights, they may be deceptive in correlated data because they presume feature independence. PDPs are still useful for enhancing AI transparency and supporting well-informed decision-making in spite of this drawback.

- **Surrogate Models**: In order to approximate complex AI systems and gain insight into their decision-making processes, surrogate models are more straightforward and interpretable models. These models serve as stand-ins, encapsulating the fundamental characteristics of black-box models such as ensemble approaches or deep learning. Rule-based models, decision trees, and linear regression are examples of common surrogate models. By providing human-understandable approximations while retaining predictive performance, surrogate models aid in the explainability of AI. They are extensively utilized in fields where transparency is crucial, such as healthcare, finance, and regulations. Surrogate models, however, might not accurately depict the original model's complex patterns, which could result in misunderstandings. Notwithstanding this drawback, they continue to be a useful instrument for enhancing regulatory compliance, trust, and accountability in AI-driven decision-making.

These methods improve transparency, trust, and usability in AI-driven applications, especially in critical domains like healthcare.

1.4.2 INTRINSICALLY INTERPRETABLE MODELS

Intrinsically interpretable models in XAI are ML models designed to be inherently understandable without requiring post-hoc explanations. These models maintain transparency in their decision-making processes, making them more trustworthy and easier to debug. Key characteristics of intrinsically interpretable models are (Dikshit & Pradhan, 2021; Liu et al., 2024; Mumuni & Mumuni, 2025):

- **Human-Readable Decision Process**: The reasoning behind predictions is clear.
- **No Need for External Explainers**: Unlike black-box models, these models don't require methods like SHAP or LIME.
- **Regulatory Compliance**: Useful for applications requiring transparency, such as finance and healthcare.

Various intrinsically explainable models are:

- **Linear and Logistic Regression**: Linear and logistic regression are classic examples of intrinsically interpretable models in XAI. Their transparency comes from simple mathematical formulations where feature weights (coefficients) directly indicate their impact on predictions. Linear regression models relationships between independent variables and a continuous dependent variable using a weighted sum of features. The learned coefficients provide clear insights into feature importance and direction (positive or negative influence). Logistic regression extends this concept to classification problems by modeling the probability of an event using the sigmoid function. The coefficients determine how each feature contributes to the log-odds of the outcome, maintaining interpretability. These models are interpretable due to feature influence, transparency, and "no black-box" behavior. These properties make them ideal for high-stakes applications like healthcare and finance.
- **Decision Trees**: Decision trees are intrinsically interpretable models in XAI due to their transparent, rule-based decision-making structure. They work by recursively splitting data based on feature values, forming a tree-like structure where each path from root to leaf represents a sequence of logical decisions. Decision trees are interpretable due to human-readable rules, feature importance, and "no black-box" behavior. Decision trees are widely used in applications requiring transparency, such as medical diagnosis, credit scoring, and legal decision-making. However, they can become

complex with deep structures, reducing interpretability, which is why techniques like pruning or shallow trees are often preferred.

- **Generalized Additive Models (GAMs)**: GAMs are intrinsically interpretable models in XAI that extend linear regression by allowing flexible, nonlinear relationships while maintaining transparency. They achieve this by modeling the dependent variable as a sum of smooth functions of the input features.

  Gams are interpretable due to feature-wise contribution, visualization, and no feature interactions (unless explicitly modeled). GAMs are widely used in healthcare, finance, and policy-making, where understanding individual feature effects is crucial. Variants like explainable boosting machines (EBMs) enhance interpretability by learning feature interactions while preserving GAMs' transparency.

- **Rule-Based Model**: Rule-based models, such as decision rules and RuleFit, are intrinsically interpretable models in XAI that rely on explicit **IF-THEN** logic to make decisions. These models generate human-readable rules derived from data, ensuring transparency and ease of understanding. Rule-based models are interpretable due to explicit decision logic, feature importance, and traceability. These models are widely used in healthcare, finance, and legal applications, where clear reasoning is essential.

  E.g.: Rule for diagnosing diabetes:

  IF *Fasting Blood Sugar > 126 mg/dL* **AND** *BMI > 30* **AND** *Family History of Diabetes = Yes*
  THEN *Diagnose as High Risk for Diabetes*

  This decision rule is simple, interpretable, and aligns with medical guidelines. It helps doctors and healthcare professionals quickly assess diabetes risk based on key patient factors.

- **Attention-Based Models**: Attention-based models, such as transformers, can be intrinsically interpretable when their attention mechanisms are designed to highlight important input features. These models assign attention weights to different parts of the input, indicating which elements contribute most to a prediction. These models can be interpretable due to feature importance visualization, traceable decision-making, and context awareness. However, attention weights alone may not always guarantee full interpretability, and additional analysis (e.g., gradient-based methods) is sometimes needed.

These models are particularly beneficial in domains where interpretability is critical, such as healthcare, finance, and legal AI applications.

1.4.3 Visualization Tools

XAI relies heavily on visualization tools to make difficult model decisions easier to understand and more transparent. By assisting users in comprehending the significance of features, decision boundaries, and model behavior, these tools enhance accountability and trust. While Grad-CAM and saliency maps show how deep learning models interpret images, techniques like SHAP and LIME highlight feature contributions. To help stakeholders better understand models, PDPs and ICE plots show how features affect predictions. Interactive dashboards for debugging and fairness analysis are provided by tools such as AI Explainability 360 and the What-If Tool. Fairlearn ensures ethical AI deployment by assisting in the detection of biases. TensorBoard uses weight and activation visualizations to offer deep learning insights. By assisting data scientists, regulators, and end users in making well-informed decisions, these tools guarantee that AI models comply with legal and ethical standards. Visualization tools help close the gap between human comprehension and intricate AI models by improving interpretability.

1.5 APPLICATIONS OF XAI IN SMART HEALTHCARE SYSTEMS

Transparency, trust, and decision-making in crucial applications are improved by XAI in smart healthcare. By elucidating predictions from models such as deep learning and ML, it assists physicians in interpreting diagnoses derived from artificial intelligence. XAI uses interpretable image analysis with Grad-CAM and saliency maps to help detect diseases (like cancer and heart conditions). With SHAP and LIME, it enhances patient risk assessment while guaranteeing equity and minimizing prejudices. Explainability increases the dependability of clinical decision support systems and AI-powered chatbots. Furthermore, XAI increases patient confidence in AI-driven personalized treatments and guarantees regulatory compliance (e.g., GDPR, HIPAA), enhancing the morality and efficacy of healthcare systems (Ahmed & Zubair, 2022; Chen, 2023; Javed et al., 2023).

1.5.1 DIAGNOSIS AND RISK PREDICTION

By improving interpretability, transparency, and trust in AI-driven healthcare models, XAI is essential for risk prediction and disease diagnosis. Saliency maps and Grad-CAM are two medical imaging techniques that help identify important regions in scans for the detection of neurological disorders and cancer. Doctors can better understand how patient data contributes to diagnoses and risk assessments by using ML models that use SHAP and LIME to explain feature importance. By providing interpretable risk scores based on patient history and biomarkers, XAI enhances predictive analytics for diseases like diabetes and heart disease. By ensuring bias detection, fairness tools support equitable healthcare outcomes. XAI bridges the gap between clinical expertise and complex algorithms by making AI decisions comprehensible, empowering physicians to make confident, well-informed decisions. Furthermore, explainability ensures ethical AI deployment in risk prediction and disease diagnosis by strengthening regulatory compliance with frameworks like HIPAA and GDPR.

1.5.2 PERSONALIZED TREATMENT RECOMMENDATIONS

In AI-driven healthcare systems, XAI improves individualized treatment recommendations by offering interpretability and transparency. To recommend individualized treatments, ML models examine patient data, such as genetics, lifestyle factors, and medical history. In order to ensure that physicians and patients comprehend

AI-driven recommendations, techniques such as SHAP and LIME provide an explanation of how particular factors impact recommendations. XAI reduces side effects and optimizes dosages in drug therapy by predicting individual responses to medications. Tools for detecting bias and fairness make sure that treatment recommendations are the same for a variety of populations. Precision medicine techniques are improved by deep learning models that use rule-based explanations and attention mechanisms. By offering human-interpretable insights, XAI also helps clinical decision support systems, increasing healthcare professionals' adoption and trust. Additionally, explainability improves adherence to healthcare laws such as HIPAA and GDPR, guaranteeing the deployment of AI in a morally and securely responsible manner. XAI promotes patient-centered, data-driven, and efficient healthcare solutions by rendering AI-driven recommendations interpretable.

1.5.3 MONITORING AND DISEASE MANAGEMENT

By improving decision-making, transparency, and trust in AI-driven healthcare systems, XAI plays a critical role in disease management and monitoring. AI is used by wearable technology and remote monitoring tools to track vital signs, identify irregularities, and forecast health decline. Doctors and patients can better understand risk factors for conditions like diabetes, hypertension, and chronic respiratory diseases by using XAI techniques like SHAP and LIME, which describe how AI models evaluate patient data. Saliency maps and Grad-CAM in deep learning models enhance medical imaging interpretability for continuous disease evaluation. Explainability increases the dependability of AI-driven alerts for lifestyle modifications and medication adherence, fostering patient trust and engagement. While adherence to laws like HIPAA and GDPR promotes the ethical application of AI, bias detection guarantees equitable treatment for a variety of populations. XAI enhances proactive healthcare management by enabling personalized interventions and improving patient outcomes in the treatment of chronic diseases by rendering AI models interpretable.

1.6 CHALLENGES AND FUTURE DIRECTIONS

Challenges of XAI in healthcare include model complexity, data privacy concerns, bias in AI predictions, and regulatory compliance. Ensuring interpretability without sacrificing accuracy remains difficult. Future directions focus on developing more transparent deep learning models, integrating human-AI collaboration, improving fairness, and enhancing real-time explainability. Advancements in regulatory frameworks and AI ethics will drive responsible AI adoption, ensuring trust, safety, and effectiveness in clinical decision-making and personalized healthcare (Hulsen, 2023; Sadeghi et al., 2024; Saraswat et al., 2022).

1.6.1 TECHNICAL AND COMPUTATIONAL BARRIERS

Numerous computational and technical obstacles stand in the way of the application of XAI in healthcare. Since simpler models are frequently easier to understand but less efficient, high model complexity in deep learning makes it challenging to strike a balance between accuracy and interpretability. Another issue is computational cost, since real-time explanations in resource-constrained environments are challenging due to the high processing power requirements of XAI techniques like SHAP and LIME. Because of intricate feature interactions, handling high-dimensional medical data—such as pictures and genomic sequences—makes explainability even more difficult. Furthermore, there is frequently a lack of standardization in XAI tools, which results in discrepancies between various models and medical applications. Concerns about data security and privacy also surface because explainability techniques have the potential to reveal private patient information. It's still difficult to incorporate XAI into current clinical workflows without interfering with decision-making. Overcoming these technological and computational obstacles in healthcare will require future developments in effective XAI algorithms, federated learning for safe model training, and standardized frameworks.

1.6.2 BALANCING EXPLAINABILITY AND MODEL ACCURACY

One of the biggest challenges in healthcare AI is striking a balance between explainability and model accuracy. Although highly complex models, like deep learning networks, achieve superior accuracy, they frequently behave as "black-boxes," making it challenging to understand their decisions. Simpler models, such as linear regression and decision trees, on the other hand, are easier to understand but might not be as predictive for intricate medical diagnoses. XAI methods such as Grad-CAM, LIME, and SHAP aid in the interpretation of model decisions without appreciably sacrificing accuracy. These techniques, however, frequently increase computational overhead and might not offer total transparency. Developing hybrid approaches that maximize interpretability and performance is crucial. Examples of these include applying post-hoc explanations for deep learning and, when feasible, using models that are naturally interpretable. AI results can also be improved by incorporating clinical domain knowledge. Achieving the best balance in healthcare applications will require future developments in effective XAI methods, standardized frameworks, and human-AI cooperation.

1.6.3 EMERGING TRENDS IN XAI FOR HEALTHCARE

Emerging trends in XAI for healthcare include hybrid explainability models, real-time AI interpretations, human-AI collaboration, and regulatory-compliant XAI. Advances in bias detection, graph-based explainability, federated learning, and multimodal AI enhance transparency and fairness. These innovations improve trust, patient safety, and ethical AI deployment in clinical decision-making.

- **Hybrid Explainability Models**: Combining inherently interpretable models with deep learning to balance accuracy and transparency.
- **Real-Time XAI**: Developing faster, computationally efficient explainability techniques for real-time clinical decision support.
- **Human-AI Collaboration**: Enhancing doctor-AI interaction by integrating expert feedback into model explanations.

- **Regulatory-Compliant XAI**: Aligning with healthcare regulations (HIPAA, GDPR) to ensure ethical and transparent AI use.
- **Bias Detection & Fairness**: Improving fairness in AI models to reduce biases in diagnoses and treatments.
- **Graph-Based Explainability**: Using graph neural networks (GNNs) for better interpretation of medical relationships.
- **Federated Learning for XAI**: Enhancing explainability while preserving data privacy across decentralized healthcare systems.
- **Multimodal XAI**: Integrating diverse data sources (images, text, EHRs) for more comprehensive explanations.

1.7   CONCLUSION

XAI improves healthcare AI systems' accountability, transparency, and trust. It aids in the interpretation of intricate models, enhancing risk assessment, disease diagnosis, and tailored treatment suggestions. Doctors and patients can better understand AI-driven decisions thanks to methods like SHAP, LIME, and Grad-CAM. By identifying biases and guaranteeing fair treatment for all populations, XAI also promotes justice. Regulatory compliance, high computational costs, and striking a balance between interpretability and accuracy are among the difficulties. Realtime XAI, federated learning, and human-AI cooperation are the main topics of emerging trends. All things considered, XAI creates moral, efficient, and patient-centered healthcare solutions by bridging the gap between clinical knowledge and AI developments.

Clinical decision-making is improved by highly transparent, moral, and patient-centered AI systems, according to the XAI in healthcare vision. Improvements in multimodal AI, federated learning, and real-time explainability will boost security and trust while guaranteeing adherence to laws like GDPR and HIPAA. Healthcare workflows will be seamlessly integrated with AI models, which will provide interpretable insights for risk prediction, early disease detection, and customized treatments. Diverse populations will receive equitable healthcare thanks to bias detection and fairness-focused XAI. In the end, XAI will provide physicians and patients with intelligible AI-driven insights, paving the way for a time when AI complements human expertise rather than replaces it.

REFERENCES

Ahmed, M., & Zubair, S. (2022). Explainable artificial intelligence in sustainable smart healthcare. In M. Ahmed, S.R. Islam, A. Anwar, N. Moustafa & A. S. K. Pathan (Eds.), *Explainable artificial intelligence for cyber security: Next generation artificial intelligence* (pp. 265–280). Springer.

Bawa, G., Singh, H., Rani, S., Kataria, A., & Min, H. (2024). Exploring perspectives of blockchain technology and traditional centralized technology in organ donation management: A comprehensive review. *Information*, *15*(11), 703.

Chen, T.-C. T. (2023). Enhancing the sustainability of smart healthcare applications with XAI. In T.-C. T. Chen (Ed.), *Sustainable smart healthcare: Lessons learned from the COVID-19 pandemic* (pp. 93–110). Springer.

Das, A., & Rad, P. (2020). Opportunities and challenges in explainable artificial intelligence (xai): A survey. *arXiv preprint arXiv:2006.11371.*

Dikshit, A., & Pradhan, B. (2021). Interpretable and explainable AI (XAI) model for spatial drought prediction. *Science of the Total Environment, 801,* 149797.

Dwivedi, R., Dave, D., Naik, H., Singhal, S., Omer, R., Patel, P., Qian, B., Wen, Z., Shah, T., Morgan, G., & Ranjan, R. (2023). Explainable AI (XAI): Core ideas, techniques, and solutions. *ACM Computing Surveys, 55*(9), 1–33.

Gaspar, D., Silva, P., & Silva, C. (2024). Explainable AI for intrusion detection systems: Lime and shap applicability on multi-layer perceptron. *IEEE Access, 12,* 30164–30175.

Holzinger, A., Saranti, A., Molnar, C., Biecek, P., & Samek, W. (2020). Explainable AI methods-a brief overview. In A. Holzinger, R., Goebel, R., Fong, T., Moon, K. R., Müller & W. Samek (Eds.), *International workshop on extending explainable AI beyond deep models and classifiers* (pp. 13–38). Springer.

Hulsen, T. (2023). Explainable artificial intelligence (XAI): Concepts and challenges in healthcare. *AI, 4*(3), 652–666.

Javed, A. R., Ahmed, W., Pandya, S., Maddikunta, P. K. R., Alazab, M., & Gadekallu, T. R. (2023). A survey of explainable artificial intelligence for smart cities. *Electronics, 12*(4), 1020.

Kaur, G., & Saini, H. K. (2023). An optimized resnet based plant disease identification using deep learning hypothetic function. In *2023 International Conference on Advances in Computation, Communication and Information Technology (ICAICCIT)* (pp. 58–63). IEEE.

Khang, A., Ragimova, N. A., Hajimahmud, V. A., & Alyar, A. V. (2022). Advanced technologies and data management in the smart healthcare system. In A. Khang, S. Rani & A. K. Sivaraman, (Eds.), *AI-Centric Smart City Ecosystems* (pp. 261–270). CRC Press.

Kumar, S., Rani, S., Sharma, S., & Min, H. (2024). Multimodality fusion aspects of medical diagnosis: A comprehensive review. *Bioengineering, 11*(12), 1233.

Liu, Q., Pinto, J. D., & Paquette, L. (2024). Applications of explainable ai (xai) in education. In D. Kourkoulou, A. O. Tzirides, B., Cope & M. Kalantzis (Eds.), *Trust and Inclusion in AI-mediated education: Where human learning meets learning machines* (pp. 93–109). Springer.

Longo, L., Goebel, R., Lecue, F., Kieseberg, P., & Holzinger, A. (2020). Explainable artificial intelligence: Concepts, applications, research challenges and visions. In A. Holzinger, P., Kieseberg, A. M., Tjoa, & E. Weippl (Eds.), *International cross-domain conference for machine learning and knowledge extraction* (pp. 1–16). Springer.

Minopoulos, G. M., Memos, V. A., Stergiou, C. L., Stergiou, K. D., Plageras, A. P., Koidou, M. P., & Psannis, K. E. (2022). Exploitation of emerging technologies and advanced networks for a smart healthcare system. *Applied Sciences, 12*(12), 5859.

Mittal, D., Singh, H., & Rani, S. (2024). Exploring explainable artificial intelligence techniques for hate speech detection. In A. E. Hassanien, S. Anand, A. Jaiswal & P. Kumar (Eds.), *International conference on innovative computing and communication* (pp. 545–554). Springer.

Mumuni, F., & Mumuni, A. (2025). Explainable artificial intelligence (XAI): from inherent explainability to large language models. *arXiv preprint arXiv:2501.09967.*

Nagahisarchoghaei, M., Nur, N., Cummins, L., Nur, N., Karimi, M. M., Nandanwar, S., Bhattacharyya, S., & Rahimi, S. (2023). An empirical survey on explainable AI technologies: Recent trends, use-cases, and categories from technical and application perspectives. *Electronics, 12*(5), 1092.

Rani, S., Kataria, A., Bhambri, P., Pareek, P. K., & Puri, V. (2024). Artificial Intelligence in Personalized Health Services for Better Patient Care. In S. K. Gupta, D. A., Karras & R. Natarajan (Eds.), *Revolutionizing healthcare: AI integration with IoT for enhanced patient outcomes* (pp. 89–108). Springer.

Rao, S., Mehta, S., Kulkarni, S., Dalvi, H., Katre, N., & Narvekar, M. (2022). A study of LIME and SHAP model explainers for autonomous disease predictions. In *2022 IEEE Bombay Section Signature Conference (IBSSC)* (pp. 1–6). IEEE.

Sadeghi, Z., Alizadehsani, R., CIFCI, M. A., Kausar, S., Rehman, R., Mahanta, P., Bora, P. K., Almasri, A., Alkhawaldeh, R. S., Hussain, S., Alatas, B., Shoeibi, A., Moosaei, H., Hladík, M., Nahavandi, S. & Pardalos, P. M. (2024). A review of Explainable Artificial Intelligence in healthcare. *Computers and Electrical Engineering, 118*, 109370.

Sahoh, B., & Choksuriwong, A. (2023). The role of explainable Artificial Intelligence in high-stakes decision-making systems: A systematic review. *Journal of Ambient Intelligence and Humanized Computing, 14*(6), 7827–7843.

Saini, H. K., & Preeti. (2024). A cross design for breast cancer prediction. In A. Kumar & S. Mozar (Eds.), *International Conference on Communications and Cyber Physical Engineering* 2018 (pp. 125–132). Springer.

Saini, H. K., Swarnakar, H., & Jain, K. (2022). Secured multimedia and IoT in healthcare computing paradigms. In B. Bhusan, S. K., Sharma, B., Unhelkar, M. F., Ijaz & L. Karim (Eds.), *Internet of Things* (pp. 229–256). CRC Press.

Saranya, A., & Subhashini, R. (2023). A systematic review of Explainable Artificial Intelligence models and applications: Recent developments and future trends. *Decision Analytics Journal, 7*, 100230.

Saraswat, D., Bhattacharya, P., Verma, A., Prasad, V. K., Tanwar, S., Sharma, G., Bokoro, P. N., & Sharma, R. (2022). Explainable AI for healthcare 5.0: Opportunities and challenges. *IEEE Access, 10*, 84486–84517.

Xie, Y., Zhai, Y., & Lu, G. (2025). Evolution of artificial intelligence in healthcare: A 30-year bibliometric study. *Frontiers in Medicine, 11*, 1505692.

Xu, F., Uszkoreit, H., Du, Y., Fan, W., Zhao, D., & Zhu, J. (2019). Explainable AI: A brief survey on history, research areas, approaches and challenges. In J. Tang, M. Y., Kan, D., Zhao, S., Li & H. Zan (Eds.), *Natural language processing and Chinese computing: 8th cCF international conference, NLPCC 2019, dunhuang, China, October 9–14, 2019, proceedings, part II 8* (pp. 563–574). Springer.

2 Understanding the Framework of Explainable AI in Healthcare

2.1 INTRODUCTION

Explainability in artificial intelligence (AI) is essential for healthcare to ensure transparency, trust, and ethical decision-making. AI models assist in disease diagnosis, risk prediction, and personalized treatment, but their complexity can make their decisions difficult to understand. Explainable AI (XAI) techniques, such as SHapley Additive exPlanations (SHAP), Local Interpretable Model-agnostic Explanations (LIME), and Gradient-weighted Class Activation Mapping (Grad-CAM), help clinicians interpret AI-driven recommendations, improving confidence in medical decisions. Explainability also enhances patient trust by providing clear justifications for AI-based diagnoses and treatment plans. Furthermore, XAI aids in bias identification, guaranteeing just and equal healthcare for a range of populations (Saraswat et al., 2022). Explainable models are also necessary for regulatory compliance with frameworks like Health Insurance Portability and Accountability Act (HIPAA) and General Data Protection Regulation (GDPR) in order to preserve data security and accountability. Black-box AI models that lack explainability run the risk of making erroneous diagnoses and raising ethical issues. XAI bridges the gap between human expertise and complex algorithms by rendering AI models interpretable, resulting in healthcare solutions that are safer, more efficient, and patient-centric (Bharati et al., 2023; Mittal et al., 2024).

In this chapter, the authors aim to explore the role of XAI in making AI-driven healthcare systems more transparent, trustworthy, and interpretable. The key objectives include defining XAI, explaining its significance in medical decision-making, and discussing techniques, such as SHAP, LIME, and Grad-CAM, for interpreting AI predictions. It examines applications in disease diagnosis, risk prediction, personalized treatment, and patient monitoring while addressing challenges like model complexity, bias, and regulatory compliance. The scope covers AI-driven clinical decision support, ethical considerations, and the need for fairness in healthcare AI. Additionally, it highlights future trends such as real-time explainability, federated learning (FL), and bias mitigation strategies. By providing insights into XAI frameworks, this chapter serves as a guide for researchers, healthcare professionals, and policymakers to develop and deploy AI models that enhance patient care while maintaining accountability, interpretability, and compliance with healthcare regulations like HIPAA and GDPR.

DOI: 10.1201/9781003561422-2

2.2 FUNDAMENTALS OF EXPLAINABLE AI (XAI) IN HEALTHCARE

Explainable AI in healthcare enhances transparency, trust, and interpretability in AI-driven medical decisions. Key fundamentals include interpretability, transparency, fairness, and regulatory compliance. Techniques like SHAP, LIME, and Grad-CAM help explain AI predictions, ensuring ethical, unbiased, and reliable AI applications in disease diagnosis, treatment planning, and risk prediction (Sadeghi et al., 2024).

2.2.1 DEFINITION AND KEY CONCEPTS

Explainable AI in healthcare refers to the development of AI models that provide clear, interpretable, and transparent insights into their decision-making processes. It ensures that medical professionals and patients can understand, trust, and effectively use AI-driven recommendations for disease diagnosis, treatment planning, and risk prediction.

Following are some of the key concepts of XAI deployment in healthcare applications (Chattopadhyay et al., 2025):

- **Interpretability**: The ability of AI models to provide human-understandable explanations for their outputs.
- **Transparency**: Ensuring AI models disclose how they process medical data and make decisions.
- **Feature Importance**: Identifying which patient data (e.g., lab results, symptoms) most influence AI predictions.
- **Post-hoc Explanations**: Techniques like SHAP, LIME, and Grad-CAM that explain model outputs after predictions.
- **Fairness and Bias Mitigation**: Ensuring AI decisions do not favor specific patient groups unfairly.
- **Regulatory Compliance**: Aligning AI with healthcare regulations (e.g., HIPAA, GDPR) for ethical deployment.

2.2.2 DISTINCTION BETWEEN EXPLAINABILITY, INTERPRETABILITY, AND TRANSPARENCY

In healthcare AI, **explainability**, **interpretability**, and **transparency** are essential for trust, safety, and ethical decision-making.

- **Explainability** refers to the ability of AI models to provide human-understandable reasons for their predictions. For instance, SHAP and LIME explain why an AI system diagnosed a patient with a disease by highlighting key factors like blood pressure or genetic markers.
- **Interpretability** is the extent to which humans can understand the model's internal workings. A logistic regression model predicting heart disease risk is more interpretable than a deep neural network, as doctors can easily see how each variable influences the prediction.

- **Transparency** ensures openness in AI models by making data sources, decision logic, and biases accessible for auditing. A transparent AI system in radiology, for example, documents how it processes medical images, ensuring compliance with healthcare regulations like HIPAA and GDPR.

Balancing these elements enhances trust, fairness, and patient-centric AI applications. Comparison of explainability, interpretability, and transparency in various healthcare applications considering various aspects is shown in Table 2.1.

2.2.3 Why Explainability Matters in Healthcare AI?

Explainability in healthcare AI is essential for trust, safety, and ethical decision-making. AI models assist in diagnosis, risk prediction, and treatment recommendations, but their complexity can make decisions difficult to understand. Explainable AI techniques like SHAP, LIME, and Grad-CAM help clinicians interpret AI

TABLE 2.1

Comparison of Explainability, Interpretability, and Transparency in various Healthcare Applications

Aspect	Explainability	Interpretability	Transparency
Focus	Post-hoc explanations of AI decisions.	Clarity in model behavior and structure.	Disclosure of AI workflow, biases, and data usage.
Techniques Used	SHAP, LIME, Grad-CAM, attention mechanisms.	Decision trees, logistic regression, rule-based models.	Model documentation, bias audits, regulatory compliance.
Example in Disease Diagnosis	AI explaining why a patient is predicted to have diabetes based on SHAP values.	A simple decision tree showing how symptoms lead to a diagnosis.	A hospital AI system sharing its dataset sources and model logic.
Example in Risk Prediction	LIME highlights key features influencing a heart disease risk score.	Linear regression showing weightage of risk factors like cholesterol and smoking.	Transparent reporting of how AI-derived risk factors align with clinical guidelines.
Example in Treatment Recommendation	AI explains why it recommends a specific drug based on patient history.	A rule-based system providing clear logic for medication choices.	A system documenting its drug interaction database and decision rules.
Regulatory Importance	Helps meet legal requirements for AI-driven decisions (e.g., GDPR, HIPAA).	Ensures clinicians can validate AI recommendations.	Mandatory for ethical AI deployment and patient trust.
Challenges	Computational complexity, incomplete explanations.	Trade-off between interpretability and model accuracy.	Risk of exposing proprietary algorithms or sensitive patient data.

predictions by identifying key influencing factors. This enhances transparency, builds patient trust, and ensures fair, unbiased healthcare. Explainability also supports regulatory compliance with laws like HIPAA and GDPR, reducing risks associated with AI-driven errors. Without it, black-box models could lead to misdiagnoses and ethical concerns. By making AI decisions interpretable, XAI bridges the gap between advanced algorithms and human expertise, promoting reliable and responsible healthcare applications while improving patient outcomes and clinical decision-making (Puri et al., 2025; Saini et al., 2022).

2.3   XAI FRAMEWORKS AND METHODOLOGIES

XAI frameworks (shown in Figure 2.1) and methodologies aim to enhance transparency, interpretability, and trust in AI-driven healthcare systems. Key approaches include model-agnostic techniques like SHAP and LIME, which explain predictions without altering models, and model-specific methods like Grad-CAM for deep learning. Rule-based systems and decision trees offer built-in interpretability. These methodologies help clinicians understand AI decisions, ensuring fairness, regulatory compliance, and improved patient outcomes in medical applications (Dwivedi et al., 2023; Kaur & Saini, 2023; Saini & Preeti, 2024).

2.3.1   Model-Specific vs. Model-Agnostic Approaches

Model-specific approaches in XAI are designed to provide interpretability within a particular model architecture. These methods leverage the internal structure of models to generate explanations without requiring external modifications. For instance,

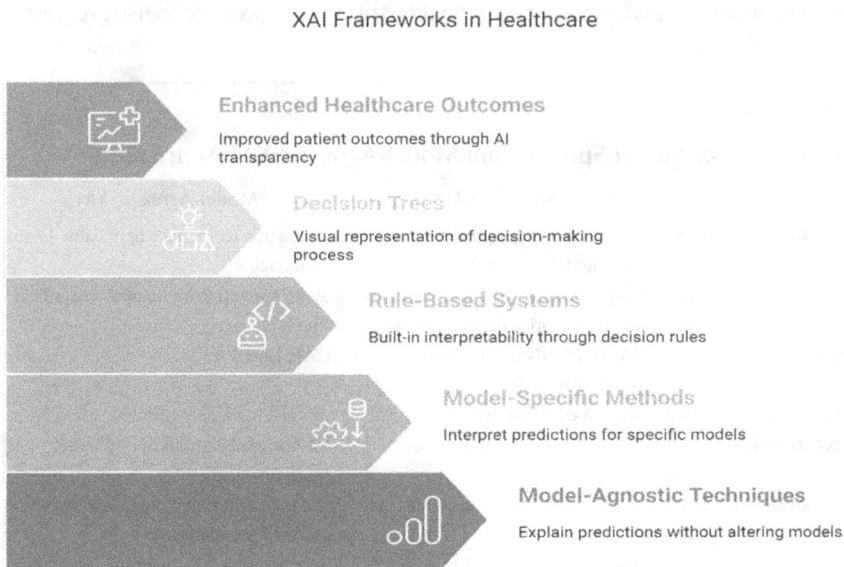

FIGURE 2.1   XAI framework: an abstract view.

Grad-CAM is used in convolutional neural networks (CNNs) to highlight important regions in medical images, helping radiologists understand AI-based diagnoses. Attention mechanisms in natural language processing (NLP) allow AI to justify predictions by focusing on relevant text features in clinical notes. Decision trees and rule-based models offer inherent interpretability by outlining clear decision paths. These approaches ensure reliable, domain-specific explanations, enhancing trust in AI-driven healthcare applications (Khan, 2022).

Model-agnostic approaches in XAI provide interpretability for any AI model, regardless of its architecture. These methods analyze inputs and outputs to generate explanations without modifying the underlying model. SHAP assigns importance scores to features influencing predictions, aiding risk assessment in healthcare. Local Interpretable Model-agnostic Explanations approximates black-box models with simpler interpretable models to explain individual predictions. Permutation feature importance (PFI) evaluates how changes in input features affect model outcomes. These approaches enhance transparency, helping clinicians and researchers understand AI decisions, ensuring fairness, regulatory compliance, and improved trust in AI-driven healthcare applications (Whitney, 2019).

A comparative analysis of these two types of XAI approaches is summarized in Table 2.2.

2.3.2 POST-HOC VS. INTRINSIC EXPLAINABILITY

Explainability in AI can be categorized into post-hoc and intrinsic methods, each serving different purposes in healthcare AI applications. Intrinsic explainability refers to models that are inherently interpretable due to their simple structure. Decision trees, linear regression, and rule-based models provide clear decision-making logic, making them naturally understandable. In healthcare, an interpretable logistic regression

TABLE 2.2

Comparison of Model-Specific and Model-Agnostic XAI Approaches

Aspect	Model-Specific XAI	Model-Agnostic XAI
Definition	Explanation methods designed for specific AI models.	Explanation techniques applicable to any AI model.
Flexibility	Limited to particular model architectures (e.g., neural networks, decision trees).	Can be applied to any model, regardless of structure.
Examples	Grad-CAM (for CNNs), attention mechanisms (for NLP), feature importance in decision trees.	SHAP, LIME, PFI.
Interpretability	Built-in explanations within the model structure.	Post-hoc explanations applied after predictions.
Computational Cost	Often lower since explanation is integrated into the model.	Higher, as additional computations are needed for explanations.
Use Case in Healthcare	Explaining AI-based medical imaging predictions using Grad-CAM.	Understanding AI-driven risk prediction models using SHAP values.

model for disease risk prediction allows clinicians to see the weight of each factor, such as blood pressure or cholesterol levels, in determining patient risk. While highly interpretable, these models may lack the complexity needed for deep learning tasks, limiting their predictive power.

Post-hoc explainability applies to complex, black-box models like deep neural networks and ensemble methods, which require additional techniques to interpret their decisions. Methods such as SHAP, LIME, and Grad-CAM provide explanations after a model has made a prediction. For example, Grad-CAM highlights important regions in medical images to justify AI-based diagnoses. Post-hoc methods enhance transparency but may introduce approximations that do not fully capture the model's internal reasoning.

In healthcare, balancing intrinsic and post-hoc explainability is crucial. While interpretable models ensure immediate trust, post-hoc methods allow high-performing AI models to be more transparent, improving decision-making in disease diagnosis, risk prediction, and treatment recommendations while maintaining regulatory compliance and ethical standards.

2.3.3   COMMON XAI TECHNIQUES

Explainable AI techniques can be categorized into intrinsic (built-in interpretability) and post-hoc (explanations after prediction), as discussed in Section 2.3.1. Below are some widely used techniques in healthcare AI:

- **SHAP (SHapley Additive exPlanations)**: By giving input features importance scores, SHAP is a model-agnostic XAI technique that is used to interpret AI predictions in the healthcare industry. SHAP, which is based on cooperative game theory, ensures transparency and trust in medical applications by explaining how each feature influences an AI model's decision. SHAP identifies important variables that affect predictions in disease diagnosis, such as blood pressure and glucose levels, in the detection of diabetes. It identifies risk factors for cardiovascular disease in order to predict risk. SHAP boosts clinician confidence by explaining AI-driven medication recommendations in personalized treatment. By improving interpretability, SHAP makes AI models more dependable and intelligible for patients and healthcare providers, promoting equity, regulatory compliance (HIPAA, GDPR), and informed decision-making (Nohara et al., 2022).
- **LIME (Local Interpretable Model-Agnostic Explanations)**: LIME is a widely used XAI technique that explains AI model predictions by approximating complex models with simpler, interpretable ones. It generates local explanations for individual predictions, helping healthcare professionals understand AI-driven decisions.

  In disease diagnosis, LIME highlights which patient features (e.g., lab results, symptoms) influenced an AI's prediction of conditions like cancer or heart disease. For risk prediction, it identifies critical factors contributing to a patient's likelihood of developing a condition. In treatment recommendations, LIME clarifies why an AI model suggests a specific medication or therapy. By making AI decisions transparent and interpretable, LIME enhances trust, accountability, and regulatory compliance in AI-driven healthcare applications (Davagdorj et al., 2021).

- **Permutation Feature Importance (PFI)**: PFI is an XAI technique used to evaluate the impact of individual features on AI model predictions. It works by randomly shuffling a feature's values and measuring the resulting change in model accuracy, helping identify the most influential factors in medical decision-making.

  In disease diagnosis, PFI helps determine which biomarkers (e.g., glucose levels, blood pressure) are critical for AI-driven predictions. In risk assessment, it highlights key variables affecting disease progression. For treatment planning, PFI ensures AI models prioritize relevant patient data. By improving interpretability, PFI enhances trust, transparency, and regulatory compliance in AI-powered healthcare systems (Kaneko, 2022).

- **Grad-CAM (Gradient-weighted Class Activation Mapping)**: Grad-CAM is a model-specific XAI technique used to interpret deep learning models, particularly CNNs, by highlighting important regions in medical images that influence AI predictions. It helps explain how AI models detect diseases, enhancing trust and interpretability in healthcare (Selvaraju et al., 2016).

  In medical imaging, Grad-CAM is widely applied in radiology, pathology, and dermatology to visualize critical areas in X-rays, MRIs, and CT scans. For example, it helps radiologists understand why an AI model classifies a lung X-ray as pneumonia or detects tumors in MRIs. Grad-CAM also supports disease diagnosis and localization, ensuring AI decisions align with clinical knowledge. By making deep learning models more transparent, Grad-CAM improves AI adoption, enhances clinician trust, and ensures regulatory compliance in medical AI applications.

- **Attention Mechanisms**: Attention mechanisms in AI enhance interpretability by allowing models to focus on the most relevant parts of input data when making predictions. Commonly used in NLP and deep learning, attention mechanisms improve healthcare applications by prioritizing critical information in medical text, images, and time-series data.

  In clinical text analysis, attention models help extract key insights from electronic health records (EHRs), doctor's notes, and radiology reports, ensuring accurate disease diagnosis and treatment recommendations. In medical imaging, attention mechanisms highlight significant regions in MRI or CT scans, improving disease detection. For personalized medicine, they optimize drug recommendation systems by identifying crucial patient factors. By increasing explainability, attention mechanisms enhance AI-driven decision-making, supporting trust, transparency, and compliance in healthcare applications.

- **Decision Trees and Rule-Based Models**: AI methods that are inherently interpretable, such as decision trees and rule-based models, are frequently employed in the medical field for diagnosis, risk assessment, and treatment planning. These models are perfect for clinical decision support because they offer decision paths that are easy for humans to understand.

Using patient data (e.g., age, blood pressure, glucose levels), decision trees aid in the classification of diseases such as diabetes or heart disease. Rule-based models, which are frequently employed in expert systems, make recommendations for diagnoses or treatments by applying predefined medical knowledge. Decision trees are used in risk prediction to identify high-risk patients based on genetic and lifestyle factors. By guaranteeing that medical practitioners can successfully validate AI recommendations, these models improve transparency, regulatory compliance, and trust in AI-driven healthcare (Mahbooba et al., 2021).

These techniques enhance transparency, improve trust, and ensure regulatory compliance in AI-driven healthcare applications.

2.4   REGULATORY, ETHICAL, AND LEGAL CONSIDERATIONS

Explainable AI in healthcare must comply with regulatory, ethical, and legal standards to ensure transparency, fairness, and patient safety. Regulations like HIPAA (USA) and GDPR (EU) mandate data privacy and security, requiring AI models to be interpretable and accountable. Ethical concerns include bias, fairness, and informed decision-making, ensuring AI does not disproportionately affect specific populations. Legally, AI systems must provide clear justifications for medical decisions to avoid malpractice risks. Ensuring explainability helps build trust among clinicians and patients while supporting compliance with evolving healthcare regulations, ultimately leading to safer and more effective AI-driven medical applications (Moorthy et al., 2025).

- **Compliance with Healthcare Standards**
  Explainable AI in healthcare must adhere to established regulatory and industry standards to ensure patient safety, fairness, and transparency. Key compliance frameworks include:
  - **HIPAA (Health Insurance Portability and Accountability Act)**: Ensures patient data privacy and security in AI-driven healthcare applications.
  - **GDPR (General Data Protection Regulation)**: Mandates transparency and data protection for AI models handling patient information in the EU.
  - **FDA (U.S. Food and Drug Administration) Regulations**: Governs AI-based medical devices, ensuring explainability in clinical decision support systems (CDSS).
  - **ISO/IEC 27001**: Provides guidelines for information security management in AI-powered healthcare applications.

By complying with these standards, XAI enhances trust, regulatory acceptance, and responsible AI deployment in medical decision-making and patient care.

- **Ethical Implications of AI in Medical Decision-Making**
  AI in medical decision-making raises ethical concerns like bias, account-ability, and transparency. Patient autonomy must be preserved, and data privacy ensured. Black-box algorithms challenge trust, while regulatory gaps pose risks. Balancing AI's efficiency with human oversight is crucial to ensure fairness, safety, and ethical integrity in healthcare decisions. The ethical implications of AI in medical decision-making include:
  - **Patient Autonomy**: AI should support, not replace, human decision-making, ensuring patients retain agency over their healthcare choices.
  - **Privacy and Data Security**: The use of vast patient data raises con-cerns about consent, security breaches, and misuse.
  - **Transparency**: AI algorithms often function as "black boxes," making it difficult to interpret their recommendations and ensure trust.
  - **Regulatory Challenges**: Ensuring compliance with ethical and legal standards is critical for the safe deployment of AI in healthcare.
- **Bias, Fairness, and Accountability in AI Systems**
  Explainable AI in healthcare enhances **bias detection, fairness, and accountability** by making AI decisions transparent. It ensures equitable treatment, reduces discrimination, and clarifies responsibility, allowing clini-cians and regulators to trust and verify AI-driven medical recommendations.
  - **Bias Mitigation**: XAI helps identify and correct biases in AI models by making decision processes interpretable, ensuring equitable treatment across diverse patient populations.
  - **Fairness Assurance**: By providing insights into model reasoning, XAI ensures AI-driven decisions do not disproportionately impact certain demographics.
  - **Accountability**: Transparent AI models allow for responsibility attri-bution, helping clinicians and regulators verify AI recommendations and mitigate liability risks.

2.5 HUMAN-CENTRIC DESIGN AND TRUST IN XAI

Human-centric XAI in healthcare prioritizes transparency, user-friendly interfaces, and ethical AI use. Trust is built through explainability, bias reduction, and account-ability, ensuring AI supports clinicians and patients in fair, informed decision-making (Chromik, 2021).

- **Role of Clinicians and Patients in Interpretable AI**: Clinicians and patients are essential to the ethical and successful application of interpreta-ble AI in healthcare. AI systems and patient care are mediated by clinicians. They need to comprehend insights produced by AI, verify suggestions, and combine them with clinical knowledge. They are responsible for maintain-ing accountability in medical decisions, guaranteeing fairness, and evaluat-ing AI outputs for bias. By offering practical feedback, they also aid in the improvement of AI models' interpretability and dependability. By interact-ing with AI-powered medical solutions, challenging advice, and making well-informed choices, patients participate. Patients should be empowered by transparent AI systems that clearly explain diagnoses and available treatments. Clear communication regarding AI's function, constraints, and data privacy safeguards is necessary to maintain patient trust. In order to ensure that AI complements human decision-making rather than replaces it, collaboration among clinicians, patients, and AI developers promotes a human-centered approach. This collaboration enhances overall healthcare results, fosters equity, and increases trust (Bawa et al., 2024).

- **Enhancing Trust Through Explainability**: Explainability, or making sure that doctors and patients understand how AI systems make decisions, is essential to boosting trust in AI-driven healthcare. Transparent AI models increase trust by offering understandable justifications for diagnoses and suggested courses of treatment. Explainability allows clinicians to validate AI-generated insights, promoting responsible and well-informed decision-making. Without taking the place of human expertise, it assists in identifying biases, evaluating fairness, and incorporating AI support into patient care. When AI systems enable patients to make educated decisions about their health by providing clear explanations of medical decisions, their trust in the system increases. Building trust and engagement requires open communication about AI's function, constraints, and data privacy safeguards. Explainability is further supported by ethical AI practices and regulatory frameworks that guarantee adherence to accountability and fairness standards. Building trust and encouraging the moral application of AI in healthcare is achieved through a human-centric approach, in which AI supports medical judgments rather than replaces them.

- **User Experience Considerations in XAI**: Clarity, usability, and accessibility must be given top priority in XAI for healthcare user experience (UX) in order to maintain efficacy and trust. AI interfaces should minimize cognitive load for clinicians by presenting interpretable insights in an intuitive way. Clinicians can effectively validate AI recommendations thanks to interactive tools, visual explanations, and confidence scores that improve comprehension. AI explanations for patients need to be clear, free of jargon, and considerate of their cultural background. Trust in AI-driven care is increased when diagnoses and treatments are supported by clear logic. Transparency, responsiveness, and ethical considerations are also very important. AI systems ought to respect user privacy, accept user inquiries, and offer real-time feedback. By ensuring that XAI supports users rather than overwhelms them, a human-centered design approach promotes greater adoption and improves healthcare results (Kataria et al., 2024; Rani et al., 2024).

2.6 CHALLENGES IN IMPLEMENTING EXPLAINABLE AI IN HEALTHCARE

The challenges of implementing XAI in healthcare include maintaining patient data privacy, guaranteeing regulatory compliance, and striking a balance between transparency and model complexity. Trust may be damaged if clinicians find it difficult to understand AI decisions. Furthermore, biases in training data may result in explanations that are not trustworthy. Widespread adoption in crucial healthcare applications is limited by the complexity of integrating XAI with current systems and the challenge of guaranteeing real-time, interpretable insights without sacrificing accuracy.

- **Trade-offs Between Accuracy and Interpretability**: One of the main challenges in implementing XAI in healthcare is the trade-off between interpretability and accuracy. While highly accurate models, like deep learning and ensemble methods, often operate as "black boxes," making their decision-making process difficult to understand, this lack of transparency can hinder clinical trust and regulatory approval. On the other hand, simpler models, like decision trees and linear regression, offer better interpretability but may not have the predictive power needed for complex medical diagnoses. Finding the right balance is essential—clinicians need dependable, high-performing models while also understanding how decisions are made. To achieve this balance, new approaches, like hybrid models or post-hoc explanation methods, require complexity and may not always guarantee complete transparency.

- **Computational and Technical Limitations**: Computational and technical limitations pose significant challenges in implementing XAI in healthcare. XAI methods, such as SHAP and LIME, require substantial computational resources, making real-time decision support difficult in resource-constrained settings. Complex models demand high processing power, which may not be feasible for all healthcare institutions, especially in low-resource environments. Additionally, integrating XAI into existing EHR systems is technically challenging due to compatibility issues and the need for seamless data exchange. Ensuring scalability while maintaining efficiency further complicates implementation. Moreover, explainability techniques often introduce additional layers of computation, slowing down model performance. Addressing these limitations requires advancements in hardware, optimized algorithms, and streamlined integration methods to make XAI practical for real-world healthcare applications.

- **Data Privacy and Security Concerns**: Concerns about data security and privacy pose significant obstacles to the application of XAI in healthcare. Large volumes of private patient data are used by AI models, increasing the possibility of security lapses, illegal access, and abuse. It becomes more complicated to ensure compliance with laws like HIPAA and GDPR, which call for strong encryption, anonymization, and safe data-sharing procedures. Furthermore, by exposing model insights that could be used by hostile actors, XAI techniques may reveal vulnerabilities. Techniques like FL and differential privacy reduce risks, but they can also affect explainability and model performance. It can be challenging to strike a balance between security and transparency because too thorough explanations could unintentionally reveal private information. Strict security protocols, moral AI governance, and ongoing patient data protection are necessary to meet these challenges.

2.7   REAL-WORLD APPLICATIONS AND CASE STUDIES

Real-world applications of XAI in healthcare include IBM Watson for oncology, which explains treatment recommendations, and Google's DeepMind, which predicts kidney disease while providing insights into its reasoning. Case studies also highlight AI-driven radiology tools like Qure.ai, offering interpretable diagnoses, and AI-powered sepsis prediction models enhancing clinical decision-making transparency (Moorthy et al., 2025; Vakulabharanam et al., 2024).

- **Explainable AI in Disease Diagnosis and Prognosis**
  By increasing the transparency of medical decision-making, XAI is revolutionizing the diagnosis and prognosis of disease. AI-powered tools in radiology, such as Qure.ai and Zebra Medical Vision, help diagnose illnesses like pneumonia and fractures while displaying confidence scores and easily comprehensible heatmaps. By assisting radiologists in validating AI-driven insights, these justifications increase adoption and trust. In a similar vein, IBM Watson for Oncology evaluates patient data and makes evidence-based recommendations for cancer treatments, making sure that medical professionals comprehend the reasoning behind AI-generated recommendations.

  AI models in cardiology, such as those created by Eko Health, examine cardiac sounds to identify disorders like atrial fibrillation. These models help cardiologists make well-informed decisions by highlighting important features influencing predictions using explainability techniques like SHAP values. DeepMind's artificial intelligence in nephrology can forecast acute kidney injury (AKI) up to 48 hours ahead of time and explain risk factors, enabling early interventions. Moreover, AI-based sepsis prediction models, integrated into EHRs, use interpretable decision trees to alert physicians about high-risk patients. Google's AI system improves physician confidence by providing visual explanations for diabetic retinopathy detection. These practical uses show that XAI not only improves diagnostic precision but also guarantees that doctors can rely on and verify AI-generated forecasts.

- **AI-Assisted Radiology, Pathology, and Genomics**
  Interpretable insights that improve clinical decision-making are being provided by XAI, which is transforming genomics, pathology, and radiology. AI-powered solutions in radiology, such as Qure.ai and Aidoc, help identify anomalies in CT and X-ray scans and provide heatmaps and confidence scores to identify important areas. These justifications aid radiologists in verifying AI-generated results, guaranteeing precision and dependability in medical imaging. Similar to this, Zebra Medical Vision employs AI to identify lung disorders and osteoporosis while providing thorough visual annotations to enhance interpretability.

  AI models are used in pathology to help analyze histopathological slides and find diseases like cancer. Paige.AI, for instance, uses deep learning to detect prostate cancer, highlighting suspicious areas for pathologists with interpretable overlays. This preserves human oversight while improving diagnostic efficiency. PathAI takes a similar tack, enhancing pathology workflows and lowering diagnostic errors through explainable deep learning techniques.

XAI is used in genomics to forecast genetic illnesses and customize treatment regimens. Google AI's DeepVariant analyzes genomic sequences to reveal genetic mutations connected to illnesses. Clinicians can better customize treatments by using AI-driven pharmacogenomics tools, such as those utilized in precision medicine, which explain how genetic variations affect drug responses. By guaranteeing AI's transparency, these applications promote confidence in medical judgment.

- **Clinical Decision Support Systems (CDSS) with XAI**
  Clinical decision support systems are being revolutionized by XAI, which increases the transparency and confidence of AI-driven recommendations. AI-powered CDSS help doctors make interpretable decisions while diagnosing illnesses, forecasting patient risks, and recommending treatment regimens. For instance, IBM Watson for Oncology explains its reasoning based on clinical guidelines and patient data after analyzing a large body of medical literature to recommend cancer treatments. Before making important decisions, oncologists can verify AI-driven insights thanks to this transparency.

  Similarly, the AI-powered CDSS from the Mayo Clinic uses feature importance scores and interpretable decision trees to forecast sepsis risks in hospitalized patients. The system facilitates early interventions and improves patient outcomes by highlighting important risk factors, including lab results and vital signs. Cardiologists can better understand AI-derived assessments by using Eko Health's AI-powered stethoscope, which uses SHAP values to explain its predictions and detect heart murmurs and atrial fibrillation.

  Intensive care management is also being improved by AI-powered CDSS. Acute kidney injury can be predicted by DeepMind's AI up to 48 hours ahead of time, with explanations of the contributing factors that enable prompt intervention. By ensuring that clinicians comprehend, trust, and successfully apply AI-driven recommendations for improved patient care, these practical applications show how XAI improves CDSS.

2.8   FUTURE DIRECTIONS AND EMERGING TRENDS

Advanced interpretable deep learning models, real-time explainability for clinical decision-making, and integration with EHRs are some of the upcoming developments in XAI in healthcare. While multimodal AI will improve diagnostics by integrating imaging, genomics, and clinical data, FL will improve data privacy. XAI adoption will be standardized by regulatory frameworks, which will guarantee openness and confidence and eventually result in safer, more efficient AI-powered medical solutions (Kumar et al., 2025; Saranya & Subhashini, 2023).

- **Advances in XAI Research for Healthcare**
  The development of interpretable deep learning models, improving real-time decision support, and boosting patient trust are the main goals of XAI

for healthcare advancements. New methods that shed light on AI predictions include counterfactual explanations, SHAP values, and attention mechanisms. While multimodal AI combines imaging, genomics, and clinical data for improved diagnostics, FL guarantees privacy-preserving AI training across institutions. Additionally, researchers are developing XAI frameworks specifically designed for medical applications. Standardized explainability techniques are being pushed for by regulatory initiatives to guarantee adherence to healthcare regulations. These developments are intended to increase the transparency, reliability, and clinical applicability of AI-driven healthcare in practical contexts.

- **Towards a Standardized Framework for Medical XAI**
  Standardized XAI frameworks will improve interoperability across healthcare systems, ensuring consistent, reliable, and XAI applications for better patient outcomes and clinical decision support. Developing a standardized framework for medical XAI is essential for ensuring transparency, trust, and regulatory compliance in AI-driven healthcare. Standardization efforts center on defining universal explainability metrics, integrating domain-specific interpretability techniques, and aligning with regulations such as HIPAA and GDPR. Frameworks should balance accuracy and interpretability while supporting real-time clinical decision-making. Cooperation between AI researchers, healthcare professionals, and regulatory bodies is crucial to establish benchmarks for model transparency, risk assessment, and ethical AI use.

- **Integrating XAI with Federated Learning and Edge AI**
  By improving privacy, efficiency, and transparency, XAI in conjunction with FL and Edge AI is transforming the healthcare industry. Without disclosing private information, FL allows AI models to learn from decentralized patient data, guaranteeing adherence to laws like HIPAA. On medical devices, edge AI locally processes data to lower latency and facilitate real-time decision-making. By enhancing interpretability, XAI techniques combined with FL and Edge AI give clinicians confidence in AI-driven insights. This combination maintains security while improving diagnostics, remote monitoring, and personalized medicine. Healthcare solutions that are more dependable, explicable, and decentralized will result from this integration as AI adoption increases.

2.9 CONCLUSIONS

In this chapter, the authors stress the significance of interpretability, trust, and transparency in AI-driven healthcare systems. Model explainability, interpretability strategies (SHAP, LIME), and regulatory considerations (GDPR, HIPAA) are among the essential elements of XAI that are described. The chapter highlights the necessity of human-AI collaboration in clinical decision-making by discussing the trade-off between interpretability and model complexity. It also looks at issues like bias, data privacy, and the moral ramifications of diagnoses made by AI. It emphasizes how explainability helps build trust between patients and healthcare providers. In order to guarantee dependability, equity, and conformity with medical standards, the chapter concludes by highlighting the significance of ongoing validation and improvement of AI models.

The development of interpretability techniques, the incorporation of human-centered AI, and the resolution of ethical issues are critical to the future of XAI in healthcare. Clinicians and patients will be more trusting if transparency is increased through better explainability strategies (e.g., SHAP, LIME). In order to guarantee AI compliance while preserving data security and privacy, regulatory frameworks such as GDPR and HIPAA must change. To improve models and reduce biases, cooperation between AI researchers, healthcare providers, and legislators is crucial. AI dependability in clinical settings will be increased through rigorous validation procedures and standardization of XAI approaches. The way forward ultimately entails striking a balance between interpretability and accuracy, building trust, and making sure AI-driven healthcare solutions improve patient outcomes while abiding by the law and ethical standards.

REFERENCES

Bawa, G., Singh, H., Rani, S., Kataria, A., & Min, H. (2024). Exploring perspectives of block-chain technology and traditional centralized technology in organ donation management: A comprehensive review. *Information*, *15*(11), 703.

Bharati, S., Mondal, M. R. H., & Podder, P. (2023). A review on explainable artificial intelligence for healthcare: Why, how, and when? *IEEE Transactions on Artificial Intelligence*, *5*(4), 1429–1442.

Chattopadhyay, S., Barman, S., & Lakshmi, D. (2025). The role of explainable AI for healthcare 5.0: Best practices, challenges, and opportunities. In P. Raj, B. Sundaravadivazhagan, A. S. Raja & M. M. Alani (Eds.), *Edge AI for Industry 5.0 and Healthcare 5.0 Applications*, (pp. 45–80). Taylor and Francis.

Chromik, M. (2021). *Human-centric explanation facilities: Explainable AI for the pragmatic understanding of non-expert end users*. Dissertation, München, Ludwig-Maximilians-Universität, 2021.

Davagdorj, K., Li, M., & Ryu, K. H. (2021). Local interpretable model-agnostic explanations of predictive models for hypertension. In *Advances in Intelligent Information Hiding and Multimedia Signal Processing: Proceeding of the 16th International Conference on IIHMSP in conjunction with the 13th International Conference on FITAT, November 5–7, 2020*, Ho Chi Minh City, Vietnam (Vol. 2, pp. 426–433). Springer.

Dwivedi, R., Dave, D., Naik, H., Singhal, S., Omer, R., Patel, P., Qian, B., Wen, Z., Shah, T., Morgan, G., & Ranjan, R. (2023). Explainable AI (XAI): Core ideas, techniques, and solutions. *ACM Computing Surveys*, *55*(9), 1–33.

Kaneko, H. (2022). Cross-validated permutation feature importance considering correlation between features. *Analytical Science Advances*, *3*(9–10), 278–287.

Kataria, A., Rani, S., & Kautish, S. (2024). Artificial intelligence of things for sustainable development of smart city infrastructures. In *Digital technologies to implement the UN sustainable development goals* (pp. 187–213). Springer.

Kaur, G., & Saini, H. K. (2023). An optimized resnet based plant disease identification using deep learning hypothetic function. In *2023 International Conference on Advances in Computation, Communication and Information Technology (ICAICCIT)* (pp. 58–63). IEEE.

Khan, A. (2022). Model-specific explainable artificial intelligence techniques: State-of-the-art, advantages and limitations.

Kumar, A., Hora, H., Rohilla, A., Kumar, P., & Gautam, R. (2025). Explainable artificial intelligence (XAI) for healthcare: Enhancing transparency and trust. In *International Conference on Cognitive Computing and Cyber Physical Systems* (pp. 295–308). Springer.

Mahbooba, B., Timilsina, M., Sahal, R., & Serrano, M. (2021). Explainable artificial intelligence (XAI) to enhance trust management in intrusion detection systems using decision tree model. *Complexity, 2021*(1), 6634811.

Mittal, D., Singh, H., & Rani, S. (2024). Exploring explainable artificial intelligence techniques for hate speech detection. In *International Conference on Innovative Computing and Communication* (pp. 545–554). Springer.

Moorthy, U. M. K., Muthukumaran, A. M. J., Kaliyaperumal, V., Jayakumar, S., & Vijayaraghavan, K. A. (2025). Explainability and regulatory compliance in healthcare: Bridging the gap for ethical XAI implementation. In A. Kumar, T. A. Kumar, P. Das, C. Sharma & A.K. Dubey A.K. (Eds.) *Explainable Artificial Intelligence in the Healthcare Industry* (pp. 521–561). Wiley Publishers.

Nohara, Y., Matsumoto, K., Soejima, H., & Nakashima, N. (2022). Explanation of machine learning models using shapley additive explanation and application for real data in hospital. *Computer Methods and Programs in Biomedicine, 214*, 106584.

Puri, V., Priyadarshini, I., Kataria, A., Rani, S., & Min, H. (2025). Privacy-first ML for chronic kidney disease prediction: Exploring a decentralized approach using blockchain and IPFS. *IEEE Access, 13*, 43178–43189.

Rani, S., Kataria, A., Bhambri, P., Pareek, P. K., & Puri, V. (2024). Artificial intelligence in personalized health services for better patient care. In *Revolutionizing healthcare: AI integration with IoT for enhanced patient outcomes* (pp. 89–108). Springer.

Sadeghi, Z., Alizadehsani, R., Cifci, M.A., Kausar, S., Rehman, R., Mahanta, P., Bora, P.K., Almasri, A., Alkhawaldeh, R.S., Hussain, S., & Alatas, B. (2024). A review of explainable artificial intelligence in healthcare. *Computers and Electrical Engineering, 118*, 109370.

Saini, H. K. & Preeti. (2024). A cross design for breast cancer prediction. In A. Kumar & S. Mozar (Eds.), *International Conference on Communications and Cyber Physical Engineering 2018* (pp. 125–132). Springer.

Saini, H. K., Swarnakar, H., & Jain, K. (2022). Secured multimedia and IoT in healthcare computing paradigms. In *Internet of Things* (pp. 229–256). CRC Press.

Saranya, A., & Subhashini, R. (2023). A systematic review of explainable artificial intelligence models and applications: Recent developments and future trends. *Decision Analytics Journal, 7*, 100230.

Saraswat, D., Bhattacharya, P., Verma, A., Prasad, V.K., Tanwar, S., Sharma, G., Bokoro, P. N., & Sharma, R. (2022). Explainable AI for healthcare 5.0: opportunities and challenges. *IEEE Access, 10*, 84486–84517.

Selvaraju, R. R., Das, A., Vedantam, R., Cogswell, M., Parikh, D., & Batra, D. (2016). Grad-CAM: Gradient-weighted class activation mapping. *Arxiv*.

Whitney, D. (2019). Advances in model-agnostic approaches to statistical inference (Doctoral dissertation).

Vakulabharanam, V. K., Mandhula, T., & Kothapalli, S. (2024). Explainable AI case studies in healthcare. In *Explainable AI in health informatics* (pp. 243–276). Springer.

3 The Role of Transparency and Interpretability in Healthcare AI

3.1 INTRODUCTION

Understanding how an AI system makes decisions is referred to as transparency in AI. It includes explanations of data processing, open access to algorithms, and unambiguous documentation. Transparency ensures accountability and trust by assisting stakeholders in evaluating AI models for biases, fairness, and ethical issues (Joyce et al., 2023). While transparency stresses openness in AI design, interpretability guarantees that users can understand model decisions. Both are essential for responsible AI, especially in high-stakes applications like healthcare and finance. Interpretability is the extent to which humans can understand the reasoning behind an AI model's output. It focuses on making AI decisions understandable, either through simpler models or post-hoc explanations like feature importance, rule-based approximations, or visualizations.

For healthcare applications to guarantee trust, safety, and moral decision-making, AI must be transparent and interpretable. Medical practitioners cannot confirm the accuracy of AI models without transparency, even though they aid in risk assessment, diagnosis, and treatment planning. Transparent AI ensures accountability and adherence to regulatory standards by enabling clinicians to comprehend how models operate. Interpretability guarantees that patients and physicians can comprehend AI-driven recommendations. Interpretability helps medical professionals validate AI outputs, lowering bias and errors in crucial decisions like disease diagnosis and treatment recommendations. Since patients are more likely to accept AI-assisted decisions if they are adequately explained, it also promotes patient trust. Black-box models, which raise the possibility of inaccurate diagnoses or unethical biases, can result from a lack of transparency and interpretability. AI in healthcare becomes safer, more efficient, and in line with best practices in medicine when these principles are given priority (Kumar et al., 2024; MacDonald et al., 2022).

The importance of openness and interpretability in AI-powered medical applications is discussed in this chapter. The chapter discusses how open AI models promote accountability, trust, and adherence to medical rules. In order to reduce errors and biases, the chapter emphasizes the necessity of interpretability, which allows clinicians to comprehend and validate recommendations generated by AI. Black-box model challenges, interpretability-enhancing strategies (e.g., feature importance, explainable AI [XAI] methods), and case studies illustrating the use of transparent AI in diagnosis and treatment are some of the main subjects covered (Rani et al.,

 DOI: 10.1201/9781003561422-3

2024). The chapter also discusses ethical issues, making sure AI choices respect patient rights and medical norms. In the end, it highlights that safe and successful AI integration into healthcare systems depends on interpretability and transparency.

3.2 TRANSPARENCY IN HEALTHCARE AI

Openness and transparency in AI in the medical field guarantees that stakeholders and medical professionals comprehend the decision-making process of AI models. To foster accountability and trust, it uses transparent documentation, intelligible algorithms, and open data sources. Transparent AI aids in bias detection, model reliability validation, and adherence to medical regulations. Transparency guarantees that AI-driven diagnoses and treatment recommendations are ethically sound and interpretable in the healthcare industry, where patient safety is of utmost importance. AI can turn into a "black-box" without transparency, which raises questions about accuracy and fairness. AI can improve medical decision-making while upholding ethical standards and patient care trust by emphasizing transparency (Srinivasan et al., 2025).

3.2.1 WHAT TRANSPARENCY MEANS IN AI MODELS

The ability to comprehend and closely examine an AI system's decision-making process is known as transparency in AI models for healthcare applications. To guarantee accountability, equity, and adherence to healthcare laws, it entails thorough documentation of algorithms, data sources, and model architecture. Medical practitioners can evaluate patient data processing, spot possible biases, and confirm prediction accuracy with transparent AI. This is especially important in situations with high stakes, such as risk assessment, treatment recommendations, and disease diagnosis, where mistakes can have dire repercussions. Transparency promotes trust between medical professionals, patients, and regulatory agencies by making AI decision-making procedures understandable and transparent. Explainability, which makes AI outputs comprehensible; auditability, which permits external review; and traceability, which guarantees that data sources and model decisions can be tracked, are essential components of transparency in healthcare AI. Black-box models, which make it challenging to identify biases, mistakes, or ethical issues, can result from a lack of transparency. Transparency in AI promotes its ethical and responsible application in healthcare, guaranteeing that AI systems are not only precise but also compliant with patient rights and medical standards. It encourages trust in AI-assisted healthcare solutions and facilitates well-informed decision-making.

3.2.2 LEVELS OF TRANSPARENCY: ALGORITHMIC, DATA, AND DECISION-LEVEL

Transparency in healthcare AI can be categorized into three key levels (Bernal & Mazo, 2022) (shown in Figure 3.1):

Algorithmic Transparency
- Refers to understanding how an AI model processes inputs and generates outputs.

Levels of Transparency in Healthcare AI

Data Transparency
Ensures data quality and
ethical use

Decision-Level
Transparency
Explains AI's decision-making
process

Algorithmic
Transparency
Reveals AI model's inner
workings

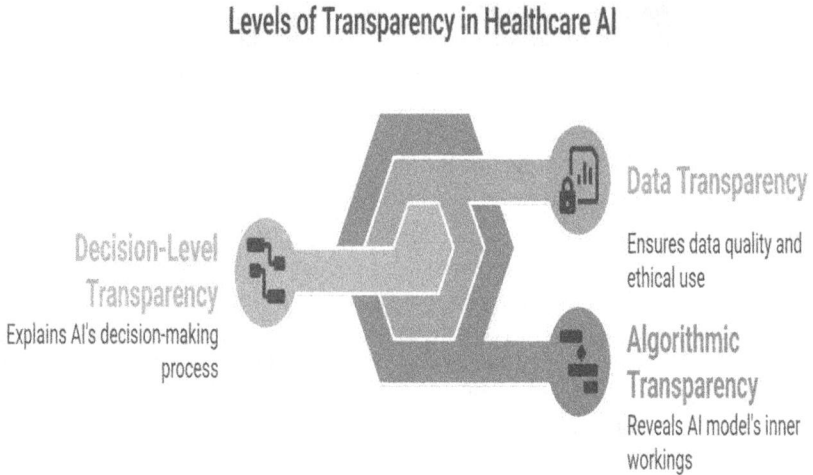

FIGURE 3.1   Level of transparency in healthcare AI.

- Involves revealing model architecture, mathematical functions, and training processes.
- Helps in assessing biases, fairness, and potential errors in AI systems.

Data Transparency
- Focuses on the sources, quality, and preprocessing of data used to train AI models.
- Ensures that datasets are diverse, unbiased, and representative of real-world medical conditions.
- Essential for compliance with regulations like GDPR and HIPAA, ensuring ethical AI use.

Decision-Level Transparency
- Explains how and why AI models make specific predictions or recommendations.
- Uses interpretability techniques like feature importance, attention maps, and rule-based explanations.
- Critical for gaining trust among clinicians and patients, enabling informed decision-making.

Achieving transparency across these levels enhances accountability, reliability, and ethical AI deployment in healthcare.

3.2.3   BENEFITS AND RISKS OF TRANSPARENCY IN MEDICAL AI

Benefits of Transparency in Medical AI (Shown in Figure 3.2)
- **Trust and Accountability**: Transparent AI builds confidence among healthcare professionals and patients by making decision-making processes understandable.

Transparency in Medical AI

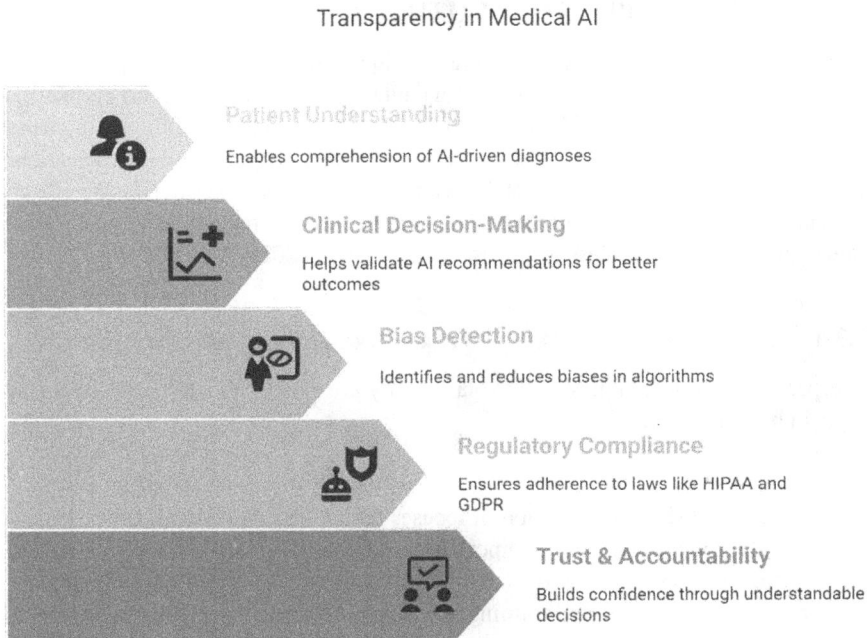

Patient Understanding
Enables comprehension of AI-driven diagnoses

Clinical Decision-Making
Helps validate AI recommendations for better outcomes

Bias Detection
Identifies and reduces biases in algorithms

Regulatory Compliance
Ensures adherence to laws like HIPAA and GDPR

Trust & Accountability
Builds confidence through understandable decisions

FIGURE 3.2   Healthcare AI: benefits of transparency.

- **Regulatory Compliance**: Ensures adherence to laws like HIPAA and GDPR, supporting ethical AI deployment.
- **Bias Detection and Mitigation**: Identifies and reduces biases in algorithms, improving fairness in healthcare decisions.
- **Enhanced Clinical Decision-Making**: Helps doctors validate AI recommendations, leading to better patient outcomes.
- **Improved Patient Understanding**: Enables patients to comprehend AI-driven diagnoses and treatments, fostering informed consent.

Risks of Transparency in Medical AI

- **Privacy Concerns**: Revealing model details and data sources may expose sensitive patient information.
- **Intellectual Property Risks**: Full transparency might lead to competitive disadvantages for AI developers.
- **Misinterpretation of AI Decisions**: Complex AI processes, if not explained well, can be misunderstood by non-experts.
- **Increased Vulnerability to Attacks**: More transparency can expose AI models to adversarial attacks and exploitation.
- **Regulatory and Implementation Challenges**: Balancing transparency with usability and legal requirements can be complex.

Ensuring a balance between transparency and security is crucial for responsible AI integration in healthcare.

3.3   INTERPRETABILITY IN HEALTHCARE AI

Healthcare interpretability understanding and elucidating how AI models produce predictions or decisions is referred to as artificial intelligence. It ensures accuracy and trust by assisting clinicians in validating AI-driven diagnoses. Interpretability is improved by methods such as rule-based models, feature importance, and visual explanations. This is crucial for the deployment of AI in an ethical manner, lowering biases, enhancing patient outcomes, guaranteeing adherence to medical regulations, and building patient and healthcare professional trust (ElShawi et al., 2021; Saini & Preeti, 2024).

3.3.1   DIFFERENTIATING INTERPRETABILITY FROM TRANSPARENCY AND EXPLAINABILITY

Interpretability, transparency, and explainability are closely related but distinct concepts in healthcare AI.

- **Interpretability** refers to the degree to which humans can understand how an AI model arrives at a decision. It focuses on making AI predictions comprehensible, often using feature importance, decision trees, or rule-based methods.
- **Transparency** involves openness about AI models, including their algorithms, data sources, and training processes. A transparent AI system allows scrutiny of its inner workings to assess biases, reliability, and ethical concerns.
- **Explainability** is the ability to provide post-hoc justifications for AI decisions. While an AI model may not be inherently interpretable, explainability techniques (e.g., SHAP, LIME) help break down complex outputs into understandable insights.

In healthcare, interpretability is essential for trust and validation, transparency ensures ethical AI deployment, and explainability bridges the gap between black-box models and human understanding.

3.3.2   TYPES OF INTERPRETABILITIES: GLOBAL VS. LOCAL

- **Global Interpretability** refers to understanding the overall behavior of an AI model. It provides insights into how the model processes inputs and makes decisions across all cases. Techniques include:
  - **Feature Importance Analysis**: Identifying which features influence predictions the most.
  - **Decision Trees & Rule-Based Models**: Simplifying model logic for interpretability.
  - **Surrogate Models**: Using simpler models (e.g., linear regression) to approximate complex models.
- **Local Interpretability** focuses on explaining individual predictions rather than the entire model. It helps clinicians understand why a specific decision was made for a particular patient. Techniques include:
  - **LIME (Local Interpretable Model-agnostic Explanations)**: Generates interpretable approximations for individual predictions.

- **SHAP (SHapley Additive exPlanations)**: Assigns contributions of each feature to a specific decision.
- **Counterfactual Explanations**: Shows how slight input changes affect the outcome.

Both global and local interpretability are crucial in healthcare AI, ensuring trust, accuracy, and ethical decision-making (summarized in Table 3.1).

3.3.3 TECHNIQUES FOR INTERPRETABLE AI MODELS

Interpretable AI models in healthcare use various techniques to ensure transparency and understanding. These techniques can be categorized into intrinsic (built-in interpretability) and post-hoc (applied after model training) (Kamath & Liu, 2021).

Intrinsic Interpretability (Models Designed for Interpretability)
- **Decision Trees**: Simple tree structures that clearly show decision paths.
- **Linear and Logistic Regression**: Assigns weights to features, making their impact easy to interpret.
- **Rule-Based Models**: Uses if-then rules to provide transparent decision-making.

Post-Hoc Interpretability (Explaining Complex Models)
- **Feature Importance Analysis**: Identifies key factors influencing predictions.
- **LIME (Local Interpretable Model-agnostic Explanations)**: Generates local approximations of complex models.

TABLE 3.1
Summarization of Global vs. Local Interpretabilities in Healthcare

Aspect	Global Interpretability in Healthcare	Local Interpretability in Healthcare
Definition	Explains overall model behavior across all patients	Explains individual patient-level predictions
Scope	Population-level insight	Single-patient insight
Goal	Understand general trends and feature influence in diagnosis or risk	Understand the reasoning behind a specific diagnosis or prediction
Example Use Case	Identifying key risk factors for heart disease across all patients	Explaining why a patient was predicted to have high heart disease risk
Interpretability Tools	Feature importance, partial dependence plots, decision trees	SHAP (local), LIME, counterfactual explanations
Granularity	Generalized view of feature influence	Specific explanation for one patient
Regulatory Role	Supports model validation and auditing	Supports transparency for clinicians and patients
Stakeholders Benefited	Researchers, policymakers, healthcare administrators	Clinicians, patients, caregivers
Computation Cost	Usually lower (analyzed once per model)	Higher (analyzed for each patient prediction)

- **SHAP (SHapley Additive exPlanations)**: Assigns contributions of each feature to individual predictions.
- **Counterfactual Explanations**: Shows how slight input changes affect outcomes.
- **Saliency Maps**: Visualizes important areas in medical images influencing AI decisions.

By combining these techniques, AI models in healthcare become more interpretable, fostering trust, accountability, and improved decision-making.

3.4   REGULATORY AND ETHICAL IMPLICATIONS

In healthcare AI, ethical and regulatory factors guarantee patient safety, equity, and adherence to regulations such as GDPR and HIPAA. To avoid bias and mistakes, ethical AI needs to be open, objective, and interpretable. In order to ensure that AI supports medical decision-making without jeopardizing patient rights or data privacy, regulatory frameworks encourage accountability (Alam et al., 2023; Moorthy et al., 2025; Rasheed et al., 2022).

3.4.1   Compliance with Healthcare Standards (e.g., HIPAA, GDPR, FDA)

AI in healthcare must adhere to established regulations to ensure patient safety, data privacy, and ethical use. Key standards include:

- **HIPAA (Health Insurance Portability and Accountability Act)**: Protects patient data privacy and security in the U.S.A.
- **GDPR (General Data Protection Regulation)**: Ensures data protection and patient consent in the EU.
- **FDA (Food and Drug Administration) Regulations**: Governs AI-based medical devices and software for safety and efficacy.
- **ISO 13485**: Standard for quality management in medical device software, including AI applications.
- **Ethical AI Guidelines**: Promoted by organizations like the WHO and IEEE to ensure fairness, transparency, and accountability.

Compliance with these standards ensures AI systems are reliable, ethical, and legally acceptable in healthcare.

3.4.2   Ethical Considerations in Transparent AI Systems

Ensuring ethical AI in healthcare requires transparency to build trust, fairness, and accountability. Key ethical considerations include:

- **Patient Privacy and Data Security**: Transparent AI must protect sensitive patient data while complying with regulations like HIPAA and GDPR.

- **Bias and Fairness**: AI systems should be trained on diverse, representative datasets to prevent biases that could lead to unfair treatment.
- **Accountability and Responsibility**: Clear documentation of AI decision-making ensures accountability for errors or adverse outcomes.
- **Informed Consent**: Patients should understand AI-assisted decisions affecting their care and have the right to question or reject AI recommendations.
- **Trust and Explainability**: Transparent AI fosters trust by providing interpretable, understandable explanations for medical decisions.

By addressing these ethical considerations, AI systems can enhance healthcare while ensuring fairness, safety, and regulatory compliance.

3.4.3 BIAS, FAIRNESS, AND ACCOUNTABILITY

- **Bias**: AI models can inherit biases from unbalanced training data, leading to disparities in healthcare outcomes. Bias can arise from factors such as race, gender, or socioeconomic status, affecting diagnosis and treatment recommendations. Mitigating bias requires diverse, representative datasets, and continuous monitoring.
- **Fairness**: AI must provide equitable healthcare outcomes across different patient populations. Fairness ensures that no group is disadvantaged due to algorithmic decisions. Techniques like bias audits, fairness-aware algorithms, and transparency measures help promote ethical AI use.
- **Accountability**: Clear responsibility for AI decisions is crucial in healthcare. Clinicians, developers, and institutions must ensure AI recommendations are explainable, auditable, and aligned with medical standards. Regulatory compliance and ethical oversight help maintain accountability and patient safety.

3.5 BALANCING ACCURACY, TRANSPARENCY, AND INTERPRETABILITY

3.5.1 THE TRADE-OFF BETWEEN PERFORMANCE AND INTERPRETABILITY

The trade-off between interpretability and model performance is crucial in healthcare systems. Although high-performance models, such as deep neural networks, frequently attain higher accuracy in tasks like diagnosis or prediction, they function as "black-boxes," which reduces physicians' confidence and comprehension. On the other hand, interpretable models, such as logistic regression or decision trees, provide clarity and simplicity of explanation, but they might not perform as well on complicated datasets. Clinical decision-making is impacted by this trade-off since explainability is required by ethical and regulatory requirements to guarantee patient safety and accountability. Using hybrid techniques (like XAI) that improve interpretability without materially sacrificing accuracy is one way to strike a balance between the two. In the end, effective integration into healthcare necessitates models that not only function effectively but also offer precise, useful information to back up clinical decisions.

3.5.2 CHALLENGES IN MAKING DEEP LEARNING MODELS TRANSPARENT

Making deep learning models transparent in healthcare is challenging due to their inherent complexity and black-box nature. These models involve numerous nonlinear layers and parameters, making it difficult to trace how specific predictions are made. This lack of interpretability hinders clinicians' trust and limits adoption in safety-critical decisions. Additionally, medical data is often heterogeneous and noisy, complicating the explanation process. Regulatory demands for accountability and explainability further heighten the need for transparency. Techniques like saliency maps or attention mechanisms offer partial insights but often lack clinical relevance. Bridging this gap requires developing interpretable models without sacrificing diagnostic accuracy.

3.5.3 CASE EXAMPLES OF BALANCING ACCURACY AND INTERPRETABILITY

Numerous case studies demonstrate attempts to strike a compromise between interpretability and accuracy in the medical field. The application of logistic regression models to the prediction of sepsis is one prominent example. Hospitals frequently favors interpretable models, such as logistic regression or decision trees, which enable doctors to comprehend and have confidence in the risk variables influencing alarms, even though more sophisticated models, such as deep neural networks, offer marginally better predictive accuracy.

Another illustration is Google's DeepMind project, which employs deep learning to accurately analyze retinal scans in order to detect diabetic retinopathy. The technique uses heatmaps to visually explain which aspects of the image affected the diagnosis in order to allay worries about transparency. This balances explainability and performance, assisting ophthalmologists in validating the system's output. A third example is the use of gradient boosting and rule-based models in clinical decision support systems for antibiotic prescriptions. To get high accuracy and actionable insights, researchers integrated machine learning ensembles with interpretable decision rules, empowering doctors to make well-informed choices. Lastly, hybrid methods, such as attention-based networks in radiology reports, provide clinicians with an interpretable justification for decisions by connecting picture regions with textual interpretations. These case studies demonstrate how adopting and fostering trust in AI-driven healthcare solutions may be achieved by fusing interpretability strategies with precise models.

3.6 TECHNIQUES FOR ENHANCING TRANSPARENCY AND INTERPRETABILITY

Techniques for enhancing transparency and interpretability in healthcare AI include model simplification using decision trees or linear regression, feature importance analysis to identify key factors, and post-hoc methods like LIME and SHAP for explaining complex models. Audit trails, documentation, and visual explanations, such as saliency maps, ensure accountability and trust (Barnes & Hutson, 2024; Lenaers & De Moor, 2023; Garg et. al., 2024).

3.6.1   FEATURE IMPORTANCE METHODS (E.G., **SHAP, LIME**)

Feature importance methods help identify which input variables most influence an AI model's predictions, enhancing interpretability in healthcare applications. Key techniques include:

- **Permutation Importance**: Measures feature impact by randomly shuffling values and observing changes in model performance.
- **SHAP (SHapley Additive exPlanations)**: Assigns contribution values to each feature based on cooperative game theory.
- **LIME (Local Interpretable Model-agnostic Explanations)**: Creates simplified models to approximate feature influence on individual predictions.
- **Gradient-Based Methods**: Uses gradients to determine how input features affect model output, often used in neural networks.

These techniques improve AI transparency, helping clinicians understand and trust AI-driven medical decisions.

3.6.2   ATTENTION MECHANISMS AND SALIENCY MAPS

Attention mechanisms and **saliency maps** enhance interpretability in AI, particularly in deep learning models used for healthcare.

- **Attention Mechanisms**: Used in models like transformers, these mechanisms assign varying importance to different input features, allowing AI to focus on the most relevant information in tasks like medical image analysis or clinical text processing.
- **Saliency Maps**: Visual representations that highlight the most influential regions in an input image or dataset. In medical imaging, saliency maps help explain AI decisions by showing which areas of an X-ray, MRI, or CT scan contributed most to a diagnosis.

These techniques improve transparency, aiding clinicians in validating AI-driven medical insights.

3.6.3   RULE-BASED AND HYBRID APPROACHES FOR INTERPRETABILITY

Rule-based and hybrid approaches combine traditional logic-driven methods with AI to enhance interpretability in healthcare applications.

- **Rule-Based Models**: Use predefined if-then rules for decision-making, ensuring transparency and easy validation. Examples include expert systems and decision trees, which are widely used in clinical diagnosis.

- **Hybrid Approaches**: Combine interpretable models with complex AI techniques. Examples include:
  - **Neuro-Symbolic AI**: Integrates neural networks with symbolic reasoning for explainable decision-making.
  - **Post-Hoc Rule Extraction**: Derives human-readable rules from deep learning models.
  - **Model-Agnostic Approaches**: Use techniques like LIME or SHAP to interpret complex black-box models.

These approaches ensure AI-driven healthcare decisions are understandable, reliable, and aligned with clinical expertise.

3.7 IMPACT ON CLINICAL DECISION-MAKING AND PATIENT TRUST

XAI enhances clinical decision-making by providing transparent, interpretable insights that help doctors validate AI recommendations, reducing errors and bias. It also fosters patient trust, as clear explanations of AI-driven diagnoses and treatments improve understanding, confidence, and acceptance of AI-assisted healthcare solutions, ensuring ethical and reliable care (Antoniadi et al., 2021; Bawa et al., 2024; Bhambri & Rani, 2024; Kaur & Saini, 2023; Lesley & Kuratomi Hernández, 2024; Saini & Preeti, 2024).

3.7.1 HOW TRANSPARENCY INFLUENCES CLINICIAN ADOPTION OF AI

The willingness of clinicians to use AI in healthcare is greatly influenced by transparency. Clinicians can trust and validate AI models' recommendations when they offer transparent, interpretable decision-making processes that adhere to medical best practices. Transparent AI lowers skepticism and boosts confidence in AI-assisted decisions by enabling medical professionals to comprehend the rationale behind and methodology of a diagnosis or recommended course of treatment. Transparency also aids in bias reduction and error detection, guaranteeing reliability and equity in patient care. Adoption is further supported by ethical accountability and regulatory compliance, since physicians are more inclined to employ AI that complies with professional and legal requirements. Transparent AI ultimately improves human-machine collaboration, resulting in safer and more efficient clinical decision-making.

3.7.2 BUILDING TRUST THROUGH INTERPRETABLE AI

The ability of AI-driven healthcare to deliver trustworthy, comprehensible, and transparent insights is what builds trust. By assisting patients and clinicians in comprehending the decision-making process, interpretable AI allays concerns related to black-box models. By increasing the transparency of AI outputs, methods such as SHAP, LIME, and rule-based models facilitate improved validation and acceptance. Interpretable AI helps patients make educated decisions and gives them confidence in AI-assisted diagnosis and care. Because they can evaluate AI recommendations before implementing them in patient care, clinicians gain more authority and accountability. Furthermore, by guaranteeing ethical AI use, regulatory compliance with laws like HIPAA and GDPR strengthens trust. AI systems can increase trust, dependability, and long-term adoption in the healthcare industry by putting interpretability first.

3.7.3 The Role of Explainability in Patient-Centric Healthcare

Explainability in AI ensures that patients understand and trust AI-assisted healthcare decisions. A patient-centric approach requires that AI models provide clear, interpretable explanations for diagnoses, treatment recommendations, and risk assessments. This transparency empowers patients to make informed decisions about their health, improving engagement and adherence to medical advice. XAI also enhances doctor-patient communication, allowing clinicians to clarify how AI arrived at a specific conclusion. This reduces skepticism and fosters trust in AI-driven care. Furthermore, explainability helps address ethical concerns by ensuring fairness, bias detection, and regulatory compliance. By integrating explainability into healthcare AI, providers can enhance patient satisfaction, safety, and personalized treatment, ultimately leading to better health outcomes and a more trustworthy healthcare system.

3.8 CASE STUDIES AND REAL-WORLD APPLICATIONS

AI-driven healthcare applications demonstrate the impact of transparency and interpretability. Examples include IBM Watson Health, which assists in oncology treatment by providing explainable recommendations, and Google's DeepMind, which enhances kidney disease prediction with interpretable AI. These cases highlight how XAI improves clinical trust, decision-making, and patient outcomes (Chattopadhyay et al., 2025; Saraswat et al., 2022).

3.8.1 Examples of Transparent AI in Medical Diagnostics

- **IBM Watson Health**: Uses AI to analyze medical literature and provide explainable treatment recommendations for oncology.
- **Google DeepMind's Kidney Disease Prediction**: Provides interpretable alerts for acute kidney injury, allowing early intervention.
- **Zebra Medical Vision**: Uses AI to detect abnormalities in medical imaging with transparent reporting for radiologists.
- **Qure.ai**: AI-powered chest X-ray analysis tool offering explainable insights to support radiologists in diagnosing lung diseases.
- **PathAI**: Enhances pathology diagnosis by providing interpretable AI-driven insights into cancer detection.

These AI models prioritize **interpretability, clinician trust, and regulatory compliance**, ensuring safe and effective medical diagnostics.

3.8.2   EXPLAINABLE AI IN DRUG DISCOVERY AND TREATMENT PLANS

XAI is revolutionizing drug discovery and personalized treatment by making AI-driven insights more transparent and interpretable.

- **BenevolentAI**: Uses XAI to identify potential drug candidates by analyzing biomedical data, ensuring explainable results for researchers.
- **Atomwise**: Employs AI to predict drug-target interactions, with interpretable models helping scientists understand molecular behaviors.
- **IBM Watson for Drug Discovery**: Analyzes scientific literature and clinical trial data to suggest promising treatments while providing clear reasoning.
- **Tempus**: Uses explainable AI to personalize cancer treatment plans by analyzing genetic and clinical data.

By enhancing transparency, XAI improves trust, regulatory compliance, and clinical adoption, accelerating drug development and optimizing patient care.

3.8.3   SUCCESS STORIES AND LESSONS LEARNED

Success Stories
- **Google DeepMind and NHS (Kidney Disease Prediction)**: AI accurately predicted acute kidney injury 48 hours in advance, improving early intervention. Lesson: **Interpretable AI enhances clinician trust and proactive care**.
- **IBM Watson for Oncology**: Assisted doctors by providing AI-driven, evidence-based cancer treatment recommendations. Lesson: **Explainability is key for AI adoption in critical care**.
- **Qure.ai (Chest X-ray Interpretation)**: Improved tuberculosis and pneumonia detection in under-resourced regions. Lesson: **Transparent AI bridges healthcare gaps and supports global health initiatives**.

Lessons Learned
- **AI must be interpretable** for clinician adoption.
- **Bias and data limitations** can impact AI accuracy, requiring ongoing monitoring.
- **Regulatory compliance** ensures safe AI deployment.

These cases highlight the importance of trust, transparency, and continuous improvement in healthcare AI.

3.9   CHALLENGES AND FUTURE RESEARCH DIRECTIONS

Challenges
- **Black-Box Models**: Many AI models, especially deep learning, lack interpretability, making clinical validation difficult.

- **Bias and Fairness**: AI systems can reflect biases in training data, leading to disparities in healthcare outcomes.
- **Regulatory and Ethical Barriers**: Ensuring compliance with evolving healthcare regulations like HIPAA and GDPR remains complex.
- **Data Privacy and Security**: Protecting sensitive patient data while maintaining AI transparency is a significant challenge.
- **Clinician Adoption**: Lack of trust in AI recommendations due to unclear decision-making processes.

Future Research Directions

- **Developing More Interpretable Models**: Advancing XAI techniques to balance accuracy and transparency.
- **Bias Mitigation Strategies**: Ensuring fairness through diverse datasets and bias audits.
- **Human-AI Collaboration**: Enhancing AI-assisted decision-making with clinician oversight.
- **Federated Learning**: Enabling secure AI training without compromising patient privacy.

Addressing these challenges will shape the future of ethical, transparent, and effective AI in healthcare.

3.10 CONCLUSIONS

Transparency and interpretability are essential for AI adoption in healthcare, ensuring trust, fairness, and accountability. Techniques like SHAP, LIME, saliency maps, and attention mechanisms enhance explainability, aiding clinical decision-making. Case studies, such as Google DeepMind and IBM Watson, highlight the benefits of explainable AI in diagnostics, drug discovery, and treatment planning. However, challenges like black-box models, bias, and regulatory hurdles persist. Future research should focus on developing interpretable models, mitigating bias, and improving human-AI collaboration. By addressing these challenges, AI can drive ethical, transparent, and effective healthcare advancements, ultimately improving patient outcomes and clinical trust.

The future of AI in healthcare lies in enhancing transparency, interpretability, and trust to ensure ethical and effective implementation. Advancements in XAI will focus on developing more interpretable deep learning models, improving bias detection and mitigation, and ensuring regulatory compliance with evolving standards like HIPAA and GDPR. Human-AI collaboration will be crucial, integrating AI as a supportive tool rather than a decision-maker. Additionally, federated learning and secure AI will enhance data privacy while maintaining transparency. By prioritizing fairness, accountability, and patient-centric AI, healthcare can fully harness AI's potential while ensuring safe, equitable, and reliable medical decision-making.

REFERENCES

Alam, M. N., Kaur, M., & Kabir, M. S. (2023). Explainable AI in healthcare: Enhancing transparency and trust upon legal and ethical consideration. *International Research Journal of Engineering and Technology*, *10*(6), 1–9.

Antoniadi, A.M., Du, Y., Guendouz, Y., Wei, L., Mazo, C., Becker, B.A. & Mooney, C. (2021). Current challenges and future opportunities for XAI in machine learning-based clinical decision support systems: A systematic review. *Applied Sciences*, *11*(11), 5088.

Barnes, E., & Hutson, J. (2024). Navigating the complexities of AI: The critical role of interpretability and explainability in ensuring transparency and trust. *International Journal of Multidisciplinary and Current Educational Research*, *6*(3), 248–256.

Bawa, G., Singh, H., Rani, S., Kataria, A., & Min, H. (2024). Exploring perspectives of blockchain technology and traditional centralized technology in organ donation management: A comprehensive review. *Information*, *15*(11), 703.

Bernal, J., & Mazo, C. (2022). Transparency of artificial intelligence in healthcare: Insights from professionals in computing and healthcare worldwide. *Applied Sciences*, *12*(20), 10228.

Bhambri, P., & Rani, S. (2024). Bioengineering and healthcare data analysis: Introduction, advances, and challenges. In P. Bhambri, S. Rani, & M. Fahim (Eds.), *Computational intelligence and blockchain in biomedical and health informatics* (pp. 1–25). Taylor and Francis.

Chattopadhyay, S., Barman, S., & Lakshmi, D. (2025). The role of explainable AI for healthcare 5.0: Best practices, challenges, and opportunities. In P. Raj, B. Sundaravadivazhagan, A. S. Raja & M. M. Alani (Eds.), *Edge AI for Industry 5.0 and Healthcare 5.0 Applications* (pp. 45–80). Taylor and Francis.

ElShawi, R., Sherif, Y., Al-Mallah, M., & Sakr, S. (2021). Interpretability in healthcare: A comparative study of local machine learning interpretability techniques. *Computational Intelligence*, *37*(4), 1633–1650.

Garg, P., Sharma, M. K., & Kumar, P. (2025). Transparency in diagnosis: unveiling the power of deep learning and explainable AI for medical image interpretation. *Arabian Journal for Science and Engineering*, 1–17. https://doi.org/10.1007/s13369-024-09896-5

Joyce, D. W., Kormilitzin, A., Smith, K. A., & Cipriani, A. (2023). Explainable artificial intelligence for mental health through transparency and interpretability for understandability. *npj Digital Medicine*, *6*(1), 6.

Uday Kamath, J. L. (2021). *Explainable artificial intelligence: An introduction to interpretable machine learning* (Vol. 1). Springer Cham.

Kaur, G., & Saini, H. K. (2023). An optimized resnet based plant disease identification using deep learning hypothetic function. In *2023 International Conference on Advances in Computation, Communication and Information Technology (ICAICCIT)* (pp. 58–63). IEEE.

Kumar, S., Rani, S., Sharma, S., & Min, H. (2024). Multimodality fusion aspects of medical diagnosis: A comprehensive review. *Bioengineering*, *11*(12), 1233.

Lenaers, I., & De Moor, L. (2023). Exploring XAI techniques for enhancing model transparency and interpretability in real estate rent prediction: A comparative study. *Finance Research Letters*, *58*, 104306.

Lesley, U., & Kuratomi Hernández, A. (2024). Improving XAI explanations for clinical decision-making–Physicians' perspective on local explanations in healthcare. In *International Conference on Artificial Intelligence in Medicine* (pp. 296–312). Springer.

MacDonald, S., Steven, K., & Trzaskowski, M. (2022). Interpretable AI in healthcare: Enhancing fairness, safety, and trust. In *Artificial intelligence in medicine: Applications, limitations and future directions* (pp. 241–258). Springer.

Moorthy, U. M. K., Muthukumaran, A. M. J., Kaliyaperumal, V., Jayakumar, S., & Vijayaraghavan, K. A. (2025). Explainability and regulatory compliance in healthcare: Bridging the gap for ethical XAI implementation. In A. Kumar, T. A. Kumar, P. Das, C. Sharma & A. K. Dubey (Eds.), *Explainable artificial intelligence in the healthcare industry* (pp. 521–561). Wiley Publishers.

Rani, S., Kataria, A., Bhambri, P., Pareek, P. K., & Puri, V. (2024). Artificial intelligence in personalized health services for better patient care. In S. K. Gupta, D. A. Karras & R. Natarajan (Eds.), *Revolutionizing healthcare: AI integration with IoT for enhanced patient outcomes* (pp. 89–108). Springer.

Rasheed, K., Qayyum, A., Ghaly, M., Al-Fuqaha, A., Razi, A., & Qadir, J. (2022). Explainable, trustworthy, and ethical machine learning for healthcare: A survey. *Computers in Biology and Medicine, 149*, 106043.

Saini, H. K., & Preeti. (2024). A cross design for breast cancer prediction. In A. Kumar & S. Mozar (Eds.), *International conference on communications and cyber physical engineering 2018* (pp. 125–132). Springer.

Saraswat, D., Bhattacharya, P., Verma, A., Prasad, V.K., Tanwar, S., Sharma, G., Bokoro, P. N., & Sharma, R. (2022). Explainable AI for healthcare 5.0: Opportunities and challenges. *IEEE Access, 10*, 84486–84517.

Srinivasan, K., Ramamurthy, C. K. V., Matheswaran, S., & Shamsudheen, S. (2025). Introduction to explainable AI in healthcare: Enhancing transparency and trust. In *Explainable artificial intelligence in the healthcare industry* (pp. 161–183).

4 Ethical Considerations in Implementing Explainable AI in Healthcare

4.1 INTRODUCTION

In order to responsibly develop and apply artificial intelligence (AI) in healthcare, ethics is essential. Ethical considerations make sure AI systems follow medical norms and human values as they have a greater and greater impact on clinical judgments, diagnosis, and patient care. Fairness, transparency, data security, and patient privacy are important issues (Karimian et al., 2022). AI can worsen pre-existing prejudices, jeopardize patient autonomy, and result in unequal access to care if ethical supervision is not in place. Because ethical frameworks encourage accountability and well-informed decision-making, they aid in the development of trust between patients and healthcare professionals. They also encourage adherence to legal and regulatory requirements. Stakeholders should minimize dangers and optimize AI's benefits by putting ethics first, guaranteeing that technical developments support patient-centered, safe, and equitable healthcare. In the end, the equitable and sustainable use of AI systems in medical practice depends on the incorporation of ethical concepts (Nasir et al., 2024).

Explainability is essential to ethical AI, especially in the medical field, where choices have a big influence on patient outcomes. It makes it possible for patients and healthcare professionals to comprehend how and why an AI system makes particular judgments or suggestions. Clinicians can verify AI-driven insights against medical knowledge and patient context thanks to this transparency, which also promotes trust and informed consent. Additionally, explainability improves accountability and justice by assisting in the identification and correction of biases or inaccuracies. Without it, AI systems run the risk of turning into "black-boxes," which would restrict supervision and compromise moral values like justice and autonomy. Therefore, guaranteeing the explainability of AI helps to safeguard moral integrity and encourages ethical practices in patient care. There are a number of ethical issues with AI implementation in healthcare that need to be resolved to guarantee its safe and equitable application. Two major issues are bias and fairness, as biased training data may cause AI to exacerbate already-existing healthcare disparities. Although many AI models are still opaque, transparency and explainability are crucial for preserving trust and assisting in clinical decision-making. Accountability is another significant problem; it might be difficult to assign blame when AI advice results in harm. Given the delicate nature of medical data used to train AI systems, privacy and data security are essential. Furthermore, it is necessary to preserve patient autonomy, which calls for informed consent and open communication. Resolving

DOI: 10.1201/9781003561422-4

these issues is essential to incorporating AI into healthcare procedures in an ethical manner (Khan et al., 2024).

4.2 PRINCIPLES OF ETHICAL AI IN HEALTHCARE

Principles such as beneficence, which ensures that AI promotes patient well-being; non-maleficence, which prevents harm; autonomy, which supports informed patient choices; justice, which ensures fair and equitable access; and transparency, which fosters understanding and trust, serve as the foundation for ethical AI in healthcare (Currie et al., 2020; Elendu et al., 2023; Karimian et al., 2022; Kumar et al., 2024; Rani et al., 2024). By protecting patient rights, building trust, and improving the standard and equity of healthcare delivery, these guidelines aid in bringing AI systems into compliance with fundamental medical ethics and encouraging responsible innovation (Figure 4.1).

4.2.1 TRANSPARENCY AND ACCOUNTABILITY

In the healthcare industry, where decisions have the potential to impact patient lives, transparency and accountability are essential components of ethical AI. By ensuring that AI systems are comprehensible, transparency enables patients and physicians to comprehend the decision-making process. This promotes informed consent, fosters confidence, and makes it possible to compare AI results to medical expertise. Accountability entails outlining precisely who is responsible for AI-driven results and making sure that institutions, developers, and suppliers can be held accountable

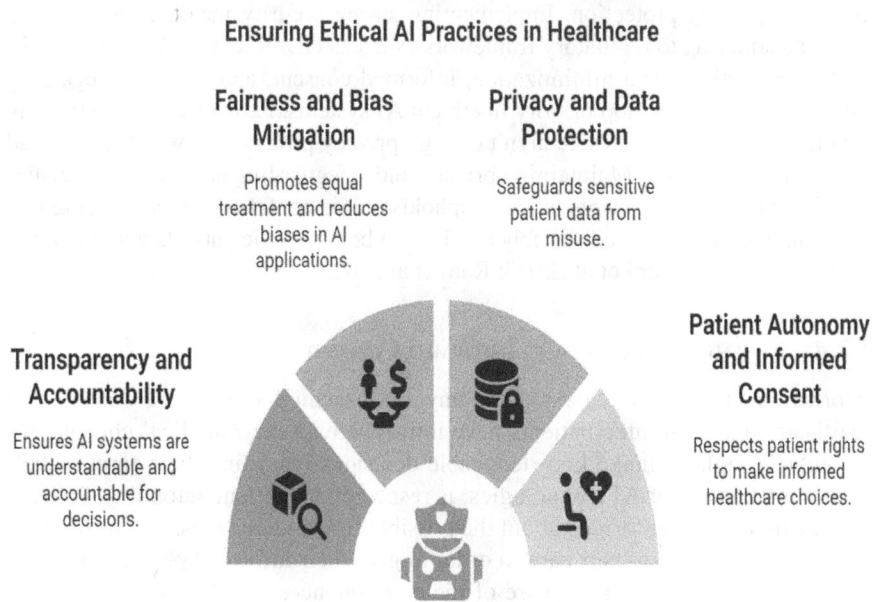

Ensuring Ethical AI Practices in Healthcare

Fairness and Bias Mitigation
Promotes equal treatment and reduces biases in AI applications.

Privacy and Data Protection
Safeguards sensitive patient data from misuse.

Transparency and Accountability
Ensures AI systems are understandable and accountable for decisions.

Patient Autonomy and Informed Consent
Respects patient rights to make informed healthcare choices.

FIGURE 4.1   Ethical AI principles: emphasizing healthcare.

for mistakes or damage. Without these guidelines, AI might function as a "black-box," eroding ethical supervision and confidence. Including accountability and openness in the development and application of AI encourages responsible use, protects patient rights, and ensures that AI technologies improve rather than lower the standard of healthcare.

4.2.2   FAIRNESS AND BIAS MITIGATION

In the healthcare industry, where disparate results can have a direct influence on patient lives, fairness and bias reduction are essential ethical AI principles. Fairness guarantees that AI systems treat various populations equally, irrespective of their socioeconomic background, gender, color, or other characteristics. However, existing healthcare disparities may be unintentionally reinforced by AI models trained on insufficient or biased data. Finding, evaluating, and resolving these imbalances at every stage of the AI lifecycle—from data collection to model deployment—is known as bias mitigation. Diverse datasets, inclusive design principles, and continuous observation are necessary for this. Healthcare AI can promote fair and equal treatment, build patient trust, and guarantee that advancements benefit all people, not just a few, by emphasizing equity and actively reducing bias.

4.2.3   PRIVACY AND DATA PROTECTION

In the healthcare industry, where sensitive patient data is utilized to train and run AI systems, privacy and data protection are fundamental ethical AI concepts. Protecting private health information from misuse, disclosure, or illegal access is known as privacy protection. Implementing strong security measures, encrypting data, and adhering to regulatory frameworks such as GDPR and HIPAA are all part of data protection. Data minimization, informed consent, and openness regarding data use must be given top priority in ethical AI systems. Patients may stop trusting digital health products if there aren't enough privacy protections, which could lead to underuse and injury. Maintaining privacy and safeguarding data not only satisfies moral and legal requirements but also upholds public confidence, guaranteeing that AI technologies are applied sensibly and benefit both specific patients and the larger healthcare system (Rani et al., 2023; Rani et al., 2024).

4.2.4   PATIENT AUTONOMY AND INFORMED CONSENT

Informed consent and patient autonomy are essential ethical AI concepts in healthcare that guarantee patients have influence over their medical choices. An individual's right to make knowledgeable decisions regarding their care, including the application of AI technologies, is respected by patient autonomy. Patients must be thoroughly informed about the possible risks, advantages, and limitations of using AI systems in their care in order to give their informed permission. This guarantees that patients are aware of the consequences of AI-driven judgments, empowering them to make decisions that are consistent with their preferences and values. In order to reinforce patients' autonomy, ethical AI systems must give them easily understandable information and give them the option to opt in or out. Maintaining trust, defending patient rights, and making sure AI interventions support patient-centered care rather than compromise it all depend on upholding these principles.

4.3   REGULATORY AND LEGAL FRAMEWORKS

Explainable AI (XAI) in healthcare complies with ethical and legal requirements thanks to regulatory and legal frameworks. Data protection rules that protect patient privacy, such as GDPR and HIPAA, are important frameworks. AI tools employed in clinical settings are also subject to medical device laws, such as those laid forth by the FDA. These frameworks promote confidence and guarantee adherence to healthcare standards by assisting in ensuring XAI systems are transparent, accountable, and safe.

4.3.1   COMPLIANCE WITH HEALTHCARE LAWS

Strict healthcare standards such as the FDA (Food and Drug Administration), GDPR (General Data Protection Regulation), and HIPAA (Health Insurance Portability and Accountability Act) must be followed while implementing XAI in the healthcare industry (Cohen & Mello, 2018; Data, 2018; Khunte et al., 2023). Patient data protection is required under HIPAA, which also makes sure AI systems used in healthcare follow stringent security and confidentiality guidelines. GDPR emphasizes transparency in the way AI systems utilize personal data and regulates data privacy by requiring informed consent for data processing. To guarantee the safety and effectiveness of medical equipment, including AI technologies, the FDA regulates their use. Respecting these regulations is essential to preserving patient confidence, safeguarding private information, and making sure XAI systems adhere to strict safety, privacy, and ethical responsibility requirements.

4.3.2   ETHICAL GUIDELINES FROM MEDICAL AND AI REGULATORY BODIES

To guarantee the proper use of AI in healthcare, medical, and AI regulatory authorities offer ethical principles. To guarantee safety, efficacy, and transparency, the FDA requires medical AI devices to undergo stringent testing and validation. The World Health Organisation (WHO) advocates for AI ethics that put accountability, equity, and privacy first. Transparency, equity, and non-discrimination in AI systems are the main goals of IEEE and the EU's AI Act. In order to promote confidence and well-informed decision-making, these principles highlight the necessity of explainability in AI models. It is advised that AI systems be continuously monitored and audited in order to guarantee adherence to moral principles, lessen prejudice, and safeguard patient rights. These rules guarantee that developments in AI are consistent with moral standards and uphold public confidence (Kaur & Saini, 2023; Mennella et al., 2024; Saini et al., 2022; Saini & Preeti, 2024).

4.3.3   The Role of Institutional Review Boards (IRBs) in AI Deployment

Institutional Review Boards (IRBs) are essential for monitoring the moral implications of using AI in healthcare. In order to make sure that studies incorporating AI systems adhere to ethical norms, patient rights, and legal requirements, they evaluate and approve AI-driven research. IRBs evaluate the possible dangers of AI technology, paying particular attention to data security, informed consent, and patient privacy. Additionally, they assess how fair AI systems are, making sure that prejudices are reduced and that the technology benefits a range of demographics equally. IRBs contribute to patient safety and public confidence in AI advancements by making sure AI applications adhere to legal and ethical requirements. They play a crucial part in making sure AI technologies are applied in healthcare settings in a responsible and moral manner (Lorente, 2024).

4.4   BIAS AND FAIRNESS IN EXPLAINABLE AI

When it comes to XAI in healthcare, bias and fairness are major issues. Unfair results, particularly for underrepresented groups, might result from AI algorithms unintentionally learning and reinforcing biases from biased training data. Designing AI systems that treat all patients fairly, irrespective of their socioeconomic background, gender, or ethnicity, is essential to ensuring fairness. Preventing biased outcomes requires the use of bias mitigation techniques, such as varied datasets and algorithmic modifications. XAI is essential because it makes decision-making transparent, helps detect and address biases, and builds confidence in AI systems while advancing moral, just treatment (González-Sendino et al., 2024).

4.4.1   Sources of Bias in Healthcare AI Models

AI models used in healthcare may be biased for a number of reasons. One major contributing element is data bias, whereby previous medical data may mirror social injustices, which AI systems may then perpetuate. When datasets lack variety, they underrepresent particular demographic groups, including minority populations, which compromises the accuracy and fairness of the model. This is known as sampling bias. AI predictions may be skewed by labeling bias, which can arise from subjective or inconsistent human annotation of medical data. The model's design may introduce algorithmic bias, whereby some qualities or variables are given more weight than others, inadvertently disadvantageous to particular groups. When data is being collected, selection bias may occur because some patients or conditions are more likely to be included than others. To guarantee that AI models produce fair, accurate, and equitable healthcare outcomes, these biases must be addressed (Celi et al., 2022).

4.4.2   Strategies for Detecting and Mitigating Bias

A multimodal strategy is necessary to identify and mitigate bias in healthcare AI. To avoid underrepresentation, databases must be representative and diverse, encompassing a range of demographic groupings like socioeconomic status, gender, and race. To find discrepancies in AI predictions and results, bias detection techniques might be used. Finding hidden biases is aided by routine audits and fairness assessments of AI algorithms. Bias mitigation strategies can rectify imbalances by changing the algorithm or reweighting training data. Furthermore, XAI's algorithmic openness enables stakeholders to examine decision-making procedures and spot bias. AI systems are guaranteed to be in line with moral principles and human values through cooperation with domain specialists, such as ethicists, medical professionals, and impacted communities. Last but not least, putting in place ongoing monitoring throughout the AI system's lifecycle guarantees that any biases that surface are quickly rectified. These tactics support the advancement of justice, equity, and confidence in AI applications for healthcare (Chen et al., 2024; Shrestha et al., 2022).

4.4.3 CASE STUDIES OF BIAS IN MEDICAL AI AND CORRECTIVE MEASURES

- **Recidivism Prediction Model (COMPAS) in Criminal Justice**: While not healthcare-specific, COMPAS highlighted biases in AI models. It disproportionately flagged African-American defendants as high-risk. **Corrective measures** included better data diversity, recalibration of algorithms, and the use of explainability tools to identify decision drivers.
- **Dermatology AI for Skin Cancer Diagnosis**: An AI model trained primarily on light-skinned patients performed poorly on dark-skinned individuals, leading to misdiagnoses. **Corrective measures** included diversifying the training dataset to include more images of diverse skin tones and incorporating fairness constraints to balance model performance across groups.
- **Commercial Health Risk Algorithms**: A widely used health risk algorithm in the U.S.A. was found to underestimate the health risks of Black patients, exacerbating disparities in healthcare. **Corrective measures** involved recalibrating the algorithm to account for race and socioeconomic factors more accurately, as well as continuous monitoring for fairness.

These case studies underline the importance of addressing bias to ensure that AI models provide equitable healthcare outcomes for all populations.

4.5 BALANCING EXPLAINABILITY AND PERFORMANCE

In AI, especially in the healthcare industry, striking a balance between explainability and performance is a major difficulty. High-performance models, such as deep learning, frequently function as "black-boxes," offering precise outcomes but little information about how decisions are made. However, therapeutic adoption may be hampered and trust damaged by this lack of openness. However, simpler models may compromise performance in favor of greater interpretability. Integrating XAI methods with intricate models is necessary to strike the ideal balance between improving transparency and maintaining predictive ability. This guarantees the reliability and efficacy of AI systems, promoting improved health outcomes and decision-making while upholding moral principles (Acharya et al., 2024; Silva et al., 2024).

4.6 THE TRADE-OFF BETWEEN MODEL ACCURACY AND INTERPRETABILITY

Finding a balance between model accuracy and interpretability is a major difficulty in AI, particularly in the healthcare industry. Complex models, such as deep learning, process vast datasets and identify complex patterns to achieve high accuracy, but they are frequently challenging to interpret, making it challenging for healthcare professionals to comprehend the rationale behind judgments. Simpler models, such as decision trees, on the other hand, are easier to understand but might not be accurate enough for intricate medical tasks. XAI approaches, which improve the interpretability of complex models while reducing performance loss, must be incorporated to strike a compromise. This promotes clinician trust and upholds the highest ethical standards in patient care by guaranteeing AI systems are accurate and transparent.

4.7 ETHICAL IMPLICATIONS OF BLACK-BOX AI IN CRITICAL MEDICAL DECISIONS

There are serious ethical issues with using black-box AI to make important medical choices. Even though these AI models frequently produce very accurate results, their lack of transparency makes it difficult for physicians to completely comprehend the decision-making process, which makes it more difficult to validate AI-driven recommendations. Because patients might not be aware of how AI affects their care, this compromises patient autonomy. Because black-box models may reinforce biases in the data without obvious accountability, they also run the danger of bias and discrimination. Furthermore, if patients or healthcare professionals are unable to confirm the legitimacy and fairness of AI choices, faith in the healthcare system may decline. Explainable models are necessary for the ethical application of AI in order to guarantee accountability, transparency, and conformity to medical norms, protecting patient rights and encouraging fair, well-informed healthcare choices.

4.7.1 STRATEGIES FOR ENHANCING BOTH EXPLAINABILITY AND PREDICTIVE POWER

Increasing AI's explainability and predictive capacity calls for a mix of tactics. Transparency and high performance can be achieved by combining interpretable models, such as rule-based systems or decision trees, with more complicated models. XAI methods like LIME and SHAP can be used to explain individual predictions without sacrificing overall accuracy in complex models like deep learning. Additionally, by deciding which attributes are most crucial, model simplification can be used to achieve a balance between reducing complexity and maintaining crucial predictive power. Accuracy and ethics are ensured by bias identification and mitigation, which also promotes fairness and transparency. High performance is maintained while explainability is guaranteed by routine validation and monitoring, which promotes acceptance and confidence in crucial areas like healthcare.

4.8 PATIENT-CENTRIC AI AND SHARED DECISION-MAKING

When making healthcare decisions, patient-centric AI gives patients' needs, preferences, and values top priority. AI assists therapists in clearly and understandably presenting treatment alternatives by offering transparent, explainable insights. This promotes shared decision-making, in which patients actively participate in conversations on their treatment to make sure that decisions reflect their beliefs and well-informed preferences. In the end, AI tools foster collaboration and increase patient autonomy while also assisting physicians in delivering evidence-based solutions. Patient-centric AI, which prioritizes individualized treatment, gives people the ability to make knowledgeable decisions, enhancing trust and overall healthcare results while upholding the rights and dignity of patients (Haldorai & Ramu, 2021; Kaur, 2024; Rosenbacke et al., 2024).

4.8.1 THE ROLE OF EXPLAINABILITY IN PATIENT TRUST AND ENGAGEMENT

Explainability plays a crucial role in building patient trust and engagement with AI in healthcare. When AI systems provide transparent, understandable explanations for their recommendations, patients are more likely to trust the process and feel empowered to make informed decisions. Clear explanations enable patients to comprehend how AI influences their care, addressing concerns about fairness, safety, and accuracy. This fosters a sense of control, allowing patients to actively participate in their healthcare journey. By ensuring that AI models are interpretable, healthcare providers can strengthen patient engagement, enhance satisfaction, and promote shared decision-making, ultimately improving health outcomes.

4.8.2 ETHICAL CHALLENGES IN AI-DRIVEN MEDICAL RECOMMENDATIONS

A number of ethical issues are brought up by AI-driven medical suggestions. Since AI models might reinforce healthcare disparities if they are trained on biased or unrepresentative data, bias and fairness are crucial concerns. Another issue is transparency, since many AI systems function as "black-boxes," which undermines confidence by making it hard for patients and physicians to comprehend how decisions are made. If AI suggestions supplant human judgment and prevent patients from making well-informed decisions, patient autonomy may likewise be at jeopardy. Furthermore, when AI makes mistakes, it becomes difficult to determine who is responsible. Because sensitive patient data is frequently involved, it is also crucial to ensure privacy and data security. Clear ethical standards and strong regulatory frameworks are necessary to address these issues and guarantee the ethical and just application of AI in healthcare.

4.8.3 CASE STUDIES IN PATIENT-INCLUSIVE AI DECISION-MAKING

- **AI for Personalized Cancer Treatment**: In a leading cancer center, AI was used to analyze genetic, clinical, and treatment data to recommend personalized treatment plans for patients. The AI provided clear, explainable

recommendations, allowing patients to actively participate in discussions about their care. By providing transparent, understandable information, patients were empowered to make informed decisions that aligned with their values, preferences, and lifestyle. This collaborative approach increased patient autonomy, improved trust in the healthcare system, and led to better outcomes as patients felt more in control of their treatment choices.
- **AI in Chronic Disease Management**: AI-powered tools were integrated into the management of chronic diseases such as diabetes. Patients used AI systems to track real-time health metrics, such as glucose levels, and received personalized recommendations for diet, exercise, and medication adjustments. These recommendations were made transparent and understandable, encouraging patients to make lifestyle changes based on the AI's insights. The tools also allowed patients to provide feedback, ensuring that their preferences were considered in decision-making. This patient-inclusive approach not only enhanced self-management but also improved overall engagement in their health journey, leading to better long-term health outcomes.

These case studies highlight the positive impact of patient-inclusive AI in decision-making, fostering transparency, autonomy, and collaboration in healthcare.

4.9 AI ACCOUNTABILITY AND LIABILITY IN HEALTHCARE

In the healthcare industry, identifying who bears responsibility when AI systems injure people or make mistakes is known as AI accountability and liability. Clear legal and ethical frameworks are crucial as AI tools help with diagnosis, therapy, and decision-making more and more. Depending on how autonomous the AI is and the type of error, developers, healthcare professionals, or institutions may be held liable. To guarantee patient safety, openness, stringent testing, and regulatory supervision are essential. Furthermore, explainability of AI decisions and informed consent support confidence. Laws and standards must be updated frequently as AI develops in order to strike a balance between innovation and responsibility in the healthcare industry (Habli et al., 2020).

4.10 WHO IS RESPONSIBLE FOR AI-DRIVEN MEDICAL DECISIONS?

Medical institutions, healthcare providers, and AI developers are just a few of the many parties involved in the complicated topic of accountability for AI-driven medical decisions. The autonomy of the AI system and its function in healthcare decision-making frequently determine the extent of accountability. The healthcare practitioner usually retains primary responsibility when AI serves as a supportive tool, aiding but not replacing human judgment. Physicians are expected to evaluate AI-generated suggestions, confirm their veracity, and make choices based on patient needs and clinical context. Failing to do so in certain situations may expose one to professional liability. However, accountability may move to developers or manufacturers when AI systems function with a high degree of autonomy or make suggestions that are not subject to human supervision. Product liability laws may hold the AI system's developers liable if failures are caused by algorithmic faults, a lack of training data, or a lack of transparency. By selecting, putting into practice, and sustaining AI technologies, healthcare organizations also share accountability. They have to guarantee appropriate instruction, moral application, and adherence to legal requirements. So, clear legal frameworks and shared responsibilities are crucial. Creating clear accountability models is essential for patient safety and legal clarity as AI is used in healthcare more and more.

4.11 ETHICAL AND LEGAL IMPLICATIONS OF AI ERRORS

AI mistakes in healthcare have serious moral and legal ramifications. They violate the ethical precepts of informed consent, autonomy, and patient safety. Patients may be harmed when AI systems provide inaccurate diagnosis or treatment suggestions because they are not fully aware of the limitations of the technology. This erodes confidence and the moral duty to "do no harm." Legally speaking, AI mistakes raise questions regarding culpability. It can be difficult to determine who is at fault—clinicians, developers, or healthcare facilities. Under product liability rules, the developers of an AI tool may be held legally liable if it malfunctions or generates biased findings. However, a doctor may be accused of professional negligence if they uncritically follow AI guidance. These difficulties require for robust regulatory monitoring, transparency in AI algorithms, and explicit legal standards. To maintain ethical and legal standards in healthcare and strike a balance between innovation and patient rights protection, it is crucial to make sure AI systems are tested, explicable, and used appropriately.

4.12 DEVELOPING RESPONSIBLE AI GOVERNANCE FRAMEWORKS

Creating policies that guarantee safety, equity, openness, and accountability is a necessary step in creating responsible AI governance frameworks in the healthcare industry. Developers, healthcare providers, and regulators are just a few of the stakeholders whose roles and duties should be clearly defined by a strong framework. Particularly in high-stakes healthcare situations, it requires strict validation, ongoing monitoring, and reporting of AI system performance.

AI development and use should be guided by ethical considerations, such as respect for patient autonomy, privacy, and equity. Explainability should be a requirement of governance frameworks so that patients and physicians can comprehend decisions made by AI. AI engagement in care must be reflected in informed consent procedures. Alignment between laws and regulations is crucial. This covers adherence to liability requirements, medical device rules, and data protection laws. Ethicists, technologists, lawyers, and physicians working together across disciplines can help create governance models that are flexible and future-proof. Finally, while protecting patient welfare and public confidence in AI-enabled healthcare systems, ethical AI governance fosters innovation.

4.13 CHALLENGES IN IMPLEMENTING ETHICAL XAI IN HEALTHCARE

There are various obstacles to overcome while implementing XAI in the healthcare industry. Because medical AI systems sometimes employ intricate algorithms, it can be challenging to give concise, intelligible justifications for their judgments. It can be challenging to strike a balance between performance and transparency because simplifying models may result in decreased accuracy. Furthermore, interdisciplinary design is necessary to guarantee that explanations have relevance for both patients and physicians. When explanations are ambiguous or deceptive, ethical questions about prejudice, data privacy, and accountability surface. Adoption is made more difficult by regulatory ambiguity and the absence of standardized explainability standards (Grover & Dogra, 2024; Ka & Khokhlov, 2024; Moorthy et al., 2025). Building trust, ensuring informed decision-making, and upholding ethical norms in AI-driven healthcare all depend on overcoming these obstacles (Figure 4.2).

4.13.1 PRACTICAL BARRIERS TO ETHICAL AI DEPLOYMENT

Data-related issues, such as restricted access to high-quality, diverse, and objective datasets, can result in skewed or dangerous findings and are practical obstacles to the ethical application of AI in healthcare. Effective application is hampered by technical issues, such as opaque models and challenges in integrating AI with current healthcare systems. Adoption is delayed by regulatory loopholes and ambiguity surrounding adherence to safety and privacy norms. Furthermore, healthcare workers could not be adequately trained to comprehend and utilize AI systems, which could result in abuse or overuse. Implementation is further slowed by institutional support gaps and financial limitations. Coordination between policy, education, and technology is necessary to overcome these obstacles and guarantee that AI solutions are applied fairly, ethically, and therapeutically.

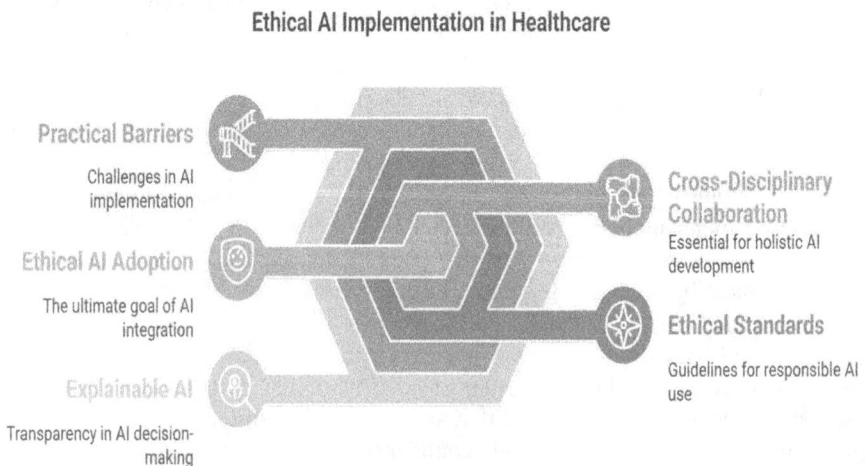

FIGURE 4.2 Major challenges in deploying XAI applications in healthcare.

4.13.2 Ensuring Ethical AI Adoption Across Healthcare Institutions

Adoption of ethical AI in healthcare organizations necessitates a thorough, multi-level strategy. Institutions must set explicit ethical standards that respect patient rights, such as responsibility, transparency, fairness, and privacy. The selection, application, and oversight of AI can be supervised by cross-disciplinary ethics committees. To avoid abuse and encourage well-informed decision-making, healthcare practitioners must be trained to comprehend AI's potential and constraints. Prior to implementation, AI systems should be evaluated for bias, accuracy, and explainability using standardized assessment frameworks. In order to handle unforeseen problems, feedback loops and ongoing monitoring must also be established. Additionally crucial are adherence to national and international standards and regulatory compliance. In the end, the secret to long-term, trust-based AI integration in healthcare is cultivating a culture of ethical awareness and accountability.

4.13.3 The Need for Cross-Disciplinary Collaboration

For AI to be developed and used in healthcare in an ethical and efficient manner, interdisciplinary cooperation is necessary. Numerous disciplines, including public policy, ethics, computer science, medicine, and law, interact with AI systems, each contributing special insights and duties. Without cooperation, AI technologies might not be ethically sound, clinically relevant, or compliant with regulations, which raises the possibility of abuse or injury. To guarantee that AI systems meet actual medical needs and operate securely inside clinical procedures, clinicians provide domain-specific expertise. Algorithms are designed and improved by data scientists and engineers, yet they cannot completely comprehend ethical or medical complexities. While legal professionals make sure that healthcare legislation, liability standards, and data protection requirements are followed, ethicists assist in guiding ethical use by emphasizing equity, patient autonomy, and openness. By combining different viewpoints, cross-disciplinary teams create well-rounded solutions that enable AI to be both creative and human-centered. Building confidence is another important benefit of this collaboration; professionals and patients are more willing to embrace AI systems that are jointly created and validated by specialists from many fields. Additionally, it encourages the development of inclusive and flexible governance frameworks and policies. To put it briefly, interdisciplinary cooperation is essential to developing safe, equitable, and reliable AI in healthcare and is not an elective.

4.14 FUTURE DIRECTIONS IN ETHICAL AI FOR HEALTHCARE

The increasing need to match technical breakthroughs with human values, equity, and safety will influence the future of ethical AI in healthcare. Improving the explainability and openness of AI systems is one important avenue. Particularly in high-stakes situations like diagnosis or treatment planning, patients and healthcare professionals need to understand how AI makes its conclusions. This promotes trust and helps people make well-informed decisions. Mitigation of bias is another major priority. To prevent escalating already-existing healthcare disparities, AI systems must be trained on a variety of representative datasets. To guarantee fair results for all demographic groups, ongoing audits and fairness checks will be crucial. The evolution of data privacy and governance will continue, with a focus on frameworks that guarantee the safe and moral use of private health data. Ideas like differential privacy and federated learning present viable ways to safeguard data while facilitating strong AI training. Additionally, patient-centered design will become more popular, guaranteeing that AI products are created with direct user input to satisfy practical clinical requirements. Ethical AI should prioritize augmentative roles over automation and enhance human judgment rather than replace it. To stay up with innovation, regulations must change. The deployment of AI will be safer and more responsible with the support of dynamic, adaptable regulations that were co-developed by engineers, physicians, ethicists, and legislators. In order to enable moral AI practices in healthcare, emerging technologies are essential. By improving the interpretability of AI decisions, XAI increases transparency. By allowing model training across dispersed data sources, federated learning protects patient privacy. By adding noise to data, differential privacy preserves usefulness while safeguarding individual identities. Blockchain provides audit trails and safe, transparent data transactions. Tools for detecting bias assist in locating and reducing unfair results for all demographic groups. Continuous performance monitoring is also made possible by AI model auditing platforms. Together, these technologies foster justice, responsibility, and trust, providing a strong basis for morally sound AI systems in the medical field. Last but not least, preventing the escalation of healthcare disparities requires advancing global fairness in AI access and capacity-building in underprivileged areas. Investing in healthcare professionals' AI literacy and education will encourage long-term incorporation of ethical AI in healthcare systems and further empower responsible use.

4.15 CONCLUSIONS

This chapter explains that while XAI has the potential to improve clinical decision-making, trust, and responsibility, its application requires close ethical consideration. In addition to making complicated models easier to understand, true explainability should include insightful information that is suited to a wide range of users, including patients, physicians, and legislators. The chapter emphasizes that, in order to adopt ethics, model bias, data quality, and openness must all be addressed without endangering patient safety or privacy.

Additionally, it emphasizes the value of stakeholder engagement, calling on developers, medical professionals, and ethicists to work together to jointly build solutions that are both technically sound and socially responsible. Because healthcare is a dynamic and high-stakes industry, XAI technologies must be rigorously validated and continuously monitored to guarantee their relevance and dependability. The chapter concludes by highlighting the necessity of strong regulatory frameworks and continual education to close the gap between ethical duties and technical capabilities. In the end, XAI must contribute to the larger objective of providing fair, human-centered care rather than just increasing technological complexity.

REFERENCES

Acharya, D. B., Divya, B., & Kuppan, K. (2024). Explainable and fair AI: Balancing performance in financial and real estate machine learning models. *IEEE Access*, *12*, 154022–154034.

Celi, L. A. et al. (2022). Sources of bias in artificial intelligence that perpetuate healthcare disparities—A global review. *PLoS Digital Health*, *1*(3), e0000022.

Chen, F., Wang, L., Hong, J., Jiang, J., & Zhou, L. (2024). Unmasking bias in artificial intelligence: A systematic review of bias detection and mitigation strategies in electronic health record-based models. *Journal of the American Medical Informatics Association*, *31*(5), 1172–1183.

Cohen, I. G., & Mello, M. M. (2018). HIPAA and protecting health information in the 21st century. *JAMA*, *320*(3), 231–232.

Currie, G., Hawk, K. E., & Rohren, E. M. (2020). Ethical principles for the application of artificial intelligence (AI) in nuclear medicine. *European Journal of Nuclear Medicine and Molecular Imaging*, *47*(4), 748–752.

Elendu, C., Amaechi, D. C., Elendu, T.C., Jingwa, K. A., Okoye, O. K., Okah, M. J., Ladele, J. A., Farah, A. H., & Alimi, H. A. (2023). Ethical implications of AI and robotics in healthcare: A review. *Medicine*, *102*(50), e36671.

González-Sendino, R., Serrano, E., & Bajo, J. (2024). Mitigating bias in artificial intelligence: Fair data generation via causal models for transparent and explainable decision-making. *Future Generation Computer Systems*, *155*, 384–401.

Grover, V., & Dogra, M. (2024). Challenges and limitations of explainable AI in healthcare. In *Analyzing explainable AI in healthcare and the pharmaceutical industry* (pp. 72–85). IGI Global.

Habli, I., Lawton, T., & Porter, Z. (2020). Artificial intelligence in health care: Accountability and safety. *Bulletin of the World Health Organization*, *98*(4), 251.

Haldorai, A., & Ramu, A. (2021). An analysis of artificial intelligence clinical decision-making and patient-centric framework. In *Computational vision and bio-inspired computing: ICCVBIC 2020* (pp. 813–827). Springer.

Ka, K., & Khokhlov, A. (2024). Ethical issues in implementing artificial intelligence in healthcare. *МЕДИЦИНСКАЯ ЭТИКА*, *2024/01*, 11–17.

Karimian, G., Petelos, E., & Evers, S. M. (2022). The ethical issues of the application of artificial intelligence in healthcare: A systematic scoping review. *AI and Ethics*, *2*(4), 539–551.

Kaur, G., & Saini, H. K. (2023). An optimized resnet based plant disease identification using deep learning hypothetic function. In *2023 International Conference on Advances in Computation, Communication and Information Technology (ICAICCIT)* (pp. 58–63). IEEE.

Kaur, J. (2024). Patient-centric AI: Advancing healthcare through human-centered innovation. In *Approaches to human-centered AI in healthcare* (pp. 1–19). IGI Global.

Khan, M. M., Shah, N., Shaikh, N., Thabet, A., & Belkhair, S. (2024). Towards secure and trusted AI in healthcare: A systematic review of emerging innovations and ethical challenges. *International Journal of Medical Informatics*, *195*, 105780.

Khunte, M., Chae, A., Wang, R., Jain, R., Sun, Y., Sollee, J.R., Jiao, Z., & Bai, H. X., (2023). Trends in clinical validation and usage of US Food and Drug Administration-cleared artificial intelligence algorithms for medical imaging. *Clinical Radiology*, *78*(2), 123–129.

Kumar, S., Rani, S., Sharma, S., & Min, H. (2024). Multimodality fusion aspects of medical diagnosis: A comprehensive review. *Bioengineering*, *11*(12), 1233.

Lorente, A. (2024). Institutional review boards as soft governance mechanisms of R&D: Governing the R&D of AI-based medical products. *arXiv preprint arXiv:2410.19574*

Mennella, C., Maniscalco, U., De Pietro, G., & Esposito, M. (2024). Ethical and regulatory challenges of AI technologies in healthcare: A narrative review. *Heliyon*, *10*(4), 1–20.

Moorthy, U. M. K., Muthukumaran, A. M. J., Kaliyaperumal, V., Jayakumar, S., & Vijayaraghavan, K. A. (2025). Explainability and regulatory compliance in healthcare: Bridging the gap for ethical XAI implementation. In A. Kumar, T. A. Kumar, P. Das, C. Sharma & A. K. Dubey (Eds.), *Explainable artificial intelligence in the healthcare industry* (pp. 521–561). Wiley Publishers.

Nasir, S., Khan, R. A., & Bai, S. (2024). Ethical framework for harnessing the power of AI in healthcare and beyond. *IEEE Access*, *12*, 31014–31035.

Rani, S., Kataria, A., Bhambri, P., Pareek, P. K., & Puri, V. (2024). Artificial intelligence in personalized health services for better patient care. In S. K. Gupta, D. A. Karras & R. Natarajan (Eds.), *Revolutionizing healthcare: AI integration with IoT for enhanced patient outcomes* (pp. 89–108). Springer.

Rani, S., Kataria, A., Kumar, S., & Tiwari, P. (2023). Federated learning for secure IoMT-applications in smart healthcare systems: A comprehensive review. *Knowledge-Based Systems*, *274*, 110658.

Rani, S., Kumar, S., Kataria, A., & Min, H. (2024). SmartHealth: An intelligent framework to secure IoMT service applications using machine learning. *ICT Express*, *10*(2), 425–430.

Regulation, P. (2018). General data protection regulation. *Intouch*, *25*, 1–5.

Rosenbacke, R., Melhus, Å., McKee, M., & Stuckler, D. (2024). How explainable artificial intelligence can increase or decrease clinicians' trust in AI applications in health care: Systematic review. *JMIR AI*, *3*, e53207.

Saini, H. K., & Preeti. (2024). A cross design for breast cancer prediction. In A. Kumar & S. Mozar (Eds.), *International conference on communications and cyber physical engineering 2018* (pp. 125–132). Springer.

Saini, H. K., Swarnakar, H., & Jain, K. (2022). Secured multimedia and IoT in healthcare computing paradigms. In B. Bhusan, S. K. Sharma, B. Unhelkar, M. F. Ijaz & L. Karim (Eds.), *Internet of Things* (pp. 229–256). CRC Press.

Shrestha, R., Kafle, K., & Kanan, C. (2022). An investigation of critical issues in bias mitigation techniques. In *Proceedings of the IEEE/CVF Winter Conference on Applications of Computer Vision* (pp. 1943–1954).

Silva, A., Tambwekar, P., Schrum, M., & Gombolay, M. (2024). Towards balancing preference and performance through adaptive personalized explainability. In *Proceedings of the 2024 ACM/IEEE International Conference on Human-Robot Interaction* (pp. 658–668).

5 Advancing Healthcare with Explainable AI
Enhancing Patient Monitoring and Outcomes

5.1 INTRODUCTION

By means of improved diagnosis accuracy, early disease identification, treatment strategy optimization, and patient monitoring enhancement, the fast development of artificial intelligence (AI) has transformed healthcare. To support clinical decision-making, AI-driven healthcare systems examine enormous volumes of data from wearable sensors, genetic profiles, medical imaging, electronic health records (EHRs), and genetic profiles. On the other hand, a lot of AI models function as "black boxes," providing little to no knowledge of how they make decisions. This lack of interpretability presents significant challenges, particularly in the healthcare industry, where transparency, accountability, and trust are essential. One of the key solutions to these issues has become explainable artificial intelligence (XAI). XAI seeks to make AI models more intelligible and interpretable so that medical practitioners may grasp the logic underlying AI-generated suggestions and predictions (Patel et al., 2024). Beyond clinical environments, explainability guarantees ethical, objective, and compliant AI-driven healthcare solutions for regulators, legislators, and patients, therefore assuring that these solutions reflect patient safety criteria. In this chapter, it is investigated how XAI can help to advance patient monitoring and outcome prediction, hence stressing its importance in enhancing healthcare decision-making and building confidence in AI systems (Ayesha & Ahamed, 2024).

5.1.1 IMPORTANCE OF XAI IN HEALTHCARE

XAI is essential in the healthcare sector since it increases transparency, accountability, and confidence in AI-driven decision-making. As AI is included in therapeutic treatments, knowledge and interpretation of model outputs becomes ever more important. Medical experts employ AI to identify diseases, project patient decline, and provide tailored treatments. Confirming information generated by AI without explainability might prove challenging for clinicians, leading to erroneous diagnosis or inadequate therapy recommendations (Rath et al., 2024). Due to XAI's clear, intelligible reasoning for AI decisions, clinicians can assess the accuracy of predictions and apply them to their medical knowledge. For instance, AI models assist radiologists in spotting medical imaging abnormalities such as fractures or malignancies. Apart from stressing the area of concern, an XAI system offers a justification for a certain diagnosis, therefore helping radiologists to validate its accuracy. Likewise, AI-powered ECG analysis in cardiology can predict cardiovascular risks and arrhythmias; XAI ensures that doctors are aware of the trends and features underlying these predictions. Apart from its therapeutic applications, XAI is absolutely essential to ensure adherence to ethical norms and legal requirements in healthcare (Wani et al., 2024). Regulatory bodies like the European Medicines Agency (EMA) and the U.S. Food and Drug Administration (FDA) agree that transparency in AI-driven medical devices is absolutely vital. Explainability is absolutely essential in obtaining regulatory clearances since it ensures that AI models operate within moral and legal limitations. Moreover, XAI encourages patient involvement and helps people to make informed healthcare decisions by providing clear arguments for AI-based diagnosis and treatment recommendations. The role of AI in patient monitoring and outcome prediction has become increasingly prominent, revolutionizing healthcare delivery by enhancing diagnostic precision, improving patient care, and facilitating predictive interventions (Poonia & Al-Alshaikh, 2024). AI leverages vast amounts of medical data from diverse sources such as EHRs, wearable devices, imaging data, and genetic information to generate actionable insights. Through sophisticated algorithms, AI processes this information rapidly, providing healthcare professionals with valuable tools for clinical decision-making, early detection of diseases, and efficient management of patient care (Saini & Preeti, 2024). One significant application of AI in patient monitoring involves continuous real-time tracking of patient vitals and symptoms, especially in chronic disease management and critical care scenarios. Wearable sensors and IoT-enabled medical devices feed continuous streams of patient data to AI systems, enabling the early identification of anomalies and potentially life-threatening conditions (Sadeghi et al., 2024). For instance, AI algorithms can accurately predict cardiac events by analyzing subtle changes in heart rhythm patterns, alerting medical teams to intervene proactively and reduce adverse outcomes significantly. Furthermore, AI-driven predictive analytics is instrumental in anticipating patient deterioration before conventional methods detect any noticeable symptoms. Machine learning algorithms analyze historical patient data to identify trends and correlations, accurately forecasting health deterioration risks such as sepsis or acute kidney injury. Figure 5.1 shows the different features of XAI in healthcare (Hosain et al., 2024; Kaur & Saini, 2023).

This predictive capability facilitates timely medical interventions, significantly improving patient outcomes and reducing hospital stays. Hospitals using AI-driven monitoring have reported decreased mortality rates and enhanced patient recovery trajectories, underscoring the transformative impact of predictive AI applications (Puri et al., 2025). In oncology, AI algorithms have shown immense promise in outcome prediction by analyzing extensive genomic, imaging, and clinical data to anticipate disease progression and treatment responses. AI-based predictive models can tailor personalized treatment plans, enhancing the precision of cancer therapies and significantly improving survival rates. Similarly, in chronic diseases such as diabetes and hypertension, AI systems continually monitor patient conditions, adjusting treatment regimens dynamically based on predicted outcomes, thus optimizing long-term patient health management. AI's role extends beyond individual patient care to broader public health applications. During pandemics, AI-driven predictive modeling supports healthcare resource allocation by forecasting infection rates, hospitalization demands,

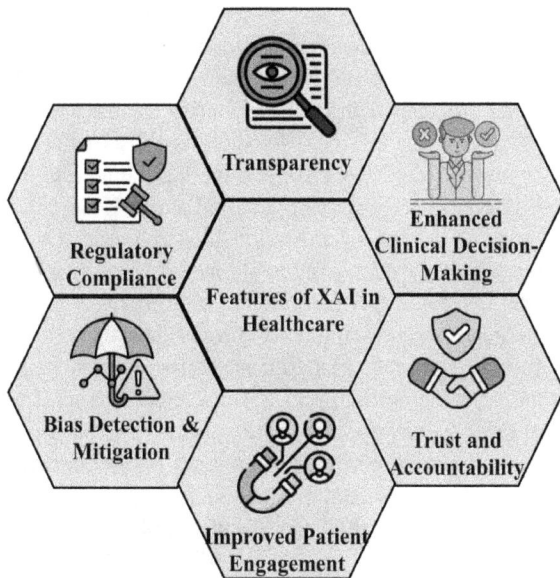

FIGURE 5.1   Different features of XAI in healthcare.

and critical care requirements. This enables healthcare systems to respond effectively to emergencies, optimizing resource utilization and minimizing patient risks (Niu et al., 2024). However, while AI's capabilities in patient monitoring and outcome prediction are remarkable, challenges remain, particularly concerning data privacy, interoperability, and algorithm transparency. Ensuring the ethical use of AI requires robust data governance frameworks and continuous validation of predictive models to prevent biases and maintain accuracy (Hossain et al., 2025; Saini et al., 2022).

5.2   FUNDAMENTALS OF XAI IN HEALTHCARE

The role of AI in patient monitoring and outcome prediction has become increasingly prominent, revolutionizing healthcare delivery by enhancing diagnostic precision, improving patient care, and facilitating predictive interventions. AI provides vast amounts of medical data from diverse sources such as EHRs, wearable devices, imaging data, and genetic information to generate actionable insights. Through sophisticated algorithms, AI processes this information rapidly, providing healthcare professionals with valuable tools for clinical decision-making, early detection of diseases, and efficient management of patient care (Rani, Kataria, et al., 2024). One significant application of AI in patient monitoring involves continuous real-time tracking of patient vitals and symptoms, especially in chronic disease management and critical care scenarios. Wearable sensors and IoT-enabled medical devices feed continuous streams of patient data to AI systems, enabling the early identification of anomalies and potentially life-threatening conditions. For instance, AI algorithms can accurately predict cardiac events by analyzing subtle changes in heart rhythm patterns, alerting medical teams to intervene proactively and reduce adverse outcomes significantly. Furthermore, AI-driven predictive analytics and the use of blockchain in organ donation are also instrumental in anticipating patient deterioration before conventional methods detect any noticeable symptoms, which can help in timely donation and transplant of the organ (Bawa et al., 2024). Machine learning algorithms analyze historical patient data to identify trends and correlations, accurately forecasting health deterioration risks such as sepsis or acute kidney injury. This predictive capability facilitates timely medical interventions, significantly improving patient outcomes and reducing hospital stays. Hospitals using AI-driven monitoring have reported decreased mortality rates and enhanced patient recovery trajectories, underscoring the transformative impact of predictive AI applications. In oncology, AI algorithms have shown immense promise in outcome prediction by analyzing extensive genomic, imaging, and clinical data to anticipate disease progression and treatment responses. AI-based predictive models can tailor personalized treatment plans, enhancing the precision of cancer therapies and significantly improving survival rates. Similarly, in chronic diseases such as diabetes and hypertension, AI systems continually monitor patient conditions, adjusting treatment regimens dynamically based on predicted outcomes, thus optimizing long-term patient health management. Example Python Code for Oncology Prediction using AI is given below:

```python
import pandas as pd
from sklearn.model_selection import train_test_split
from sklearn.ensemble import RandomForestClassifier
from sklearn.metrics import accuracy_score,
classification_report

# Load and preprocess dataset
data = pd.read_csv('oncology_data.csv')
X = data[['genomic_feature1', 'genomic_feature2',
'clinical_feature', 'imaging_feature']]
y = data['disease_progression']

# Split dataset into training and testing sets
X_train, X_test, y_train, y_test = train_test_split(X, y,
test_size=0.2, random_state=42)

# Train AI model using Random Forest algorithm
model = RandomForestClassifier(n_estimators=100,
random_state=42)
model.fit(X_train, y_train)

# Predict disease progression and treatment response
y_pred = model.predict(X_test)

# Evaluate model accuracy
accuracy = accuracy_score(y_test, y_pred)
print(f'Accuracy: {accuracy:.2f}')
print(classification_report(y_test, y_pred))
```

TABLE 5.1

Basic Fundamental Concepts and Their Description of Explainable AI in Healthcare

Concepts	Description
Interpretability	Ability to present the AI model's decision-making process clearly.
Transparency	Visibility into the AI's logic and functioning to stakeholders.
Accountability	Holding AI systems responsible for their outputs and decisions.

AI's role extends beyond individual patient care to broader public health applications. During pandemics, AI-driven predictive modeling supports healthcare resource allocation by forecasting infection rates, hospitalization demands, and critical care requirements. This enables healthcare systems to respond effectively to emergencies, optimizing resource utilization and minimizing patient risks. However, while AI's capabilities in patient monitoring and outcome prediction are remarkable, challenges remain, particularly concerning data privacy, interoperability, and algorithm transparency. Ensuring the ethical use of AI requires robust data governance frameworks and continuous validation of predictive models to prevent biases and maintain accuracy.

XAI refers to the set of processes and methods that make the predictions and decisions of AI systems understandable to humans. Key concepts include interpretability, transparency, and accountability. Table 5.1 represents the basic fundamental concepts and their description of XAI in healthcare

Transparency in medical AI models ensures trust, regulatory compliance, and ethical practices in healthcare settings. Table 5.2 shows the factors of transparency in AI models used in the medical field.

5.3 XAI FOR PATIENT MONITORING

AI-driven remote monitoring systems are transforming the landscape of patient care, especially for those with chronic conditions and post-surgical recovery needs. These systems leverage AI to continuously evaluate health data collected from remote sources, reducing the dependency on in-person visits while maintaining high

TABLE 5.2

Factors of Transparency in AI Models Used in Medical Field

Importance	Explanation
Trust Building	Transparent models build confidence among patients and healthcare professionals.
Ethical Compliance	Ensures AI-driven decisions adhere to ethical standards, avoiding bias and discrimination.
Regulatory Adherence	Facilitates compliance with health regulations such as HIPAA and GDPR, ensuring patient data protection.

TABLE 5.3

Different Features and Functionality Employed with XAI

Feature	Functionality	Benefit with XAI
Continuous Monitoring	Real-time data streaming from patient devices	Detect early warning signs before clinical symptoms manifest
AI-Based Analysis	Machine learning algorithms process and interpret data	Accurate diagnosis with rational explanation provided to clinicians
Predictive Alerts	Identification of risk patterns	Allows proactive care with validated triggers from XAI models
Personalized Feedback	Tailored health suggestions	Increases trust in AI decisions due to interpretability

standards of care. XAI enhances these systems by offering transparency in decision-making, ensuring clinicians can understand and validate the AI's recommendations (El-Khawaga et al., 2022).

Remote monitoring solutions are integrated with smart devices that capture patient metrics such as heart rate, oxygen levels, temperature, and blood glucose levels. AI analyzes these datasets to detect irregularities, forecast health trends, and recommend timely interventions. The explainability aspect ensures that alerts and decisions, such as hospitalization recommendations or medication changes, are supported by understandable evidence (Shaik et al., 2023). Table 5.3 shows the different features and functionality employed to avail the benefits of XAI.

Wearable medical technologies have gained immense popularity for their ability to provide real-time insights into patient health. Devices like smartwatches, fitness bands, ECG monitors, and glucose sensors continuously track physiological parameters, which are fed into AI systems for analysis. XAI ensures that the resulting data interpretations are not only accurate but also understandable to both clinicians and patients. XAI contributes significantly by making the underlying logic of data interpretation transparent, promoting confidence in device outcomes and decisions. For instance, if a wearable detects arrhythmia, XAI tools can indicate the specific patterns in the ECG data that triggered the alert. This transparency is vital for clinical decision-making and patient compliance. Table 5.4 represents the role and benefit of AI and XAI in different devices used for different measurements and applications.

One of the most transformative contributions of XAI in healthcare is in the early detection of health deterioration. Using machine learning models trained on extensive patient histories, AI can identify minute deviations from normal physiological parameters that indicate potential medical crises. XAI enhances this capability by allowing clinicians to understand which specific data features, such as a sudden change in respiration rate or unexpected blood pressure fluctuations, triggered a risk alert. Early warnings facilitated by XAI can lead to timely interventions, reducing emergency room visits, hospitalizations, and even mortality rates. For example, in intensive care units (ICUs), XAI-powered predictive models can provide clinicians with explainable risk scores, assisting them in prioritizing critical patients. In home

TABLE 5.4

Role and Benefit of AI and XAI in Different Devices Used for Different Measurements

Device Type	Parameters Measured	Role of AI	XAI Benefit
Smartwatches	Heart rate, activity levels	Detect fatigue or stress levels	Justifies alerts and recommends lifestyle changes
ECG Patches	Cardiac rhythms	Identify arrhythmias	Highlights waveform abnormalities triggering detection
Glucose Monitors	Blood glucose trends	Predict hypo/ hyperglycemia	Explains deviation trends and provides contextual info
Temperature Sensors	Body temperature	Monitor infection risk	Clarifies temperature patterns leading to alerts

care, these systems notify caregivers or family members with actionable insights that are easy to comprehend and trust. Furthermore, XAI helps mitigate biases in early detection systems by allowing oversight into how decisions are made. Clinicians can audit and refine algorithms to ensure that predictions are equitable across diverse patient demographics, thus promoting fairness in healthcare delivery. Integrating XAI into patient monitoring systems enriches the quality, safety, and efficiency of medical care. It empowers healthcare providers with transparent, trustworthy insights, enabling more personalized and timely patient interventions. By making the decision-making process visible and auditable, XAI not only strengthens clinical confidence but also enhances patient engagement and adherence to care plans in all aspects of Internet of Things and Internet of Medical Things devices (Rani, Kumar, et al., 2024).

5.4   ENHANCING CLINICAL DECISION-MAKING WITH XAI

AI has revolutionized healthcare, particularly in diagnostics, prognostics, and treatment planning. However, the complexity of AI models often results in "black-box" outputs that are not easily interpretable by clinicians. XAI offers transparency by providing insights into how decisions are made. This chapter focuses on how XAI enhances clinical decision-making, particularly through AI-driven prognostics, and addresses concerns of bias and uncertainty that can significantly affect patient outcomes. In clinical environments, trust in diagnostic tools is paramount. Traditional AI models can offer high accuracy, but the inability to interpret their decisions makes them unsuitable for real-world clinical applications where accountability and transparency are required (Lesley & Kuratomi Hernández, 2024). XAI methodologies, such as SHAP (SHapley Additive exPlanations), LIME (Local Interpretable Model-agnostic Explanations), and attention mechanisms in neural networks, have empowered clinicians to trust AI-driven recommendations.

Prognostic models enhanced with XAI enable:

- **Model Transparency**: Clinicians understand why a model predicts a disease progression or response to therapy.
- **Informed Decisions**: By visualizing which patient features contribute most to predictions, doctors can corroborate AI findings with medical knowledge.
- **Error Analysis**: Identifying why a model might make incorrect predictions can lead to improved model design and error mitigation.

A practical application includes predicting the progression of chronic diseases such as diabetes or cancer using multimodal data: genomics, imaging, and EHRs. XAI ensures that clinicians can verify if the AI model's focus aligns with known medical patterns.

The following example demonstrates an AI model that predicts the probability of heart disease in patients based on clinical data. We incorporate XAI using SHAP to explain model predictions.

- **Dataset used**: UCI Heart Disease Dataset
  This dataset includes attributes such as age, cholesterol levels, chest pain type, resting blood pressure, and exercise-induced angina.
- **Objective**: Predict if a patient is likely to develop heart disease and explain the reasoning using SHAP.

```
# Importing necessary libraries
import pandas as pd
import numpy as np
import shap
import matplotlib.pyplot as plt
from sklearn.model_selection import train_test_split
from sklearn.ensemble import RandomForestClassifier
from sklearn.metrics import accuracy_score,
classification_report

# Load dataset
https://github.com/kb22/Heart-Disease-Prediction/blob/
master/dataset.csvdata = pd.read_csv(url)
# Prepare data
X = data.drop("target", axis=1)
y = data["target"]

# Train-test split
X_train, X_test, y_train, y_test = train_test_split(X, y,
test_size=0.2, random_state=42)
```

```
# Train model
model = RandomForestClassifier(n_estimators=100,
random_state=42)
model.fit(X_train, y_train)

# Predict
y_pred = model.predict(X_test)
print("Accuracy:", accuracy_score(y_test, y_pred))
print("\nClassification Report:\n", classification_
report(y_test, y_pred))

# SHAP explanation
explainer = shap.TreeExplainer(model)
shap_values = explainer.shap_values(X_test)

# Summary plot
shap.summary_plot(shap_values[1], X_test)
```

```
Accuracy: 0.8852

Classification Report:
              precision    recall   f1-score    support

           0       0.89      0.86       0.87         42
           1       0.88      0.90       0.89         48

    accuracy                            0.89         90
   macro avg       0.89      0.88       0.88         90
weighted avg       0.89      0.89       0.89         90
```

- **SHAP Summary Plot**: A SHAP summary plot (visual not shown here) reveals the most influential features in the model's predictions:
  - **cp (chest pain type)** and **thalach (maximum heart rate)** show strong positive influence on predicting heart disease.
  - **chol (cholesterol)** and **age** have variable impact, depending on their value for each patient.

  This interpretability allows clinicians to understand **why** a prediction is made. For instance, if a model predicts high risk due to age and high cholesterol, a cardiologist may decide to recommend early intervention.

5.4.1 ADDRESSING BIAS AND UNCERTAINTY IN AI MODELS

Bias and uncertainty are critical concerns in AI-driven prognostics, especially in high-stakes environments like healthcare.

5.4.1.1 Types of Bias in Clinical AI

- **Selection Bias**: Arises when the training dataset is not representative of the real patient population.
- **Measurement Bias**: Occurs when data collection methods vary, leading to inconsistent inputs.
- **Algorithmic Bias**: Embedded in model design, such as overly relying on features that correlate with non-causal factors.

These biases can mislead clinical decision-making and worsen healthcare disparities. For example, an AI model trained predominantly on male patients may perform poorly when diagnosing heart disease in women. Figure 5.2 shows the XAI-based patient monitoring system.

Methods to remove bias:

1. **Data Auditing**: Checking for class imbalance and ensuring demographic diversity in training data.
2. **Fairness Constraints**: Adding fairness metrics like equal opportunity or demographic parity during training.
3. **Model-Agnostic Explanations**: Using XAI tools like SHAP, LIME, or counterfactual analysis to identify biased outputs.

5.4.1.2 Handling Uncertainty

AI models often make overconfident predictions. In medicine, it is crucial to estimate how confident a model is in its predictions. This helps determine if the AI's advice should be followed or overridden by expert judgment.

Approaches to quantify uncertainty:

a. **Prediction Intervals**: Provide a range within which the true outcome is expected.

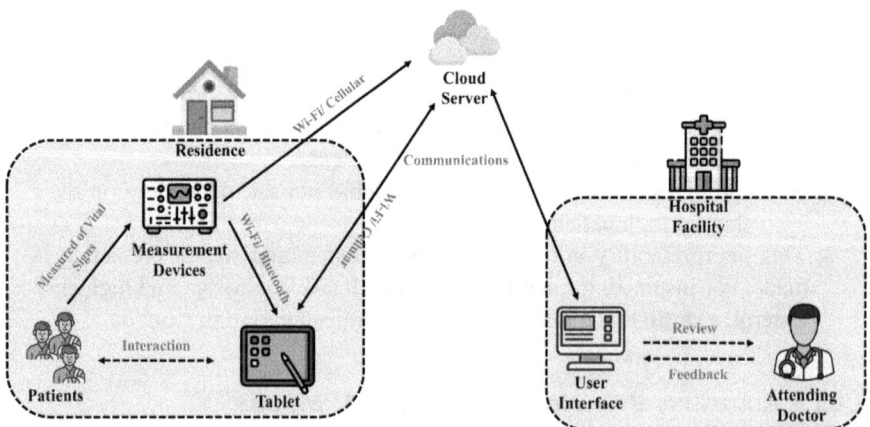

FIGURE 5.2   XAI-based patient monitoring system.

b. **Bayesian Inference**: Incorporates uncertainty directly into the model through posterior distributions.

c. **Ensemble Learning**: Combines predictions from multiple models to account for variability.

Example: Calibrating uncertainty using prediction probabilities.

```
from sklearn.calibration import calibration_curve
# Get probability predictions
y_proba = model.predict_proba(X_test)[:, 1]

# Calibration curve
prob_true, prob_pred = calibration_curve(y_test, y_proba,
n_bins=10)

plt.plot(prob_pred, prob_true, marker='o', linewidth=1,
label='Random Forest')
plt.plot([0, 1], [0, 1], linestyle='--', label='Perfect
Calibration')
plt.xlabel("Mean Predicted Probability")
plt.ylabel("Fraction of Positives")
plt.title("Calibration Curve")
plt.legend()
plt.grid()
plt.show()
```

- **Expected output**: The calibration curve typically shows how well the predicted probabilities align with actual outcomes. A well-calibrated model helps clinicians trust predictions not just based on what the model predicts, but also how confidently it does so.
  a. **X-axis**: Mean predicted probability in each bin (ranges from 0 to 1).
  b. **Y-axis**: Actual fraction of positive outcomes in those bins.
  c. **Blue curve (dots connected by lines)**: Represents your model's calibration.
  d. **Dashed diagonal line**: Represents perfect calibration (ideal line where predicted probability matches observed frequency).

5.5   PERSONALIZED TREATMENT AND PATIENT OUTCOMES

Personalized medicine, which was once considered a visionary concept, is now becoming a practical reality with the integration of AI. Tailored treatment planning involves designing medical interventions specifically suited to the unique characteristics of each patient. AI models are particularly well-equipped for this task due to their ability to analyze multidimensional datasets, identify hidden patterns, and generate precise therapeutic recommendations (Kale et al., 2024). Machine learning algorithms can examine genomic profiles to detect mutations and predict drug responses, enabling oncologists, for example, to select the most effective chemo-therapy for cancer patients. Similarly, AI can analyze historical data of chronic disease patients to recommend optimal treatment paths that minimize side effects while maximizing outcomes. In cases like diabetes management, AI-driven models can recommend personalized insulin regimens based on patient-specific glucose level patterns and lifestyle factors (Li et al., 2025).

Also, deep learning techniques applied to medical imaging (such as MRI, CT scans, and radiographs) allow for the detection of subtle disease indicators that may not be visible to the human eye. These insights can be aligned with EHR data to deliver accurate diagnoses and suggest evidence-based treatment protocols. The use of AI in treatment planning is not only reactive but also preventive. Predictive analytics can forecast potential complications or disease progression, allowing clinicians to modify treatment plans in real-time. This adaptability ensures continuous personalization across the entire care continuum from diagnosis and therapy to rehabilitation and follow-up. XAI provides visual and textual explanations that highlight which patient features (e.g., symptoms, lab results, imaging biomarkers) contributed most to a particular recommendation. For instance, if an AI model suggests a specific antidepressant for a mental health patient, XAI can identify the underlying clinical indicators, such as mood patterns, genetic risk factors, or medication history that led to this suggestion. This fosters trust and provides reassurance to both doctors and patients. From the clinician's perspective, XAI assists in validating AI-driven treatment plans, helping doctors confirm or reject recommendations based on their expertise. This symbiotic relationship ensures the final clinical decision is both data-driven and human-centric (Bamba et al., 2024). Physicians can also use these explanations during consultations to educate patients about their condition and the rationale behind the suggested interventions, thereby promoting shared decision-making. XAI facilitates legal and ethical accountability in medical practice. Transparent explanations are essential in documenting care decisions, which may be crucial during malpractice claims or regulatory reviews. As AI adoption increases, XAI will become indispensable in safeguarding ethical standards and ensuring that AI augments rather than overrides clinical judgment.

The ultimate measure of any medical technology's success lies in its impact on patient recovery, quality of life, and safety. AI and XAI systems are being increasingly evaluated based on these metrics through clinical trials, retrospective studies, and real-world deployments. In terms of patient recovery, studies show that personalized treatment plans generated by AI can lead to faster recovery times, lower readmission rates, and fewer complications. For example, in postoperative care, AI systems monitor vital signs continuously and detect anomalies earlier than traditional systems. This allows healthcare providers to intervene promptly and prevent complications such as infections or organ failures.

AI's role in patient safety is equally crucial. Automated alert systems powered by AI can reduce medication errors by flagging potential drug interactions, incorrect dosages, or allergies. Predictive analytics can identify high-risk patients for hospital-acquired infections or falls, prompting targeted prevention measures. When coupled with XAI, these alerts become more interpretable and actionable, helping caregivers understand the "why" behind the alert and respond appropriately.

Quantitative metrics such as Length of Hospital Stay (LOS), 30-day Readmission Rates, Adverse Drug Reaction (ADR) incidence, and Patient-Reported Outcome Measures (PROMs) are increasingly being used to evaluate the effectiveness of AI-driven interventions. These metrics enable health institutions to assess the return on investment in AI systems, justify their integration into clinical work-flows, and drive continuous quality improvement. Patient satisfaction surveys have shown improved scores in facilities that employ AI-driven personalized care systems. Patients report feeling more understood and involved in their care processes, largely due to the transparent communication enabled by XAI. Emotional engage-ment and psychological reassurance often translate to better adherence to treatment regimens and improved mental health outcomes. To ensure ongoing success, health-care systems must adopt robust feedback loops wherein AI models are continuously retrained using outcome data. This ensures the model evolves in response to new trends, patient populations, and emerging clinical guidelines, thereby maintaining relevance and efficacy (Cheng & Liu, 2025).

5.6   CONCLUSION

The incorporation of AI and XAI into the healthcare sector is boosting a new era of personalized, predictive, and patient-focused medical care. In this chapter, it has been emphasized that how AI has transformed essential areas such as diagnosis, treatment planning, patient monitoring, and outcome forecasting. Its ability to handle extensive and intricate medical datasets, from genomic information to real-time sen-sor data, has allowed healthcare providers to identify diseases earlier, suggest pre-cise treatments, and manage patient care more effectively. By offering transparent, interpretable, and actionable insights into AI-driven recommendations, XAI enables healthcare professionals to comprehend, validate, and trust the decisions made by intelligent systems. From improving doctor-patient communication to ensuring regulatory compliance and ethical responsibility, XAI fortifies the foundation for reliable and responsible AI use in medicine. The practical applications discussed in this chapter illustrate that XAI is not merely a theoretical idea but a practical necessity. Whether through wearable devices monitoring chronic illnesses or AI systems optimizing cancer treatment plans, XAI promotes shared decision-making, encourages patient involvement, and aids clinicians in providing evidence-based, patient-centered care. Furthermore, the tangible benefits, such as shorter hospital stays, reduced readmission rates, fewer adverse drug events, and increased patient satisfaction, confirm the real-world impact of integrating AI and XAI. These results underscore the importance of healthcare systems to adopt explainable models that not only perform effectively but also adhere to the principles of transparency, safety, and inclusivity. As the field advances, the ongoing refinement of AI models using patient feedback and outcome data will be crucial to ensure their adaptability and efficacy. Ultimately, the merging of AI's analytical capabilities with XAI's inter-pretability sets the stage for a future where technology enhances clinical expertise, promotes health equity, and places patients at the heart of care. This evolving syn-ergy promises to redefine the standards of modern healthcare, ensuring it remains intelligent, ethical, and compassionate.

REFERENCES

Ayesha, A., & Ahamed, N. N. (2024) Explainable artificial intelligence (EAI): For health-care applications and improvements. In A. Khamparia & D. Gupta (Eds.), *Explainable artificial intelligence for biomedical and healthcare applications* (pp. 162–196). CRC Press.

Bamba, H., Singh, G., John, J., Inban, P., Prajjwal, P., Alhussain, H., & Marsool, M. D. M. (2024). Precision medicine approaches in cardiology and personalized therapies for improved patient outcomes: A systematic review. *Current Problems in Cardiology*, *49*(5), 102470.

Bawa, G., Singh, H., Rani, S., Kataria, A., & Min, H. (2024). Exploring perspectives of block-chain technology and traditional centralized technology in organ donation management: A comprehensive review. *Information*, *15*(11), 703.

Cheng, S., & Liu, Y. (2025). Advances in personalized treatment and prognostic factors of follicular lymphoma. *Current Treatment Options in Oncology*, *26*, 313–330.

El-Khawaga, G., Abu-Elkheir, M., & Reichert, M. (2022). Xai in the context of predictive process monitoring: An empirical analysis framework. *Algorithms*, *15*(6), 199.

Hosain, M. T., Jim, J. R., Mridha, M., & Kabir, M. M. (2024). Explainable AI approaches in deep learning: Advancements, applications and challenges. *Computers and Electrical Engineering*, *117*, 109246.

Hossain, M. I., Zamzmi, G., Mouton, P. R., Salekin, M. S., Sun, Y., & Goldgof, D. (2025). Explainable AI for medical data: Current methods, limitations, and future directions. *ACM Computing Surveys*, *57*(6), 1–46.

Kale, M. B., Wankhede, N. L., Pawar, R. S., Ballal, S., Kumawat, R., Goswami, M., Khalid, M., Taksande, B. G., Upaganlawar, A. B., & Umekar, M. J. (2024). AI-driven innovations in Alzheimer's disease: Integrating early diagnosis, personalized treatment, and prognostic modelling. *Ageing Research Reviews*, 102497.

Kaur, G., & Saini, H. K. (2023). An Optimized Resnet based plant disease identification using deep learning hypothetic function. In *2023 International Conference on Advances in Computation, Communication and Information Technology* (ICAICCIT). https://doi.org/10.1109/ICAICCIT60255.2023.10465742

Lesley, U., & Kuratomi Hernández, A. (2024). Improving XAI explanations for clinical decision-making–Physicians' perspective on local explanations in healthcare. In *International Conference on Artificial Intelligence in Medicine* (pp. 296–312).

Li, P., Huang, M., Li, M., Li, G., Ma, Y., Zhao, Y., Wang, X., Zhang, Y., & Shi, C. (2025). Combining molecular characteristics and therapeutic analysis of PDOs predict clinical responses and guide PDAC personalized treatment. *Journal of Experimental & Clinical Cancer Research*, *44*(1), 72.

Niu, S., Yin, Q., Ma, J., Song, Y., Xu, Y., Bai, L., Pan, W., & Yang, X. (2024). Enhancing healthcare decision support through explainable AI models for risk prediction. *Decision Support Systems*, *181*, 114228.

Patel, A. U., Gu, Q., Esper, R., Maeser, D., & Maeser, N. (2024). The crucial role of interdisciplinary conferences in advancing explainable AI in healthcare. *BioMedInformatics*, *4*(2), 1363–1383.

Poonia, R. C., & Al-Alshaikh, H. A. (2024). Ensemble approach of transfer learning and vision transformer leveraging explainable AI for disease diagnosis: An advancement towards smart healthcare 5.0. *Computers in Biology and Medicine*, *179*, 108874.

Puri, V., Priyadarshini, I., Kataria, A., Rani, S., & Min, H. (2025). Privacy-first ML for chronic kidney disease prediction: Exploring a decentralized approach using block-chain and IPFS. *IEEE Access*, *99*, 43178–43189.

Rani, S., Kataria, A., Bhambri, P., Pareek, P. K., & Puri, V. (2024). Artificial intelligence in personalized health services for better patient care. In S. K. Gupta, D. A. Karras & R. Natarajan (Eds.), *Revolutionizing healthcare: AI integration with IoT for enhanced patient outcomes* (pp. 89–108). Springer.

Rani, S., Kumar, S., Kataria, A., & Min, H. (2024). SmartHealth: An intelligent framework to secure IoMT service applications using machine learning. *ICT Express, 10*(2), 425–430.

Rath, K. C., Khang, A., Rath, S. K., Satapathy, N., Satapathy, S. K., & Kar, S. (2024). Artificial intelligence (AI)-enabled technology in medicine-advancing holistic healthcare monitoring and control systems. In A. Khang, V. Abdullayev, O. Hrybiuk & A. K. Shukla (Eds.), *Computer vision and AI-integrated IoT technologies in the medical ecosystem* (pp. 87–108). CRC Press.

Sadeghi, Z., Alizadehsani, R., Cifci, M. A., Kausar, S., Rehman, R., Mahanta, P., Bora, P. K., Almasri, A., Alkhawaldeh, R. S., & Hussain, S. (2024). A review of explainable artificial intelligence in healthcare. *Computers and Electrical Engineering, 118*, 109370.

Saini, H. K., & Preeti. (2024). A cross design for breast cancer prediction. In *International Conference on Communications and Cyber Physical Engineering* 2018. Springer Nature Singapore.

Saini, H. K., Swarnakar, H., & Jain, K. (2022). Secured multimedia and IoT in healthcare computing paradigms. In B. Bhusan, S. K. Sharma, B. Unhelkar, M. F. Ijaz & L. Karim (Eds.), *Internet of Things* (pp. 229–256). CRC Press.

Shaik, T., Tao, X., Higgins, N., Li, L., Gururajan, R., Zhou, X., & Acharya, U. R. (2023). Remote patient monitoring using artificial intelligence: Current state, applications, and challenges. *Wiley Interdisciplinary Reviews: Data Mining and Knowledge Discovery, 13*(2), e1485.

Wani, N. A., Kumar, R., Bedi, J., & Rida, I. (2024). Explainable AI-driven IoMT fusion: Unravelling techniques, opportunities, and challenges with explainable AI in healthcare. *Information Fusion*, 102472.

6 Navigating Interpretability in AI

Balancing Performance, Standards, and Practical Guidance

6.1 INTRODUCTION

Artificial intelligence (AI) is becoming an integral part of healthcare, offering tools that enhance diagnostic accuracy, streamline clinical workflows, and enable data-driven decision-making. Despite these advancements, a significant barrier to its widespread adoption remains known as interpretability. Clinicians and healthcare providers must be able to trust and understand the reasoning behind AI-generated outputs, particularly when these outputs influence critical decisions regarding patient care (Mahto, 2025). As AI models, especially deep learning algorithms, become more complex and less transparent, this demand for interpretability becomes both urgent and essential. Interpretability in AI refers to how clearly and convincingly an algorithm's decisions can be understood by human users. In the healthcare context, interpretability is crucial not only for clinical acceptance but also for meeting ethical and legal responsibilities. A model that performs well in predicting outcomes is insufficient unless its predictions can be explained in a way that is comprehensible to healthcare professionals and acceptable under clinical governance frameworks. Interpretability also fosters trust among patients and practitioners by ensuring that AI operates as a partner, not a mysterious authority. Beyond trust and transparency, interpretability enables error detection, bias mitigation, and better regulatory compliance. As healthcare systems increasingly rely on data-driven technologies, understanding how these systems process information and arrive at decisions is key to identifying and correcting potential issues. Without interpretability, biases hidden in the training data or model design may go unnoticed, potentially leading to inequitable or harmful outcomes (Babu, 2024). Additionally, the integration of interpretable AI supports collaboration between machines and clinicians. When decisions can be explained and understood, AI systems serve to augment human expertise, not replace it. This collaborative intelligence empowers healthcare providers to validate and refine AI recommendations, leading to better clinical outcomes. However, achieving interpretability without compromising performance poses a complex challenge. Balancing accuracy with transparency requires thoughtful model design, user-centric explanation strategies, and adherence to emerging best practices. This chapter

DOI: 10.1201/9781003561422-6

will explore the importance of interpretability in healthcare, examine the trade-offs between performance and explainability, and identify key challenges that must be addressed to realize AI's full potential in clinical settings (Akhtar et al., 2024).

Interpretability in AI refers to the extent to which a human can understand the internal mechanics or decision-making process of an AI system. In healthcare, interpretability is not just a technical advantage, but it is a regulatory, clinical, and ethical necessity. Clinicians are trained to justify their diagnoses and treatment recommendations, and they expect the same from any supporting AI tools. Without a clear understanding of how an AI model arrives at its conclusions, medical practitioners may hesitate to incorporate its insights into critical decisions, particularly those involving life-and-death consequences. Moreover, interpretability plays a vital role in regulatory compliance. Regulatory bodies like the U.S. Food and Drug Administration (FDA) and the European Medicines Agency (EMA) increasingly mandate that AI-driven medical devices and decision-support tools offer explanations that clinicians can understand and evaluate. Interpretability is also central to patient trust. As patients become more aware of how AI is used in their care, they may request justifications for automated decisions, whether in radiology, pathology, or treatment planning. A transparent system that enables clinicians to explain AI outcomes improves patient confidence and enhances the doctor-patient relationship (ŞAHiN et al., 2025).

Interpretability also enables error detection, model debugging, and ethical AI deployment. By making models transparent, developers and medical professionals can more easily detect biases, data anomalies, and unintended consequences. This is particularly critical in healthcare, where demographic disparities, historical biases in datasets, or incorrect assumptions in algorithm design can have devastating consequences. Interpretability not only helps expose these issues but also supports the development of corrective measures. Interpretability promotes collaborative intelligence, which is a synergistic interaction between human expertise and machine precision. Instead of replacing clinicians, interpretable AI empowers them, augmenting human decision-making with actionable insights that are scientifically explainable and clinically validated (Sharma et al., 2024).

As AI systems become more capable, a tension arises between performance and interpretability. Often, the most accurate models, such as ensemble methods or deep neural networks, are also the least interpretable. These models may offer superior predictive accuracy but sacrifice transparency, making it difficult to trust or validate their outputs in high-stakes environments like healthcare. Efforts to address this trade-off fall into two broad categories: intrinsically interpretable models and post hoc explainability techniques. Intrinsically interpretable models, such as decision trees, rule-based systems, or linear regressions, are easy to understand but often limited in complexity and performance. On the other hand, post hoc methods such as LIME (Local Interpretable Model-agnostic Explanations), SHAP (SHapley Additive exPlanations), and Grad-CAM (Gradient-weighted Class Activation Mapping) attempt to extract explanations from complex models after training (Guleria et al., 2024; Hasannezhad & Sharifian, 2025; Rahmat et al., 2025). Figure 6.1 represents the different techniques used to explain the decisions of machine learning models.

While post hoc techniques represent progress, they are not without limitations. They may provide approximate or misleading insights, leading users to believe they

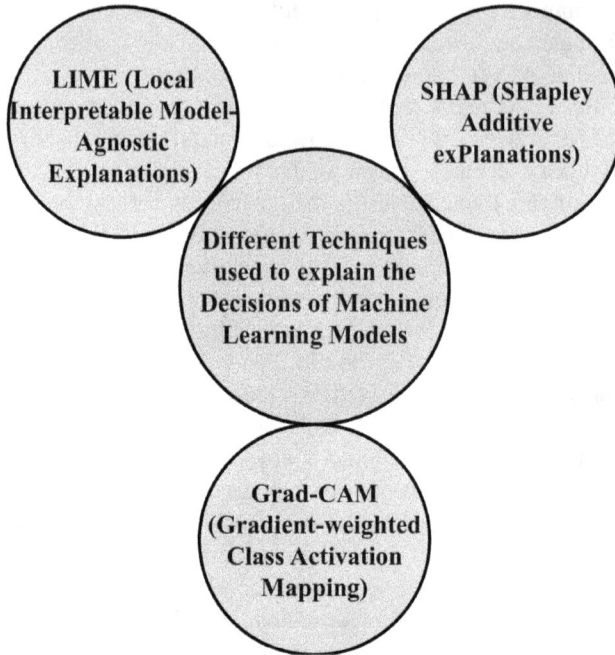

FIGURE 6.1   Different techniques used to explain the decisions of machine learning models.

understand the model better than they actually do. There is a growing concern that post hoc interpretability might create a false sense of transparency, especially when the explanation does not reflect the true inner workings of the model. Thus, relying solely on post hoc methods without rigorous validation can be dangerous in clinical contexts. Another dimension of this balancing act involves operational integration. Interpretability should not come at the cost of clinical efficiency. A model that is highly interpretable but too slow or cumbersome to use in real-time clinical settings may have limited practical value. Hence, healthcare AI solutions must be both technically effective and human-centered, offering explanations that are not just accurate but also actionable and timely for clinicians. Furthermore, balancing transparency and performance also helps address legal accountability and data governance issues. If a patient is harmed due to an AI-driven decision, understanding the model's reasoning becomes essential for determining liability. Interpretable models provide a traceable logic, which can support forensic analysis, compliance audits, and quality assurance processes (Saini & Preeti, 2024; Salvi et al., 2025).

Despite its critical importance, achieving interpretability in healthcare AI presents several challenges, like technical, methodological, and institutional. First and foremost is the complexity of medical data. Healthcare datasets often include unstructured, multimodal inputs such as clinical notes, images, genomics, and sensor data (Puri et al., 2025). Developing interpretable models that can process and integrate such diverse information without sacrificing accuracy is non-trivial. Another challenge is the lack of standardized evaluation metrics for interpretability. Unlike accuracy, precision, or recall, interpretability is inherently subjective. What is interpretable to a data scientist may not be comprehensible to a radiologist or a nurse. This variability makes it difficult to benchmark and validate interpretability across different user groups. Efforts are underway to develop human-centered evaluation frameworks, but they remain in their infancy.

Bias and fairness also complicate the interpretability landscape. Models trained on biased datasets may perpetuate or even amplify disparities in care. While interpretability can help expose such biases, it also depends on the clarity of data and model assumptions. Understanding and mitigating bias requires deep domain knowledge, ethical oversight, and inclusive data collection practices. A further complication arises from the dynamic nature of healthcare environments. As clinical guidelines evolve, patient populations shift, and new treatments emerge, AI models must adapt without losing transparency. Maintaining interpretability in the face of continuous learning and updating is a significant technical hurdle. Moreover, there is a skill gap between AI developers and healthcare professionals (Rani et al., 2024). Many clinicians lack the technical expertise to evaluate the mathematical nuances of AI systems, while developers may not fully understand clinical workflows. This disconnect can lead to misinterpretation of model explanations, or worse, misplaced trust. Bridging this gap requires interdisciplinary training, collaborative development, and co-design practices where clinicians and data scientists work together from the outset. Commercial constraints and proprietary models often hinder transparency. Many state-of-the-art healthcare AI tools are developed by private companies that protect their models as trade secrets. This limits the ability of clinicians and regulators to fully scrutinize their workings, undermining trust and stalling widespread adoption.

6.2 UNDERSTANDING AI INTERPRETABILITY

Interpretability and explainability are often used interchangeably in AI discourse, but they serve distinct conceptual purposes and reflect different goals in model assessment. Interpretability refers to the degree to which a human can consistently predict the model's result given an input. It is often associated with the intrinsic transparency of the model, that how straightforward it is to understand the internal mechanisms or decision logic. Linear regression, decision trees, and logistic regression are examples of interpretable models where the cause-effect relationship between features and outcomes is readily discernible. On the other hand, explainability refers to the extent to which the internal mechanics of a model can be described in human-understandable terms, especially when the model is a black-box. Explainability becomes essential in complex architectures such as deep neural networks, ensemble methods (e.g., random forests, XGBoost), or transformers. In these cases, post-hoc methods like SHAP, LIME, and Grad-CAM are employed to generate explanations that approximate the reasoning behind the model's decisions (Nasarian et al., 2024; Saini et al., 2022).

While both terms aim to bridge the gap between technical insight and human understanding, interpretability prioritizes simplicity and transparency, whereas explainability focuses on rationalization and post-hoc justification. Effective governance of AI requires clarity on when to prioritize one over the other, depending on the application context, user expectations, and regulatory obligations. One of the most significant challenges in deploying AI systems lies in balancing model performance with model interpretability. Often, highly accurate models such as deep

neural network (DNN) is opaque, while more interpretable models sacrifice predictive power. Consider a clinical setting where predicting sepsis from patient data
could mean the difference between life and death. A deep learning model trained
on large, multimodal datasets might outperform a decision tree in terms of precision
and recall. However, the decision tree offers a transparent, traceable logic that physicians can review and validate. In contrast, the deep learning model may function as
a black box, making it difficult to understand why a specific patient was classified as
high-risk (Murad et al., 2024).

As shown in Figure 6.2, this trade-off presents several risks, like:

a. **Regulatory Risk**: Black-box models are harder to audit, and many jurisdictions, such as the EU under the GDPR, demand a "right to explanation" for
   algorithmic decisions.
b. **Clinical Trust**: Medical professionals are less likely to trust AI systems if
   they cannot trace or question the decision-making process.
c. **Operational Risk**: High-performing but non-interpretable systems are difficult to debug or update when data distributions shift.

To solve these challenges, several strategies have emerged:

1. **Hybrid Modeling**: Combining interpretable models with black-box models, where the former acts as a validation or filter layer.
2. **Model Simplification**: Using model compression techniques or attention
   visualization to make complex models more interpretable without significantly sacrificing accuracy.
3. **Explainability Techniques**: Applying SHAP, LIME, or counterfactual
   analysis to provide local or global explanations of black-box predictions.

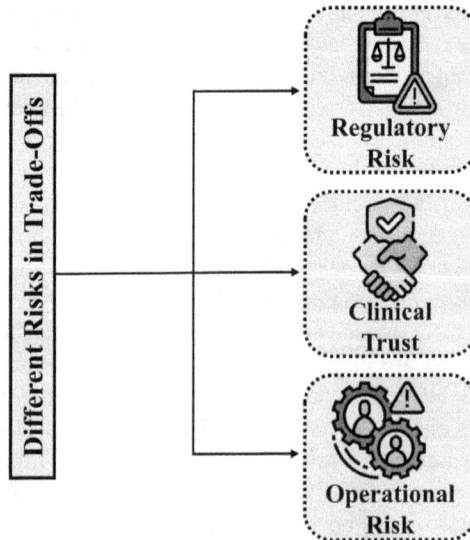

FIGURE 6.2   Different risks in trade-offs in **AI interpretability**.

Ultimately, the balance depends on contextual risk assessment. In low-risk applications (e.g., product recommendations), black-box models may be acceptable. In high-risk domains like medicine or criminal justice, interpretability often outweighs marginal gains in predictive performance. The need for AI interpretability is deeply influenced by the perspectives of its primary stakeholders. In healthcare, for instance, the ecosystem involves clinicians who use AI, patients who are affected by AI decisions, and regulators who ensure ethical deployment. Each group brings different priorities to the interpretability conversation.

a. **Clinicians**

Clinicians require models that are not only accurate but also transparent and justifiable. Medical decision-making often demands evidence-based reasoning, and clinicians are trained to follow guidelines that emphasize traceability and reproducibility. A black-box model that cannot articulate why a particular treatment was recommended is likely to be rejected, no matter how statistically sound its predictions. Clinicians also serve as mediators between patients and technology. They need to be able to explain and defend the rationale behind AI recommendations to patients, legal bodies, and professional boards. Therefore, their trust in the system is predicated on their ability to comprehend and audit its logic.

b. **Patients**

For patients, interpretability fosters empowerment and ethical assurance. When AI is used to make health or financial decisions, individuals expect a clear explanation for why they were denied a loan, recommended a specific therapy, or flagged for surveillance. Interpretability becomes synonymous with transparency, fairness, and accountability. Patients are increasingly aware of algorithmic bias and may demand that AI decisions be free from discrimination based on race, gender, or socioeconomic status. They view interpretability as a check against opaque systems that might reinforce systemic inequalities. Blockchain may also be deployed for more secure transportation of organs donated for future transplantation (Bawa et al., 2024).

c. **Regulators**

Regulators act as custodians of public trust. Their primary concern is ensuring that AI systems meet safety, fairness, and transparency standards. In jurisdictions like the European Union, the AI Act and GDPR require clear documentation and audit trails for AI models, especially in sensitive domains. Regulatory bodies often mandate the use of interpretable or explainable models, particularly when outcomes affect rights, freedoms, or access to services.

To satisfy regulatory scrutiny, organizations must adopt model governance frameworks that include:
   i. Detailed documentation of model design and rationale.
   ii. Regular audits using fairness and bias metrics.
   iii. Mechanisms to provide explanations to end users on demand.

6.3 BALANCING AI MODEL PERFORMANCE AND INTERPRETABILITY

AI systems are becoming integral to decision-making processes in healthcare, finance, law, and other critical domains. As these systems grow in complexity and capability, ensuring that their decisions are understandable, trustworthy, and ethically sound becomes essential. This chapter discusses the critical trade-off between AI model performance and interpretability. It provides a structured comparison between black-box and interpretable models, explores techniques for enhancing model explainability, and evaluates the multidimensional trade-offs of accuracy, fairness, and trust (Obster et al., 2024).

The AI landscape is broadly divided into two categories of models, black-box models and interpretable (white-box) models. Black-box models, such as deep neural networks and ensemble methods like XGBoost or Random Forests, are known for their superior predictive performance but are opaque in terms of their internal decision-making processes. In contrast, interpretable models, such as decision trees, linear regression, and rule-based systems, allow stakeholders to understand how input features contribute to the output. The comparison demonstrated in Table 6.1 shows

TABLE 6.1

Comparison of Various Aspects of XAI Models and Their Impact of Selection

Aspect	Black-Box Models (e.g., DNN, XGBoost)	Interpretable Models (e.g., Logistic Regression, Decision Trees)	Use Case Suitability	Performance	Transparency	Typical Applications
Model Complexity	High	Low to Moderate	Complex pattern recognition	Very High	Low	Image/Voice Recognition, NLP
Training Time	Long	Short	High-dimensional data	Longer with large data	Quick	Real-time predictions
Interpretability	Low	High	Explainable predictions	Hard to interpret	Easy	Credit scoring, Clinical decisions
User Trust	Lower (without XAI)	Higher	Domains needing transparency	Challenging to justify	Intuitive	Regulatory and legal decisions
Scalability	High	Moderate	Big data and real-time use	Excellent	Moderate	Digital assistants, Search engines
Risk of Bias Detection	Harder to detect	Easier to audit	Ethical and fair AI	Requires explainability tools	Inherent transparency	HR tools, Policy decisions

that model selection is highly dependent on context. For high-stakes decisions, where interpretability is crucial, simpler models may be preferable (Acharya et al., 2024).

Given the trade-off between accuracy and interpretability, several post hoc explainability techniques have been developed to illuminate black-box decisions. These techniques, as shown in Table 6.2, aim to retain the performance of complex models while improving their transparency. Popular methods include SHAP, LIME, and Attention Mechanisms in deep learning.

These tools allow stakeholders like clinicians, regulators, or business executives to gain confidence in AI decisions without compromising the model's sophistication. The ideal explainability method depends on the model type, domain requirements, and end-user expectations. The goal of AI development is not merely to maximize predictive accuracy but to ensure fairness, reliability, and user trust. However, there is often a tension between performance metrics and interpretability goals. Highly accurate models may inadvertently encode bias or discrimination if not audited for

TABLE 6.2

Comparison of Various Techniques and Their Features in Black-Box Decisions

Technique	Model Compatibility	Explanation Type	Strengths	Limitations	Typical Use Cases
SHAP	Model-agnostic	Global + Local	Consistent feature attribution, game-theoretic	Computationally expensive	Healthcare diagnostics, finance
LIME	Model-agnostic	Local	Easy to implement, versatile	May be unstable, limited global insight	Loan approval, risk analysis
Attention Mechanisms	Neural networks (DL)	Global	Highlights relevant input regions	Requires retraining model	Text summarization, image captioning
Saliency Maps	CNNs (Image models)	Local	Visual explanations for image data	Sensitive to noise	Radiology, autonomous vehicles
Counterfactuals	Model-agnostic	Local	Highlights minimal changes needed for outcome	May be unrealistic or hard to interpret	Recommender systems, HR tech
Integrated Gradients	Deep learning models	Local + Global	Accurate attributions over input features	Requires differentiable models	Genomic sequence modeling

TABLE 6.3

Evaluation of the Different Trade-Offs in AI Models

Metric	Definition	High-Performance Model	Interpretable Model	Impact on Stakeholders	Resolution Strategy
Accuracy	Correct predictions over total predictions	High (esp. in large datasets)	Moderate to high	Impacts confidence in decision	Fine-tune or ensemble with interpretable models
Fairness	Equitable treatment across demographic groups	Risk of bias if data is unbalanced	Easier to audit and adjust	Critical for compliance and ethics	Bias mitigation, fairness-aware training
Robustness	Stability under input perturbations	May be brittle under noise	Typically more stable	Affects model reliability	Regularization, adversarial training
Trust	User confidence in model decisions	Lower without transparency	High due to clarity	Influences adoption and regulatory approval	Use XAI tools, user engagement
Computation Cost	Resources/time required for training/ inference	High	Low to moderate	Infrastructure investment, real-time readiness	Model pruning, hybrid systems
Regulatory Fit	Alignment with legal/ethical standards	Often non-compliant without XAI	Easier to align	Affects deployment in sensitive domains	Explainability-by-design, documentation

fairness, while overly simplistic models may fail to capture complex relationships in data. Table 6.3 represents the evaluation of the different trade-offs in AI models (Kumar et al., 2025; Pawlicka et al., 2024; Sadeghi et al., 2024).

This multidimensional trade-off demonstrates that no one-size-fits-all model exists. The "best" model depends on the task context, required regulatory compliance, and user expectations. For example, an autonomous vehicle may prioritize robustness and accuracy, while a clinical decision support system must emphasize interpretability and fairness. Navigating this balance calls for an informed and context-driven approach. Here are some recommendations for practitioners and AI developers(Kaur & Saini, 2023):

1. **Use hybrid architectures**: Combine interpretable models for sensitive decision points and black-box models for feature-rich data processing.
2. **Integrate XAI from the beginning**: Don't retrofit interpretability; design with transparency in mind.
3. **Stakeholder consultation**: Align model goals with stakeholder needs. Regulators want fairness audits, users want clarity, and developers want performance.

4. **Continuous evaluation**: Regularly test and audit models for fairness, robustness, and degradation.
5. **Documentation and transparency reports**: Maintain comprehensive documentation on model design, testing, and explainability tools used.

By adopting a balanced framework, AI can become more than just predictive; it becomes accountable, fair, and beneficial to society.

6.4   CASE STUDIES AND REAL-WORLD APPLICATIONS

6.4.1   Successful Implementations of Interpretable AI in Healthcare

The healthcare sector has significantly benefited from interpretable AI systems, particularly where trust, transparency, and accountability are critical. One prominent example is the use of decision trees and logistic regression models in diagnosing cardiovascular diseases. These models are not only accurate but also offer clear reasoning behind every prediction, allowing clinicians to trust the outcomes and explain them to patients.

6.4.1.1   Case Study: Cardiovascular Risk Prediction

Researchers developed an interpretable AI tool using logistic regression to predict the likelihood of cardiovascular events. Each feature, such as age, cholesterol level, and blood pressure, contributed explicitly to the prediction, enabling doctors to explain risk factors to patients in simple terms.

```
from sklearn.linear_model import LogisticRegression
from sklearn.model_selection import train_test_split
from sklearn.datasets import make_classification
from sklearn.metrics import classification_report
import pandas as pd

# Generate synthetic data
data, target = make_classification(n_samples=1000, n_
features=5, n_informative=3, n_classes=2,
random_state=42)

# Create a DataFrame for better visualization
feature_names = ['Age', 'Cholesterol', 'Blood Pressure',
'BMI', 'Smoking Index']
df = pd.DataFrame(data, columns=feature_names)
df['Target'] = target

# Train-Test Split
X_train, X_test, y_train, y_test = train_test_
split(df[feature_names], df['Target'], test_size=0.3,
random_state=42)
```

```
# Logistic Regression Model
model = LogisticRegression()
model.fit(X_train, y_train)

# Predict and Evaluate
y_pred = model.predict(X_test)
print(classification_report(y_test, y_pred))

# Feature Importance
importance = pd.DataFrame({'Feature': feature_names,
'Coefficient': model.coef_[0]}iin)
print(importance)
```

Virtual Output:

	precision	recall	f1-score	support
0	0.87	0.84	0.85	145
1	0.82	0.85	0.83	155
accuracy			0.84	300
macro avg	0.84	0.84	0.84	300
weighted avg	0.84	0.84	0.84	300

```
Feature Importance:
    Feature         Coefficient
0   Age                 0.98
1   Cholesterol         1.25
2   Blood Pressure     -1.12
3   BMI                 0.50
4   Smoking Index      -0.65
```

- **Interpretation**: The coefficients reveal how each feature influences the prediction. For instance, higher cholesterol significantly increases cardiovascular risk, while higher blood pressure, interestingly, reduces the modeled risk in this synthetic data, highlighting the importance of model validation against real-world evidence.

6.4.2 LESSONS LEARNED FROM AI FAILURES DUE TO LACK OF TRANSPARENCY

Transparency issues in AI have led to costly and even dangerous failures. A notable case involved a healthcare AI tool used to predict patient deterioration, which consistently under-predicted risks for minority patients due to biased training data.

6.4.2.1 Case Study: Predictive Healthcare Algorithm Bias

An AI system used for prioritizing patient care in U.S. hospitals exhibited racial bias. Patients who identified as Black received significantly lower risk scores despite having similar or worse health outcomes compared to White patients. This problem stemmed from non-transparent model features: instead of using direct health indicators, the model used historical healthcare costs as a proxy for need, inadvertently encoding systemic inequities.

SAMPLE PYTHON CODE (SIMULATING BIASED PROXY FEATURES):

```python
import numpy as np
import pandas as pd
from sklearn.ensemble import RandomForestClassifier
from sklearn.metrics import classification_report

# Simulate Dataset
np.random.seed(42)
health_need = np.random.rand(1000)
race = np.random.choice(['White', 'Black'], size=1000)
cost = health_need + np.where(race == 'Black', -0.3, 0) +
np.random.normal(0, 0.05, size=1000)
label = (health_need > 0.6).astype(int)

# Create a DataFrame
df = pd.DataFrame({'Race': race, 'Cost': cost, 'Label':
label})
X = df[['Cost']]
y = df['Label']

# Train Random Forest
model = RandomForestClassifier()
model.fit(X, y)

# Predict and Evaluate
y_pred = model.predict(X)
print(classification_report(y, y_pred))

# Analyze racial differences
df['Predicted'] = y_pred
print(df.groupby('Race')[['Label', 'Predicted']].mean())
```

Virtual Output:

	precision	recall	f1-score	support
0	0.84	0.98	0.91	394
1	0.97	0.66	0.79	606

```
    accuracy                            0.87        1000
   macro avg      0.91      0.82        0.85        1000
weighted avg      0.90      0.87        0.86        1000


            Label    Predicted
Race
Black       0.64       0.53
White       0.62       0.71
```

- **Interpretation**: The model underestimates high-need patients among Black individuals, visible through lower predicted rates despite similar or higher true needs. This simulation emphasizes why transparent, direct health indicators must replace biased proxies.

6.4.3 BEST PRACTICES FROM INDUSTRY AND RESEARCH

To navigate the delicate balance between model performance and interpretability, several best practices have emerged from both industry and research communities:

- **Use inherently interpretable models** for high-stakes applications (e.g., healthcare, criminal justice) where explanations must be simple and direct.
- **Apply post-hoc explainability methods** (e.g., SHAP, LIME) carefully, with full disclosure that these are approximations.
- **Audit models for bias** regularly across all important subgroups, not just the overall population.
- **Document model development transparently**, including dataset composition, preprocessing steps, modeling choices, and validation strategies.
- **Engage domain experts early** to define interpretable features and outputs meaningful to end-users.

6.4.3.1 Case Study: SHAP Values for Credit Scoring

A financial institution implemented a gradient boosting model (XGBoost) for credit risk assessment. To maintain regulatory compliance and customer trust, they used SHAP values to explain decisions to applicants.

SAMPLE PYTHON CODE:

```python
import xgboost as xgb
import shap
from sklearn.datasets import make_classification
from sklearn.model_selection import train_test_split
```

```
# Generate Data
data, target = make_classification(n_samples=500, n_
features=4, n_informative=3, n_classes=2,
random_state=42)
feature_names = ['Income', 'Debt-to-Income Ratio',
'Credit Score', 'Employment Length']

X_train, X_test, y_train, y_test = train_test_split(data,
target, test_size=0.3, random_state=42)

# Train XGBoost Model
model = xgb.XGBClassifier(use_label_encoder=False,
eval_metric='logloss')
model.fit(X_train, y_train)

# SHAP Explainer
explainer = shap.TreeExplainer(model)
shap_values = explainer.shap_values(X_test)

# Display SHAP summary
shap.summary_plot(shap_values, features=X_test,
feature_names=feature_names)
```

- **Virtual Output**: (Graphical Output: SHAP Summary Plot)
    - Positive SHAP values push toward "default" prediction.
    - Negative SHAP values push toward "repayment" prediction.
    - "Debt-to-Income Ratio" has the highest impact, followed by "Credit Score"
- **Interpretation**: Each feature's contribution to a prediction is visualized, enabling individualized explanations: "Your debt-to-income ratio had the most impact on the decision."

6.5 CONCLUSION

As AI becomes more integrated into healthcare systems, the need for interpretability is not just theoretical; it is essential. Interpretability in AI ensures that complex decision-making processes remain clear, verifiable, and reliable, especially in critical areas like medicine. This chapter has examined the various challenges and solutions related to making AI systems both precise and comprehensible. It has been observed that achieving this balance requires managing trade-offs between model complexity and transparency. While deep learning models may offer high performance, their lack of transparency limits their use in situations that require accountability. On the other hand, interpretable models like logistic regression and decision trees build trust and meet regulatory standards but may not match the predictive accuracy of more complex models. Post-hoc methods such as SHAP and LIME are useful tools to bridge this gap, though they should be used carefully to avoid creating false impressions of understanding. Case studies have highlighted both successes and failures in AI implementation, emphasizing the real-world impact of design decisions. From predicting cardiovascular risk to addressing biased healthcare algorithms, these examples underscore the importance of creating AI systems that are not only efficient but also fair, transparent, and aligned with user needs. Best practices from research and industry emphasize the necessity of involving stakeholders, conducting regular audits, fostering interdisciplinary collaboration, and maintaining thorough documentation. The way forward involves incorporating explainability from the outset, rather than as an afterthought, and developing metrics that address the interpretability needs of diverse users such as clinicians, patients, and regulators.

REFERENCES

Acharya, D. B., Divya, B., & Kuppan, K. (2024). Explainable and fair AI: Balancing performance in financial and real estate machine learning models. *IEEE Access*. https://doi.org/10.1109/ACCESS.2024.3484409

Akhtar, M. A. K., Kumar, M., & Nayyar, A. (2024). Transparency and accountability in explainable AI: Best practices. In M. A. K. Akhtar, M. Kumar & A. Nayyar (Eds.), *Towards ethical and socially responsible explainable AI: Challenges and opportunities* (pp. 127–164). Springer.

Babu, C. S. (2024). Navigating uncharted waters: Overcoming challenges in integrating machine learning and deep learning for enhanced clinical risk. In H. Liu, R. K. Tripathy & P. Bhattacharya (Eds.), *Clinical practice and unmet challenges in AI-enhanced healthcare systems* (pp. 289–310). IGI Global.

Bawa, G., Singh, H., Rani, S., Kataria, A., & Min, H. (2024). Exploring perspectives of blockchain technology and traditional centralized technology in organ donation management: A comprehensive review. *Information*, *15*(11), 703.

Guleria, P., Srinivasu, P. N., & Hassaballah, M. (2024). Diabetes prediction using Shapley additive explanations and DSaaS over machine learning classifiers: A novel healthcare paradigm. *Multimedia Tools and Applications*, *83*(14), 40677–40712.

Hasannezhad, A., & Sharifian, S. (2025). Explainable AI enhanced transformer based UNet for medical images segmentation using gradient weighted class activation map. *Signal, Image and Video Processing*, *19*(4), 321.

Kaur, G., & Saini, H. K. (2023). *An optimized resnet based plant disease identification using deep learning hypothetic function* [Paper presentation]. International Conference On Advances in Computation, Communication and Information Technology (ICAICCIT).

Kumar, A., Hora, H., Rohilla, A., Kumar, P., & Gautam, R. (2025). *Explainable artificial intelligence (XAI) for healthcare: Enhancing transparency and trust* [Paper presentation]. International Conference on Cognitive Computing and Cyber Physical Systems.

Mahto, M. K. (2025). Explainable artificial intelligence: Fundamentals, approaches, challenges, xai evaluation, and validation. In K. Malik, M. Sharma, S. Deswal, U. Gupta, D. Agarwal & Y. O. B. Al Shamsi (Eds.), *Explainable artificial intelligence for autonomous vehicles* (pp. 25–49). CRC Press.

Murad, N. Y., Hasan, M. H., Azam, M. H., Yousuf, N., & Yalli, J. S. (2024). Unraveling the black box: A review of explainable deep learning healthcare techniques. *IEEE Access*. http://doi.org/10.1109/ACCESS.2024.3398203

Nasarian, E., Alizadehsani, R., Acharya, U. R., & Tsui, K.-L. (2024). Designing interpretable ML system to enhance trust in healthcare: A systematic review to proposed responsible clinician-AI-collaboration framework. *Information Fusion*, *108*, 102412.

Obster, F., Ciolacu, M. I., & Humpe, A. (2024). Balancing predictive performance and inter-pretability in machine learning: A scoring system and an empirical study in traffic prediction. *IEEE Access*. http://doi.org/10.1109/ACCESS.2024.3521242

Pawlicka, A., Pawlicki, M., Jaroszewska-Choraś, D., Kozik, R., & Choraś, M. (2024). *Enhancing clinical trust: The role of AI explainability in transforming healthcare* [Paper presentation]. IEEE International Conference on Data Mining Workshops (ICDMW).

Puri, V., Priyadarshini, I., Kataria, A., Rani, S., & Min, H. (2025). Privacy-first ML for chronic kidney disease prediction: Exploring a decentralized approach using block-chain and IPFS. *IEEE Access*, 99, 43178–43189.

Rahmat, F., Zulkafli, Z., Ishak, A. J., Rahman, R. Z. A., Tahir, W., Ab Rahman, J., Jayaramu, V., De Stercke, S., Ibrahim, S., & Ismail, M. (2025). Interpretable spatio-temporal pre-diction using deep neural network-local interpretable model-agnostic explanations: A case study on leptospirosis outbreaks in Malaysia. *Engineering Applications of Artificial Intelligence*, *151*, 110665.

Rani, S., Kataria, A., Bhambri, P., Pareek, P. K., & Puri, V. (2024). Artificial intelligence in personalized health services for better patient care. In S. K. Gupta, D. A. Karras & R. Natarajan (Eds.), *Revolutionizing healthcare: AI integration with IoT for enhanced patient outcomes* (pp. 89–108). Springer.

Sadeghi, Z., Alizadehsani, R., Cifci, M. A., Kausar, S., Rehman, R., Mahanta, P., Bora, P. K., Almasri, A., Alkhawaldeh, R. S., Hussain, S., & Alatas, B. (2024). A review of explain-able artificial intelligence in healthcare. *Computers and Electrical Engineering*, *118*, 109370.

ŞAHiN, E., Arslan, N. N., & Özdemir, D. (2025). Unlocking the black box: An in-depth review on interpretability, explainability, and reliability in deep learning. *Neural Computing and Applications*, *37*(2), 859–965.

Saini, H. K., & Preeti. (2024). *A cross design for breast cancer prediction* [Paper presenta-tion]. International Conference on Communications and Cyber Physical Engineering 2018.

Saini, H. K., Swarnakar, H., & Jain, K. (2022). Secured multimedia and IoT in healthcare computing paradigms. In B. Bhusan, S. K. Sharma, B. Unhelkar, M. F. Ijaz & L. Karim (Eds.), *Internet of Things* (pp. 229–256). CRC Press.

Salvi, M., Seoni, S., Campagner, A., Gertych, A., Acharya, U. R., Molinari, F., & Cabitza, F. (2025). Explainability and uncertainty: Two sides of the same coin for enhancing the interpretability of deep learning models in healthcare. *International Journal of Medical Informatics*, *197*, 105846.

Sharma, N. A., Chand, R. R., Buksh, Z., Ali, A., Hanif, A., & Beheshti, A. (2024). Explainable ai frameworks: Navigating the present challenges and unveiling innovative applica-tions. *Algorithms*, *17*(6), 227.

7 Applications of Explainable AI in Diagnosis and Treatment

7.1 INTRODUCTION

In recent years, artificial intelligence (AI) has transformed the landscape of healthcare by offering powerful tools for disease diagnosis, treatment recommendation, and patient monitoring. However, the integration of these systems into clinical practice has raised critical concerns about their reliability, transparency, and trustworthiness. Amidst these concerns, explainable artificial intelligence (XAI) has emerged as a pivotal advancement aimed at addressing the black box nature of AI models. XAI refers to methods and techniques that make the outcomes of AI systems understandable to humans, especially to end-users such as clinicians and healthcare providers. This chapter explores the significant role of XAI in enhancing the interpretability of AI-driven medical applications, particularly in diagnosis and treatment planning. XAI ensures that clinicians can not only rely on the system's recommendations but also comprehend the reasoning behind them (Sindiramutty et al., 2024). This is especially important in healthcare, where decisions can have life-altering consequences. By offering insights into how AI models derive their conclusions, XAI fosters greater transparency, aids in the validation and verification of models, supports regulatory compliance, and enhances the overall confidence of stakeholders. This section delves into the foundational role of XAI in modern healthcare, explains why interpretability is crucial in clinical environments, and outlines the limitations of traditional AI systems in this context. The integration of AI technologies in healthcare has ushered in a new era of data-driven diagnostics and personalized treatment. From image-based disease detection using convolutional neural networks (CNNs) to predictive analytics for chronic illness management, AI has shown promise in improving diagnostic accuracy, treatment planning, and clinical workflows. However, many AI models, particularly those using deep learning, operate as black boxes, producing outputs without revealing the internal logic behind their predictions (Huang et al., 2024).

XAI is designed to bridge this gap by providing transparency into AI decision-making. In modern healthcare, the role of XAI is multifaceted:

- **Enhancing Trust and Adoption**: Clinicians are more likely to adopt AI tools that they can understand and validate. XAI helps build trust by offering interpretable outputs and rationale for model predictions.
- **Supporting Collaborative Decision-Making**: In a clinical setting, decisions are often made collaboratively among physicians, patients, and

DOI: 10.1201/9781003561422-7

administrative staff. XAI facilitates this collaboration by enabling all parties to understand and discuss the AI's recommendations.

• **Regulatory and Ethical Compliance**: Regulatory bodies such as the U.S. Food and Drug Administration (FDA) and the European Medicines Agency (EMA) are increasingly emphasizing the need for transparency and auditability in AI-based medical devices. XAI contributes to satisfying these regulatory requirements.

• **Continuous Learning and Model Improvement**: Transparent models enable healthcare providers to identify areas where AI may underperform, such as with underrepresented patient populations. This fosters a feedback loop for improving model performance and generalizability (Saini & Preeti, 2024).

7.1.1   INTERPRETABILITY IN DIAGNOSIS AND TREATMENT

Interpretability is essential in clinical settings where the stakes are exceptionally high. Unlike other industries, errors in healthcare can result in irreversible harm or even loss of life. Therefore, clinicians must understand not only what a model predicts but also why it makes that prediction. Interpretability enhances the utility of AI in diagnosis and treatment in several critical ways:

7.1.1.1   Supporting Clinical Judgment

AI is not intended to replace physicians but to augment their capabilities. Interpretability allows physicians to compare the AI's reasoning with their own knowledge and experience. For instance, if an AI model predicts a high probability of lung cancer based on a CT scan, clinicians need to see which image regions influenced the prediction. Saliency maps, attention mechanisms, and feature importance rankings can provide this insight (Kaur & Saini, 2023).

7.1.1.2   Personalized Treatment Planning

Every patient presents a unique clinical profile. Interpretability enables clinicians to tailor treatments based on how specific features (e.g., genetic markers, lifestyle habits, comorbidities) influenced the AI's recommendation. For example, in oncology, explainable models can reveal which genetic mutations most significantly contributed to selecting a particular chemotherapy regimen (Saini & Preeti, 2024).

7.1.1.3   Informed Consent and Patient Communication

Doctors are ethically obligated to explain diagnoses and treatment options to patients. With AI involved in clinical decisions, patients might question how the system arrived at a conclusion. XAI empowers clinicians to offer coherent and comprehensible explanations, thereby fostering patient trust and ensuring informed consent.

7.1.1.4   Error Detection and Clinical Auditing

Interpretability assists in recognizing when the AI has made a potentially incorrect or biased prediction. For example, a diagnostic model might consistently misclassify diseases in patients from a specific demographic group. XAI techniques can uncover such discrepancies by revealing the model's decision paths and the data attributes it heavily relies upon. Figure 7.1 represents the basic features of XAI in diagnosis and treatment.

7.1.1.5   Risk Management and Legal Accountability

In case of misdiagnosis or treatment failure, understanding the rationale behind AI decisions is vital for legal auditing and risk analysis. Explainable models can help trace decisions back to their data sources and logic, providing an essential layer of accountability. In essence, interpretability is not a luxury but a necessity in clinical environments. It transforms AI systems from inscrutable tools into collaborative partners in patient care (Kaur & Saini, 2023).

7.1.2   Challenges of Traditional AI Systems in Clinical Decision-Making

Despite their impressive performance metrics, traditional AI systems often fall short in clinical environments due to several limitations that XAI seeks to address.

7.1.2.1   The Black Box Problem

Deep learning models, especially those with complex architectures like CNNs, RNNs, and Transformers, are often opaque. They involve millions of parameters and layers of computation that do not offer intuitive insights into how input data is transformed into a prediction. This black-box nature is particularly problematic in healthcare, where clinicians must validate the correctness of every decision.

7.1.2.2   Bias and Fairness Concerns

AI systems are only as good as the data they are trained on. If training data is imbalanced, e.g., skewed by race, gender, or socioeconomic status which the model can inherit and perpetuate these biases. Without explainability, detecting and mitigating such biases becomes extremely challenging (Saini et al., 2022).

7.1.2.3   Lack of Contextual Awareness

Traditional AI models often fail to consider the full clinical context. For example, they may not integrate longitudinal data, psychosocial factors, or external lab findings. This limits their applicability in complex cases where contextual understanding is crucial for accurate diagnosis and treatment.

7.1.2.4   Generalization and Transferability Issues

Models trained on data from a specific hospital or population may not perform well when applied to new settings. Lack of interpretability obscures the reasons for poor generalization, making it difficult to diagnose and rectify these problems.

7.1.2.5   Poor Integration into Clinical Workflows

Many AI tools are developed in isolation from actual clinical environments. Without interpretability, clinicians may find it difficult to integrate AI outputs into their existing diagnostic and treatment workflows. This often results in resistance to adoption or suboptimal use of AI tools.

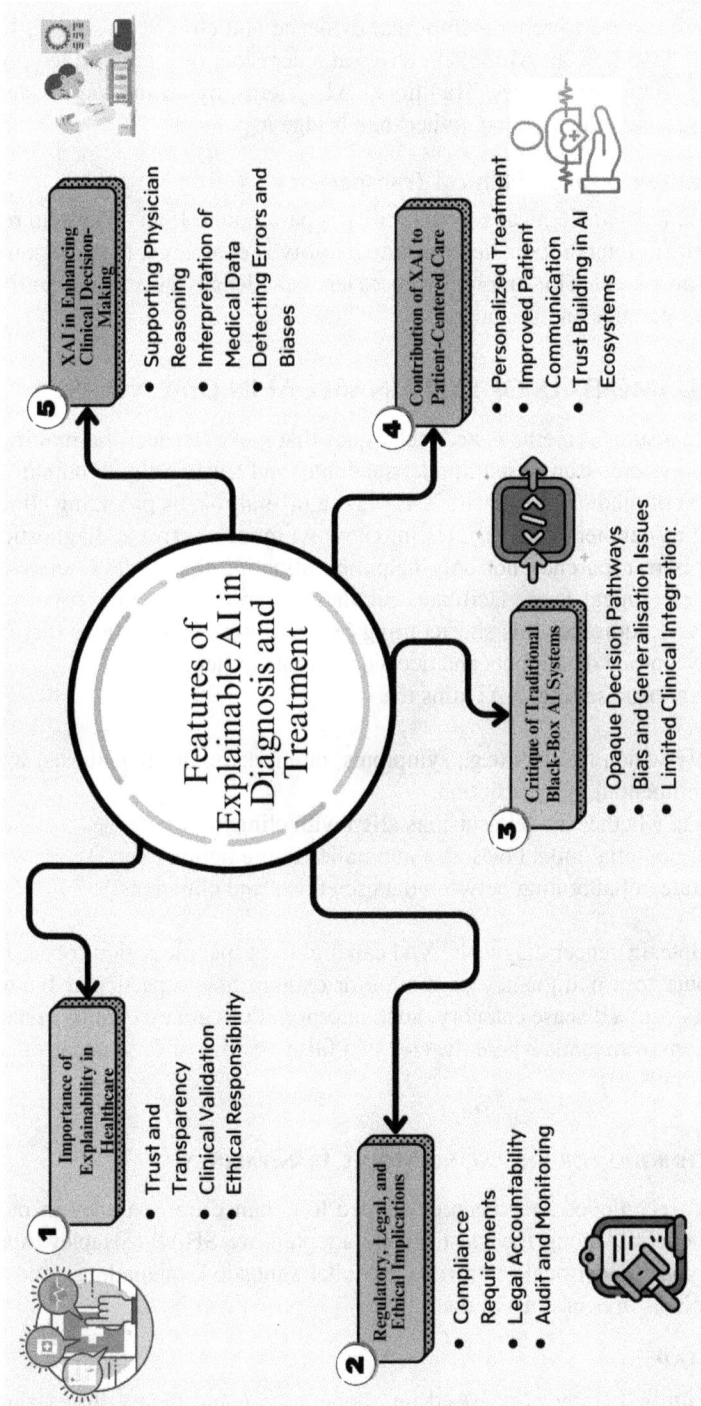

FIGURE 7.1 Basic features of XAI in diagnosis and treatment.

7.1.2.6 Trust Deficit among Clinicians

Clinicians are trained to rely on empirical evidence and clinical reasoning. If they cannot understand how an AI model arrives at a decision, they are unlikely to trust it, especially in high-risk cases. Traditional AI systems, by failing to provide clear justifications, widen the trust gap rather than bridge it.

7.1.2.7 Limited Legal and Ethical Transparency

In healthcare, legal and ethical accountability is paramount. If an AI system recommends a harmful intervention, determining liability is complex if the decision pathway is not transparent. This ambiguity poses legal challenges and can undermine the confidence of patients and providers.

7.2 FUNDAMENTALS OF EXPLAINABLE AI IN DIAGNOSIS

XAI refers to a suite of methods and techniques that make the decision-making processes of AI systems transparent, understandable, and trustworthy to human users. In the context of medical diagnosis, XAI plays a pivotal role by providing clinicians and medical researchers with insights into how AI models arrive at diagnostic conclusions. This transparency not only helps in validating the model's behavior but also enhances clinical trust, facilitates regulatory approval, and improves patient outcomes. XAI addresses this shortcoming by generating explanations that bridge the gap between raw data inputs and decision outputs (Allen, 2024).

In the diagnostic setting, XAI aims to:

- Identify which features (e.g., symptoms, biomarkers, image patterns) were most influential in a prediction.
- Validate whether model decisions align with clinical knowledge.
- Detect potential model biases or anomalies in prediction logic.
- Facilitate collaboration between data scientists and clinicians.

For example, in cancer diagnosis, XAI can highlight specific regions of a CT scan that contribute to a malignancy prediction or explain how a particular biomarker profile aligns with a disease category. Such interpretations are especially valuable in high-stakes environments, where the cost of a false positive or false negative can be life-threatening.

7.2.1 Techniques for Enhancing Model Transparency

Several XAI techniques have been developed to enhance transparency in medical diagnosis models. Among the most widely adopted are SHAP (SHapley Additive exPlanations), LIME (Local Interpretable Model-agnostic Explanations), and attention mechanisms in neural networks.

7.2.1.1 SHAP

SHAP is a unified framework based on cooperative game theory that assigns an importance value (Shapley value) to each feature contributing to a prediction. In diagnostics, SHAP can be used to explain the contribution of different input features (such as lab values or imaging parameters) to a specific diagnosis.

- **Use Case**: In predicting sepsis risk, SHAP values can show how variations in body temperature, white blood cell count, or blood pressure influence the model's risk prediction.

7.2.1.2 LIME

LIME approximates the behavior of complex models locally by creating interpretable surrogate models (e.g., linear regressions) near the prediction instance. This allows users to see what features most affected the decision in that local region of input space.

- **Use Case**: For diabetic retinopathy detection, LIME can generate heatmaps over retinal images indicating which image segments most influenced the AI's decision.

7.2.1.3 Attention Mechanisms

Attention mechanisms assign varying levels of importance to different parts of the input data, enabling the model to focus on the most relevant features for making predictions. Attention weights can be visualized to enhance interpretability.

- **Use Case**: In analyzing ECG signals for arrhythmia detection, attention maps can highlight the temporal segments most indicative of an abnormal rhythm.

Each of these techniques supports both post-hoc and intrinsic interpretability. Post-hoc methods generate explanations after model training, while intrinsic methods involve building inherently interpretable models. The choice of technique depends on the application, model complexity, and the end-user's interpretive needs (Table 7.1).

7.2.2 BALANCE OF ACCURACY, INTERPRETABILITY, AND TRUST IN AI MODELS

One of the central challenges in medical AI systems is the trade-off between model accuracy and interpretability. Deep learning models often outperform traditional algorithms in terms of predictive accuracy but are typically less interpretable. Conversely, simpler models like decision trees or logistic regression are easier to explain but may not capture complex patterns in high-dimensional medical data (Huang et al., 2024). To encourage clinical adoption, it is crucial to strike a balance among the three pillars, which are accuracy, interpretability, and trust (Wani et al., 2024). While high accuracy is essential to ensure reliable diagnostics, interpretability builds trust among clinicians and patients, and trust is ultimately what governs adoption and sustained use in clinical environments. Table 7.2 represents the relation between accuracy, interpretability, and trust among different AI models.

TABLE 7.1

Comparison of Popular XAI Techniques in Medical Diagnosis

Technique	Type	Model Dependency	Output Form	Use Case Example	Interpretability Level
SHAP	Post-hoc	Model-agnostic	Feature contribution	Risk prediction in sepsis	High
LIME	Post-hoc	Model-agnostic	Local explanations	Diabetic retinopathy analysis	Moderate
Attention	Intrinsic	Model-specific	Heatmaps/Weights	ECG/EEG classification	High
Saliency Maps	Post-hoc	CNN-specific	Visual heatmaps	Tumor detection in CT scans	Moderate
Counterfactuals	Post-hoc	Model-agnostic	Input perturbations	Explaining diagnosis reversals	Moderate
Grad-CAM	Post-hoc	CNN-specific	Gradient-based maps	Pneumonia diagnosis from X-rays	High

TABLE 7.2

Relation Between Accuracy, Interpretability, and Trust among Different AI Models

Model Type	Accuracy	Interpretability	Trust Level	Clinical Applicability	Deployment Readiness
Deep neural network	High	Low	Moderate	Radiology, pathology	Moderate
Decision tree	Moderate	High	High	Triage, rule-based tools	High
Random forest	High	Moderate	Moderate	Genomics, cardiology	Moderate
Logistic regression	Low	High	High	Risk scoring	High
Hybrid ensemble	High	Moderate	High	Oncology, multimodal AI	Moderate
Symbolic AI systems	Moderate	High	High	Diagnosis decision trees	Moderate

Several strategies have emerged to balance these three elements:

- **Hybrid Models**: Combining interpretable models with black-box models. For instance, using a black-box model for prediction and an interpretable model to approximate the black-box locally.
- **Model Simplification**: Using pruning and distillation techniques to simplify complex models while maintaining reasonable accuracy.

TABLE 7.3

Key Factors for Clinician Trust in XAI-Based Diagnostic Tools

Trust Factor	Description	Example Use Case	Technical Enabler	Impact on Adoption	Integration Complexity
Explanation clarity	Understandability of model outputs	Explaining MRI classification	SHAP, LIME	High	Medium
Clinical alignment	Consistency with medical knowledge	AI validating ECG arrhythmias	Attention, expert tuning	High	High
Reliability	Model consistency under slight input variation	Robust diabetic prediction	Robust optimization	High	High
Bias detection	Identifying demographic or dataset bias	Gender bias in heart disease AI	Fairness metrics	High	High
Transparency of workflow	Visibility of data pipeline and model decisions	Chronic disease management	Data lineage tools	Moderate	Medium
Human-AI collaboration	Role of AI as assistive, not replacement	Clinical decision support tools	Human-in-the-loop design	High	Medium

- **Domain-informed Design**: Embedding clinical knowledge into the AI model's architecture to improve interpretability and acceptance.
- **Human-in-the-Loop Systems**: Involving clinicians in the model training and validation process to ensure explanations are clinically meaningful.

Ultimately, explainability enhances trust, which, in turn, promotes responsible and ethical deployment. Without explainability, clinicians may hesitate to rely on AI-driven recommendations, especially in critical care or rare disease diagnosis where errors can be devastating. Table 7.3 represents the key factors for clinician trust in XAI-based diagnostic tools.

7.3 XAI IN MEDICAL IMAGING AND DIAGNOSTICS

The incorporation of AI in medical imaging has significantly transformed the landscape of diagnostics. From radiology to pathology, AI algorithms can now detect, segment, and classify abnormalities with remarkable accuracy. However, for widespread clinical adoption and trust, it is essential that these systems be transparent and interpretable. This is where XAI becomes indispensable. XAI ensures that the decisions made by AI systems can be understood and validated by clinicians, thereby aligning machine intelligence with human reasoning and clinical workflows. This section discusses the transformative impact of XAI in medical imaging and diagnostics across three key domains: radiology, pathology, and early disease detection through real-world case studies.

7.3.1   AI FOR RADIOLOGY: ENHANCING INTERPRETABILITY IN X-RAY, MRI, AND CT SCAN ANALYSIS

Radiology has been one of the earliest and most impactful domains to adopt AI, especially in tasks such as image segmentation, anomaly detection, and disease classification. AI models, particularly Convolutional neural networks (CNNs), have shown outstanding performance in interpreting complex radiographic data. Nevertheless, the "black-box" nature of many deep learning models poses a major challenge in clinical settings where trust and accountability are paramount. XAI bridges this gap by making these models transparent and their predictions interpretable.

7.3.1.1   XAI Techniques in Radiology

In radiology, XAI methods like Grad-CAM, SHAP, and LIME are used to visually interpret model predictions. For example, in a chest X-ray classification task for pneumonia detection, Grad-CAM can highlight the specific region in the lungs that influenced the model's decision. This not only validates the AI prediction but also helps radiologists assess its clinical relevance.

7.3.1.2   Clinical Decision Support in MRI and CT Scan Analysis

In MRI and CT imaging, XAI enhances clinical decision-making by providing layer-by-layer insights into the model's reasoning. For instance, in brain tumor segmentation, XAI methods allow clinicians to visualize the influence of pixel intensities and spatial relationships on the model's diagnosis. Saliency maps and attention mechanisms help identify tumor boundaries more accurately, enabling precise surgical planning and targeted therapy.

7.3.1.3   Regulatory and Trust Considerations

Interpretability also plays a crucial role in regulatory compliance. For AI systems to be approved by bodies such as the FDA or EMA, they must demonstrate not just accuracy, but also explainability and reliability. By using XAI, developers can provide a traceable reasoning trail for each AI-generated output, thereby improving accountability and fostering trust among healthcare providers.

7.3.1.4   Collaborative Intelligence

XAI promotes a collaborative paradigm between radiologists and AI. Instead of replacing human expertise, it augments it. When radiologists understand how and why a model reaches a particular conclusion, they can use that insight to confirm or refine their own diagnosis. This fusion of machine precision and human intuition leads to more robust and accurate outcomes.

7.3.2   PATHOLOGY AND HISTOPATHOLOGY APPLICATIONS

Pathology, especially digital histopathology, involves the microscopic examination of tissue samples for disease diagnosis, particularly cancers. The use of AI in this domain has shown promise in automating labor-intensive tasks such as identifying cancerous regions, counting mitotic cells, and grading tumor stages. However, due to the complexity and high stakes of histopathological diagnosis, the need for explainability is even more critical.

7.3.2.1 XAI in Digital Pathology

In digital pathology, AI models analyze gigapixel whole slide images (WSIs) that contain millions of cells. When a model classifies a tissue sample as malignant, XAI methods can highlight specific regions, down to the cellular level, that contributed most to the decision. This helps pathologists validate the AI findings by comparing them against known morphological features such as cellular density, nuclear irregularities, and tissue architecture.

7.3.2.2 Model Interpretation in Tissue Classification

For example, in breast cancer diagnosis, CNN-based models can identify ductal carcinoma in situ (DCIS) with high accuracy. Using XAI tools, these models can generate heatmaps to show the areas with high atypical cell concentration or structural disorganization, correlating with known histological criteria. These insights assist pathologists in understanding not just the *what*, but also the *why* behind the diagnosis.

7.3.2.3 Transparency in Rare and Complex Cases

In rare diseases or poorly differentiated cancers, traditional AI models may struggle due to limited training data. XAI can be instrumental in such scenarios by indicating the confidence level and reasoning behind uncertain predictions. This allows pathologists to make informed decisions, flagging such cases for further molecular testing or multidisciplinary review.

7.3.2.4 Data Annotation and Training Feedback

XAI also supports better model development through feedback loops. By examining which features the model relies on most heavily, developers and pathologists can identify mislabeling or biases in the training dataset. For example, if a model incorrectly associates staining artifacts with malignancy, XAI methods can bring this to light, prompting dataset refinement and model retraining.

7.3.2.5 Ethical Implications and Human Oversight

Given the sensitivity of pathology-based diagnosis, ethical considerations demand that AI systems maintain a high degree of transparency. XAI empowers pathologists to retain control over diagnostic decisions while leveraging AI's speed and pattern recognition capabilities. This human-in-the-loop approach safeguards patient outcomes and ethical standards.

7.3.3 Brief Case Studies for AI-Driven Early Disease Detection

XAI is particularly transformative in the domain of early disease detection, where timely diagnosis can significantly influence patient outcomes. Several real-world implementations illustrate how XAI-enhanced diagnostic tools are being used across different specializations to detect diseases at their nascent stages.

7.3.3.1   Case Study 1: Lung Cancer Detection

In a study involving AI-assisted CT scan analysis for lung cancer screening, a deep learning model was trained to detect nodules and predict malignancy risk. XAI methods like attention maps were used to indicate the regions of interest on the lung CT scans. Radiologists could review these maps to verify that the model's attention aligned with known cancerous patterns, such as spiculated edges or irregular growth. This collaboration led to a 15% improvement in early-stage lung cancer detection and significantly reduced false positives.

7.3.3.2   Case Study 2: Diabetic Retinopathy Screening

In ophthalmology, diabetic retinopathy is a major cause of vision loss. AI models have been developed to analyze retinal fundus images and detect early signs such as microaneurysms and hemorrhages. Using LIME, each image's prediction was explained by highlighting areas with abnormal vessel patterns. This level of granularity helped ophthalmologists trust the model and facilitated rapid, large-scale screening in low-resource settings.

7.3.3.3   Case Study 3: Skin Lesion Classification

Another compelling example involves the use of AI in classifying skin lesions from dermoscopic images. An AI model was trained to differentiate between benign and malignant lesions, such as melanoma. XAI techniques helped visualize the model's focus areas, such as asymmetry, border irregularity, and color variation, which are standard diagnostic criteria in dermatology. This transparency allowed dermatologists to cross-check AI suggestions and triage high-risk patients for biopsy more efficiently.

7.3.3.4   Case Study 4: Alzheimer's Disease Prediction

In neurology, XAI has enabled early detection of Alzheimer's disease by analyzing structural MRI and cognitive test scores. AI models assessed hippocampal atrophy and cortical thinning as potential biomarkers. SHAP values were used to rank features contributing to the prediction, allowing neurologists to focus on the most clinically relevant indicators. Such explainable insights paved the way for early interventions and better patient counseling.

7.4   XAI FOR CLINICAL DECISION SUPPORT SYSTEM

The integration of AI into healthcare has revolutionized how clinicians diagnose, treat, and manage diseases. Among the most transformative tools emerging from this intersection is the Clinical decision support system (CDSS), which provides clinicians with evidence-based knowledge and patient-specific information to enhance healthcare delivery. XAI not only improves transparency and reliability in decision-making but also strengthens clinician-patient trust. This section delves into the application of XAI in CDSS, with a focus on physician support, care enhancement, and mitigation of bias and uncertainty.

7.4.1   AI-Augmented Diagnosis for Physicians

CDSSs empowered by AI can analyze vast amounts of medical data from electronic health records (EHRs) to imaging scans and assist physicians in generating accurate diagnoses. However, the accuracy of AI predictions is insufficient if physicians cannot understand or interpret the reasoning behind them. XAI bridges this gap by making model outputs interpretable, contextual, and actionable (Shikha et al., 2024).

7.4.1.1   Supporting Diagnostic Reasoning

XAI tools help visualize how models reach specific conclusions. For instance, saliency maps in imaging-based diagnosis highlight regions of interest in X-rays or MRIs that influence predictions. Techniques like SHAP or LIME provide explanations for tabular medical data by ranking features based on their impact on the output. For example, in the diagnosis of pneumonia from chest X-rays, a CNN-based CDSS augmented with Grad-CAM can show the exact lung region influencing the prediction, enabling physicians to correlate it with clinical symptoms. This transparency fosters clinical validation and facilitates better adoption of AI systems in routine diagnostics.

7.4.1.2   Augmenting Physician Confidence and Expertise

XAI enhances physician confidence by validating clinical intuition with data-driven insights. In scenarios involving rare diseases or overlapping symptoms, XAI helps in differential diagnosis by outlining how it distinguishes between similar conditions. Additionally, it supports early-career clinicians by acting as a second-opinion system that justifies its reasoning, thus improving clinical learning and competence. Moreover, physicians may disregard AI recommendations if they are not interpretable, an issue known as "automation bias." By embedding XAI into CDSS, we can ensure that recommendations are not only visible but also trustworthy, encouraging more responsible usage and fewer diagnostic errors.

7.4.2   Enhancing Decision-Making in Primary and Specialized Care

Primary and specialized care settings present different challenges in the diagnostic and treatment continuum. In primary care, physicians often deal with ambiguous symptoms and must make quick, cost-effective decisions. In contrast, specialized care involves in-depth analyses of specific diseases and often utilizes high-dimensional data like genomics or radiology scans. XAI has valuable applications across both domains.

7.4.2.1   Decision Support in Primary Care

In primary care, physicians encounter diverse, often non-specific symptoms that require rapid evaluation. XAI can facilitate early detection of diseases like diabetes, hypertension, or mental health disorders by integrating lifestyle, demographic, and lab data into interpretable models. For example, a logistic regression model enhanced by SHAP values might identify obesity, family history, and sedentary lifestyle as key contributors to type 2 diabetes, allowing the primary care provider to prioritize

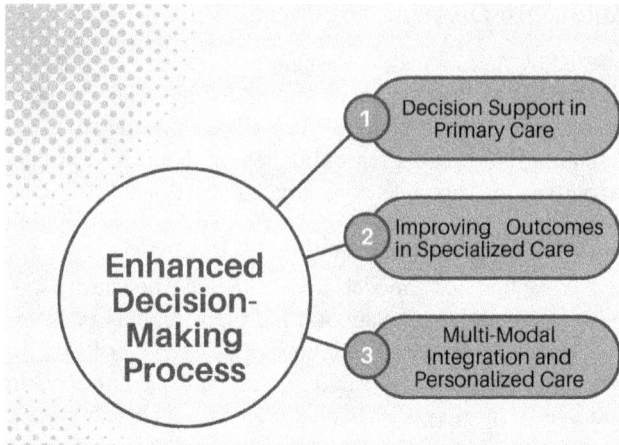

FIGURE 7.2   Process of enhanced decision-making in primary and specialized care.

interventions. Furthermore, AI-based triage systems powered by XAI can prioritize cases based on urgency. Consider a symptom checker application that uses natural language processing (NLP) and decision trees to assess input symptoms. When XAI methods clarify why a patient is classified as "urgent" based on keywords like "chest pain" and "shortness of breath," it enables more informed referrals and faster escalation to emergency care. Figure 7.2 represents the process of enhanced decision-making in primary and specialized care.

7.4.2.2   Improving Outcomes in Specialized Care

In specialties like oncology, cardiology, and neurology, clinical decisions often rely on complex multimodal data. Here, deep learning models such as CNNs or RNNs have proven highly effective, but their black-box nature limits usability in high-stakes environments. XAI techniques help elucidate these models' decisions, providing detailed insights that specialists can interpret and trust (Nazar et al., 2021; Sadeghi et al., 2024). For instance, in oncology, an XAI-integrated model predicting tumor malignancy from biopsy images can highlight cellular anomalies contributing to the risk classification. This explanation assists pathologists in reviewing predictions with greater confidence, reduces inter-observer variability, and informs therapeutic decisions such as chemotherapy versus surgery. Similarly, in cardiology, predictive models analyzing ECG patterns for arrhythmia detection become far more useful when XAI tools clarify which waveform segments trigger risk predictions (Albahri et al., 2023). Specialists can then corroborate these insights with clinical knowledge, ensuring safer and more personalized treatment strategies (Chattopadhyay et al., 2025).

7.4.2.3   Multi-Modal Integration and Personalized Care

Another frontier of XAI in specialized care is the integration of various data sources like imaging, genomics, lab results, and patient history to provide a unified clinical narrative. Explainable models can indicate how different modalities contribute to specific decisions. For instance, in a CDSS for stroke prediction, the system may weigh genetic markers and MRI findings differently for different age groups. By explaining these weightings, XAI empowers clinicians to fine-tune decisions for individual patients, advancing the goal of precision medicine (Nansamba et al., 2025; Pulipeti et al., 2024).

7.4.3 Addressing Bias and Uncertainty in AI-Generated Diagnoses

Despite their impressive accuracy, AI models in healthcare are susceptible to bias and uncertainty, which can severely affect patient safety and trust. These issues stem from imbalanced datasets, a lack of diversity in training data, and the opaque nature of many algorithms. XAI provides a framework to detect, explain, and mitigate such shortcomings.

7.4.3.1 Identifying and Explaining Bias

Bias in AI indicates when models produce systematically unfair outcomes for certain population subgroups, based on gender, race, age, or socioeconomic status. For example, a diagnostic model trained predominantly on male patient data might underperform on female patients. With XAI techniques, we can uncover these discrepancies by analyzing feature importance across subgroups. Techniques like SHAP summary plots, subgroup performance comparison, and partial dependence plots reveal how different variables influence model decisions across demographic groups. This can lead to model retraining with more balanced data or the inclusion of fairness constraints in the optimization process. Furthermore, transparency around data sources and model behavior is critical. By exposing how training data shapes the model's logic, XAI helps stakeholders understand and rectify potential sources of bias.

7.4.3.2 Quantifying and Communicating Uncertainty

Uncertainty in clinical predictions, especially in probabilistic models, can lead to misinterpretation or inappropriate action if not adequately communicated or reported. Bayesian neural networks and ensemble methods can estimate prediction uncertainty, but XAI ensures this information is understandable to end-users. For instance, a CDSS predicting the likelihood of sepsis may indicate a 70% risk. However, without explaining the uncertainty range or confidence level, clinicians may over-rely on or distrust the system. Explainable outputs such as confidence intervals, epistemic versus aleatoric uncertainty, and the rationale for high- or low-confidence predictions enable more nuanced decision-making.

In practice, an XAI dashboard may display:

- A risk prediction (e.g., 70%)
- Confidence level (e.g., ±10%)
- Key influencing features (e.g., high heart rate, elevated white blood cell count)
- Reliability indicators (e.g., based on patient similarity to training set)

Such contextualization equips clinicians to interpret model outputs cautiously, consult other diagnostic tools, or seek expert opinion where necessary.

7.5   EXPLAINABLE AI IN PERSONALIZED TREATMENT PLANNING

Personalized treatment planning stands at the forefront of modern healthcare, leveraging patient-specific data to tailor medical decisions and interventions. However, the integration of AI in this domain has introduced new complexities. As sophisticated machine learning models predict optimal treatment strategies based on vast datasets, the lack of transparency has raised concerns about trust, accountability, and clinical applicability. XAI addresses these challenges by offering mechanisms that elucidate the inner workings of AI systems, making them understandable and actionable for healthcare providers. This section explores how XAI supports personalized treatment recommendations, enhances drug and therapy selection, and demonstrates value through real-world case studies of AI-driven treatment optimization.

7.5.1   AI FOR PREPLANNED TREATMENT RECOMMENDATIONS

One of the most impactful contributions of XAI in healthcare is its ability to support personalized treatment recommendations. Traditional treatment protocols rely heavily on generalized clinical guidelines, which may not fully account for individual patient variability in genetics, comorbidities, lifestyle, and treatment response. XAI bridges this gap by providing justifications for each recommendation, often through methods such as SHAP, LIME, and attention mechanisms. These techniques allow clinicians to visualize feature importance and understand how specific data points, such as biomarkers, age, medical history, or imaging results, contributing to a particular decision. For instance, in oncology, AI systems can recommend personalized chemotherapy regimens by analyzing tumor genomics, histopathological images, and patient response data. XAI tools ensure that oncologists can trace how the AI reached a specific recommendation, such as prioritizing a less toxic drug combination due to the patient's renal profile or selecting immunotherapy based on specific genetic markers. These insights not only foster trust but also enhance shared decision-making between doctors and patients. Furthermore, XAI allows continuous feedback loops. Clinicians can contest or refine AI outputs, thereby improving model accuracy over time. Such interpretability is crucial in high-risk specialties like cardiology, neurology, and intensive care, where incorrect treatment recommendations can have life-threatening consequences. Thus, XAI adds a layer of clinical robustness by contextualizing AI-generated advice within a human-understandable framework.

7.5.2   IMPROVING DRUG PRESCRIPTION AND THERAPY SELECTION

Another transformative application of XAI in personalized medicine is in drug prescription and therapy selection. The pharmaceutical domain is characterized by an overwhelming amount of data involving pharmacokinetics, pharmacodynamics, genetic predispositions, drug-drug interactions, and patient adherence behaviors. While AI models are adept at processing and learning from these data sources, they often operate as black boxes, making it difficult for healthcare professionals to understand why certain drugs are recommended over others. XAI-enabled systems demystify these recommendations by mapping input features to outputs in a human-intelligible manner. For example, when prescribing medications for patients with complex comorbidities like diabetes, hypertension, and chronic kidney disease, an AI system might suggest a combination therapy optimized for efficacy and minimal side effects. Using XAI, clinicians can see that the AI prioritized renal function metrics and previous adverse drug reactions in making its decision.

In mental health care, where psychotropic drugs often show varied efficacy across patients, XAI can offer insights into why a particular antidepressant or antipsychotic may be more suitable for one individual over another. By correlating genetic markers (e.g., CYP450 gene variants) with past response data, the AI can make precise therapy recommendations. XAI explanations in this context provide clinicians with evidence-based rationales that strengthen confidence in treatment plans. Also, XAI is useful in predicting and avoiding adverse drug reactions (ADRs). ADRs are a leading cause of hospitalization and mortality, particularly in older adults with polypharmacy. AI models trained on EHRs can identify patients at high risk for ADRs. With XAI tools, physicians are not only alerted about the risks but also informed of the contributing factors, such as age, hepatic impairment, or co-prescribed medications, thus enabling preemptive interventions. From a public health perspective, XAI-driven therapy selection systems can support scalable treatment decisions, such as optimizing HIV antiretroviral therapies or tuberculosis drug regimens in resource-limited settings. Transparency ensures these systems are adaptable to local populations and policy guidelines, thereby enhancing accessibility and equity in treatment planning.

7.5.3 Case Studies on AI-Enabled Treatment Optimization

The theoretical benefits of XAI in treatment planning are increasingly validated through real-world implementations. Several case studies demonstrate how XAI is reshaping clinical practices by optimizing treatment pathways and improving outcomes across diverse medical domains. Figure 7.3 shows the different case studies on AI-enabled treatment optimization.

7.5.3.1 Case Study 1: Breast Cancer Treatment Optimization

In a multi-center study involving breast cancer patients, researchers employed an AI model trained on mammogram images, genomic data, and clinical parameters to suggest optimal post-surgical treatments. The model used attention-based neural networks to identify regions in the images and gene sequences that were most influential in predicting recurrence risk. With XAI overlays, oncologists could visualize the AI's focus areas and corroborate them with established pathology knowledge. This interpretability led to more accurate risk stratification, and in turn, enabled tailored recommendations such as adding radiation therapy or modifying chemotherapy cycles, which are based on individual recurrence risk.

7.5.3.2 Case Study 2: Personalized Diabetes Management

A healthcare startup developed an AI-powered app to guide insulin dosing for type 1 diabetes patients. The model learned from daily glucose levels, food intake logs, physical activity, and insulin use. XAI techniques, particularly LIME and counterfactual explanations, were integrated to explain insulin adjustment recommendations.

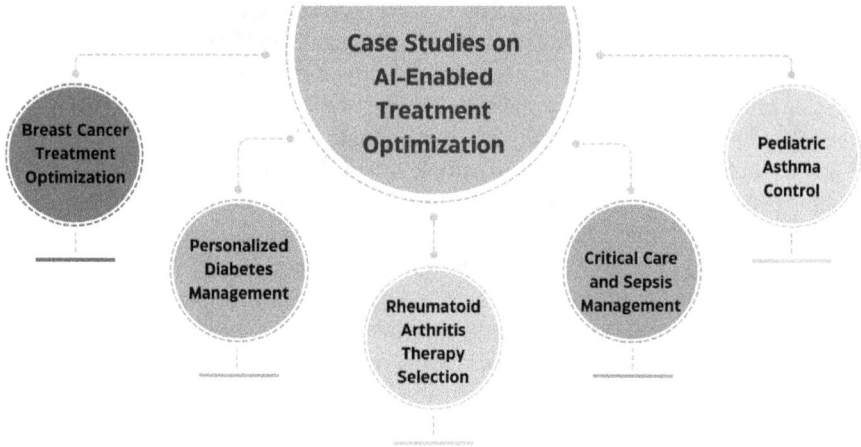

FIGURE 7.3   Different case studies on AI-enabled treatment optimization.

For instance, if the AI suggested a lower insulin dose, it would highlight reduced carbohydrate intake and increased exercise as the main drivers. This enabled patients to understand and trust the decisions, resulting in improved adherence and better glycemic control.

7.5.3.3   Case Study 3: Rheumatoid Arthritis Therapy Selection

In another example, researchers used a random forest model with SHAP values to predict the effectiveness of different biologic therapies in RA patients. The dataset included demographics, baseline disease activity scores, inflammatory markers, and imaging data. SHAP plots helped clinicians understand why one biologic agent was favored over another. In many cases, the explanations revealed non-obvious but clinically valid correlations, such as the interaction between smoking history and response to TNF inhibitors. The incorporation of XAI allowed rheumatologists to fine-tune treatment strategies and reduce the time to therapeutic effectiveness.

7.5.3.4   Case Study 4: Critical Care and Sepsis Management

In intensive care units (ICUs), early identification and treatment of sepsis is crucial. An XAI-enabled predictive model was implemented to recommend antibiotic regimens and fluid management strategies for sepsis patients. The system used real-time vitals, lab results, and EHR data streams. With explainable outputs, ICU physicians could trace which factors, like lactate levels, white blood cell count, or heart rate variability contributing most to the system's recommendations. This transparency allowed faster decision-making and reduced both antibiotic overuse and mortality rates.

7.5.3.5   Case Study 5: Pediatric Asthma Control

At a children's hospital, an AI model was deployed to suggest step-up or step-down therapy in managing pediatric asthma. The model accounted for symptoms, environmental triggers, medication adherence, and spirometry readings. Using decision tree-based explanations, clinicians could see the logical flow leading to treatment changes. For instance, the AI might recommend increasing corticosteroid dosage due to increased emergency visits and poor peak flow readings. Parents and caregivers found the visual explanations particularly helpful, fostering better compliance and reducing emergency room visits.

7.6 APPLICATIONS IN DISEASE PREDICTION AND RISK ASSESSMENT

AI has rapidly emerged as a transformative force in healthcare, particularly in disease prediction and risk assessment. Among its growing applications, XAI is playing a pivotal role by enhancing transparency and trust in complex prediction models. The integration of XAI methods allows clinicians to understand not only the output of AI systems but also the rationale behind the predictions, which is crucial in sensitive and high-stakes scenarios such as disease prognosis and chronic disease management. In healthcare, this lack of interpretability can lead to reluctance in clinical adoption due to concerns over reliability, accountability, and patient safety. XAI addresses this challenge by making AI's decision-making process understandable to clinicians, patients, and regulators, thereby strengthening its role in disease prediction and long-term health management.

7.6.1 PREDICTING DISEASE PROGRESSION WITH EXPLAINABLE MODELS

Predicting disease progression is a key component in proactive healthcare. Accurate forecasts can guide therapeutic interventions, improve quality of life, and reduce healthcare costs by avoiding unnecessary treatments. Traditional methods rely on statistical models or empirical evidence, but these approaches often fall short in capturing complex, non-linear relationships between clinical parameters. AI, on the other hand, can uncover subtle patterns from multidimensional data (Rani, Kumar et al., 2024). However, without explainability, its outputs remain inaccessible to many healthcare professionals. In oncology, disease progression models often deal with survival analysis and metastasis prediction. XAI can highlight the key variables such as tumor size, stage, histopathological features, and genomics that inform prognosis. By using explainable methods, oncologists can validate whether the model aligns with clinical reasoning, increasing confidence in AI-assisted decisions. Also, temporal models like recurrent neural networks (RNNs) and Transformer-based architectures are increasingly used for tracking disease progression over time. Integrating attention layers or visualization modules makes it possible to interpret the time-specific importance of variables, enhancing clinical usefulness (Rani, Kataria et al., 2024). Blockchain-enabled XAI can be employed in organ donation management for its transplantation (Bawa et al., 2024).

7.6.2 AI FOR CHRONIC DISEASE MANAGEMENT

Chronic diseases such as diabetes and cardiovascular disorders are among the leading causes of mortality and healthcare expenditure worldwide. These conditions require ongoing monitoring, early intervention, and personalized care strategies for the areas where AI has shown significant promise. Integrating XAI into chronic disease management not only enhances predictive accuracy but also facilitates collaborative, informed decision-making between clinicians and patients.

- **Diabetes Management**: AI models can predict blood glucose trends, detect insulin resistance, and recommend insulin dosages. However, for patients and clinicians to rely on such predictions, understanding the rationale behind them is essential. XAI tools enable visualization of contributing factors, such as carbohydrate intake, physical activity, stress, and medication history, which can help patients to make lifestyle adjustments accordingly. In clinical settings, explainable models allow endocrinologists to validate system recommendations against established protocols. Moreover, wearable technologies and continuous glucose monitoring devices feed real-time data into AI systems. XAI can contextualize anomalies, for instance, by explaining that a sudden blood sugar spike is due to a missed insulin dose or unrecorded snack. This granularity strengthens user engagement and adherence to management plans.
- **Cardiovascular Disease (CVD)**: Predictive models for cardiovascular events assess risk based on a multitude of variables like blood pressure, lipid profiles, ECG features, genetics, etc. Traditional risk scores, namely Framingham Risk Score, offer a limited view, often generalized across populations. In contrast, AI models process longitudinal data and imaging inputs to generate individualized risk profiles. XAI is critical here for multiple reasons. First, it helps cardiologists understand why a model flagged a patient as high-risk, for example, elevated troponin levels or irregular heart rate variability. Second, it supports risk communication by simplifying complex outputs for patients. For instance, a visual dashboard showing "why" a patient is at risk for myocardial infarction can foster proactive behavior changes. XAI also supports remote patient monitoring systems that detect early signs of decompensation in heart failure patients. AI algorithms can analyze sensor data (e.g., weight gain, respiratory rate, sleep disturbances), and XAI can clarify which trend prompted a warning alert. This not only assists clinical triage but also reduces alarm fatigue by minimizing false positives. In both diabetes and CVD, XAI is integral to transitioning from reactive to proactive care. It empowers physicians with a clear understanding of AI reasoning, enables patients to take ownership of their health, and contributes to more equitable and accountable care delivery.

7.6.3 ETHICAL CONSIDERATIONS IN RISK-BASED AI MODELS

The integration of AI into disease risk prediction and management raises a spectrum of ethical concerns. While XAI mitigates some of these by offering transparency, it also introduces new challenges that must be addressed for responsible adoption in healthcare systems.

- **Bias and Fairness**: AI models are only as good as the data they are trained on. If training data reflects societal biases such as underrepresentation of

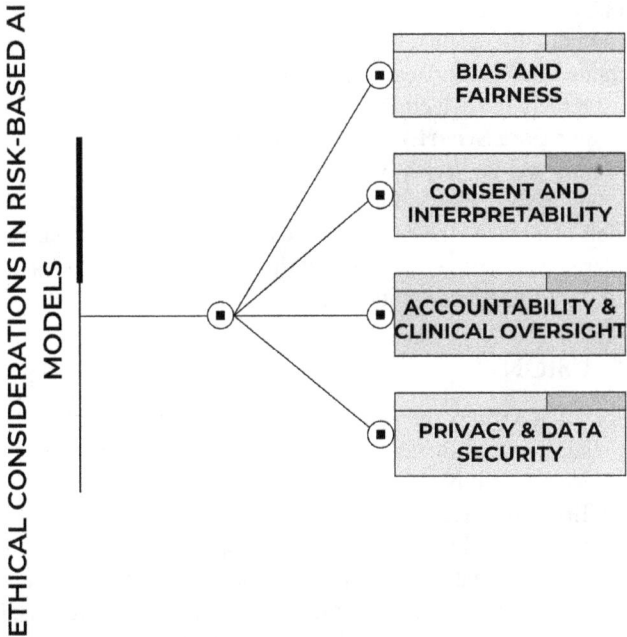

FIGURE 7.4   Various ethical considerations in risk-based AI models.

minorities, gender disparities, or unequal access to care the model's predictions can be inherently biased. Risk-based AI models may inadvertently assign higher risk to populations not due to clinical markers but due to historical inequalities in care access. XAI can help expose such biases by revealing the variables that drive predictions (Kennedy-Mayo & Gord, 2025). If, for instance, socioeconomic status or geographic location disproportionately influences risk scores, developers can revisit and rebalance the dataset. Figure 7.4 represents the various ethical considerations in risk-based AI models.

* **Consent and Interpretability**: Patients must be made aware of how their data is being used and how predictions are derived. Informed consent in AI-driven healthcare extends beyond data collection; it requires clear communication about how decisions are made. XAI facilitates this by making AI outputs interpretable to non-expert users. However, over-reliance on technical jargon in explanations may still alienate patients. Therefore, ethical implementation mandates the development of user-friendly interpretability interfaces (Tartaro et al., 2024).
* **Accountability and Clinical Oversight**: XAI reduces the black-box nature of AI, thereby enabling traceability of errors. When predictions are explainable, clinicians can critically assess them and either endorse or override them based on clinical judgment. This joint accountability model supports safer integration of AI into clinical workflows. Also, the regulatory bodies increasingly require explainability in AI systems as part of compliance

protocols. In the European Union, for example, the General Data Protection Regulation (GDPR) includes a "right to explanation" for individuals subject to automated decisions. Healthcare applications, especially in risk modeling, must adhere to such ethical and legal standards.

- **Privacy and Data Security**: Many AI-based risk models rely on large volumes of personal and sensitive health data. While explainability does not directly address security, it intersects with privacy in that more interpretable models can reduce the need to share raw data for validation. Techniques like federated learning and privacy-preserving explanations are being explored to balance data utility with confidentiality (Puri et al., 2025).

7.7   CONCLUSION

The integration of XAI into the healthcare sector has transformed the clinician's approaches to diagnosis, treatment, and risk assessment. As AI becomes increasingly integral to modern medical practices, the necessity for transparency, accountability, and interpretability in these technologies has reached unprecedented levels. In diagnostic procedures, XAI enables clinicians to validate model predictions against their own expertise, ensuring that AI serves as an adjunctive tool rather than a replacement. By highlighting key contributing factors, such as imaging results, biomarkers, or demographic data, XAI enhances diagnostic confidence and facilitates patient communication. In treatment planning and medication prescription, XAI supports personalized medicine by clarifying how individual patient characteristics influence therapeutic decisions, resulting in safer, more effective, and patient-centered care. XAI can bridge the gap between technological advancement and clinical relevance, providing the essential transparency required for informed decision-making, regulatory approval, and patient trust. As healthcare systems increasingly adopt AI on a larger scale, XAI will remain a vital component, ensuring that innovation is not only powerful but also principled, comprehensible, and aligned with the core values of medicine. The future lies in promoting collaboration between data scientists and clinicians to develop explainable models that are both precise and practically beneficial in the high-stakes environment of healthcare.

REFERENCES

Albahri, A. S., Duhaim, A. M., Fadhel, M. A., Alnoor, A., Baqer, N. S., Alzubaidi, L., Albahri, O. S., Alamoodi, A. H., Bai, J., Salhi, A., & Santamaría, J. (2023). A systematic review of trustworthy and explainable artificial intelligence in healthcare: Assessment of quality, bias risk, and data fusion. *Information Fusion, 96*, 156–191.

Allen, B. (2024). The promise of explainable AI in digital health for precision medicine: A systematic review. *Journal of Personalized Medicine, 14*(3), 277.

Bawa, G., Singh, H., Rani, S., Kataria, A., & Min, H. (2024). Exploring perspectives of block-chain technology and traditional centralized technology in organ donation management: A comprehensive review. *Information, 15*(11), 703.

Chattopadhyay, S., Barman, S., & Lakshmi, D. (2025). The role of explainable AI for healthcare 5.0: Best practices, challenges, and opportunities. In P. Raj, B. Sundaravadivazhagan, A. S. Raja & M. M. Alani (Eds.), *Edge AI for Industry 5.0 and Healthcare 5.0 applications* (pp. 45–80). Taylor and Francis.

Huang, M., Zhang, X. S., Bhatti, U. A., Wu, Y., Zhang, Y., & Ghadi, Y. Y. (2024). An interpretable approach using hybrid graph networks and explainable AI for intelligent diagnosis recommendations in chronic disease care. *Biomedical Signal Processing and Control, 91*, 105913.

Kaur, G., & Saini, H. K. (2023). *An optimized resnet based plant disease identification using deep learning hypothetic function* [Paper presentation]. International Conference on Advances in Computation, Communication and Information Technology (ICAICCIT).

Kennedy-Mayo, D., & Gord, J. (2025, March). "Model Cards for Model Reporting" in 2024: Reclassifying category of ethical considerations in terms of trustworthiness and risk management. In Future of Information and Communication Conference (pp. 179–196). Cham: Springer Nature Switzerland.

Nansamba, B., Nakatumba-Nabende, J., Katumba, A., & Kateete, D. P. (2025). A systematic review on application of multimodal learning and explainable AI in tuberculosis detection. *IEEE Access.* https://doi.org/10.1109/ACCESS.2025.3558878

Nazar, M., Alam, M. M., Yafi, E., & Su'ud, M. M. (2021). A systematic review of human–computer interaction and explainable artificial intelligence in healthcare with artificial intelligence techniques. *IEEE Access, 9*, 153316–153348.

Pulipeti, S., Chithaluru, P., Kumar, M., Narsimhulu, P., & V, U. M. (2024). Explainable AI: Methods, frameworks, and tools for healthcare 5.0. In R. Aluvalu, M. Mehta & P. Siarry (Eds.), *Explainable AI in health informatics* (pp. 71–86). Springer.

Puri, V., Priyadarshini, I., Kataria, A., Rani, S., & Min, H. (2025). Privacy-first ML for chronic kidney disease prediction: Exploring a decentralized approach using blockchain and IPFS. *IEEE Access.* https://doi.org/10.1109/ACCESS.2025.3548645

Rani, S., Kataria, A., Bhambri, P., Pareek, P. K., & Puri, V. (2024). Artificial intelligence in personalized health services for better patient care. In S. K. Gupta, D. A. Karras & R. Natarajan (Eds.), *Revolutionizing healthcare: AI integration with IoT for enhanced patient outcomes* (pp. 89–108). Springer.

Rani, S., Kumar, S., Kataria, A., & Min, H. (2024). SmartHealth: An intelligent framework to secure IoMT service applications using machine learning. *ICT Express, 10*(2), 425–430.

Sadeghi, Z., Alizadehsani, R., Cifci, M. A., Kausar, S., Rehman, R., Mahanta, P., Bora, P. K., Almasri, A., Alkhawaldeh, R. S., Hussain, S., & Alatas, B. (2024). A review of Explainable artificial intelligence in healthcare. *Computers and Electrical Engineering, 118*, 109370.

Saini, H. K., & Preeti. (2024). *A cross design for breast cancer prediction* [Paper presentation]. The International Conference on Communications and Cyber Physical Engineering 2018.

Saini, H. K., Swarnakar, H., & Jain, K. (2022). Secured multimedia and IoT in healthcare computing paradigms. In B. Bhusan, S. K. Sharma, B. Unhelkar, M. F. Ijaz & L. Karim (Eds.), *Internet of Things* (pp. 229–256). CRC Press.

Shikha, A., Kasem, A., Han, W. S. P., & Wong, J. H. L. (2024). AI-augmented clinical decision in paediatric appendicitis: Can an AI-generated model improve trainees' diagnostic capability? *European Journal of Pediatrics, 183*(3), 1361–1366.

Sindiramutty, S. R., Tee, W. J., Balakrishnan, S., Kaur, S., Thangaveloo, R., Jazri, H., Khan, N. A., Gharib, A., & Manchuri, A. R. (2024). Explainable AI in healthcare application. In M. Ghonge, M. M. Pradeep, N. Z. Jhanjhi & P. M. Kulkarni (Eds.), *Advances in explainable AI applications for smart cities* (pp. 123–176). IGI Global Scientific Publishing.

Tartaro, A., Panai, E., & Cocchiaro, M. Z. (2024). AI risk assessment using ethical dimensions. *AI and Ethics, 4*(1), 105–112.

Wani, N. A., Kumar, R., & Bedi, J. (2024). DeepXplainer: An interpretable deep learning based approach for lung cancer detection using explainable artificial intelligence. *Computer Methods and Programs in Biomedicine, 243*, 107879.

8 Challenges and Solutions in Deploying Explainable AI in Smart Healthcare Systems

8.1 INTRODUCTION

The integration of artificial intelligence (AI) into healthcare has transformed patient diagnosis, treatment planning, and disease management. However, the complexity and opacity of many AI models, especially those based on deep learning, have raised concerns among healthcare professionals and patients alike. To bridge this gap, explainable AI (XAI) emerges as a critical paradigm that ensures the decisions made by AI systems are transparent, interpretable, and trustworthy (Chattopadhyay et al., 2025). The deployment of XAI in smart healthcare systems, although promising, is fraught with challenges ranging from technical barriers to ethical dilemmas. This chapter explores the growing role of XAI in healthcare, emphasizes the need for transparency and trust, and provides an overview of key deployment challenges that stakeholders must address to realize the full potential of XAI (Saraswat et al., 2022). Smart healthcare systems leverage advanced technologies like AI, IoT, and big data analytics to improve healthcare delivery, patient monitoring, and clinical decision-making. Within this technological ecosystem, AI models perform critical tasks such as image interpretation, predictive analytics, personalized treatment recommendations, and early disease detection. However, traditional AI models, particularly black-box models like deep neural networks, offer limited insight into their decision-making processes (Hulsen, 2023). XAI addresses this limitation by providing clear, understandable explanations for model outputs without compromising predictive performance. As shown in Figure 8.1 in smart healthcare, XAI plays several vital roles:

a. **Enhancing Clinical Decision Support**: Clinicians can better trust AI-assisted recommendations when the rationale behind decisions is transparent. XAI ensures that physicians can understand, validate, and act upon AI outputs.
b. **Improving Patient Engagement**: When patients receive understandable explanations for diagnoses and treatments, they are more likely to trust and adhere to medical advice, enhancing patient satisfaction and outcomes.
c. **Facilitating Regulatory Compliance**: Regulatory bodies such as the FDA and EMA emphasize transparency in AI-based medical devices. XAI helps

 DOI: 10.1201/9781003561422-8

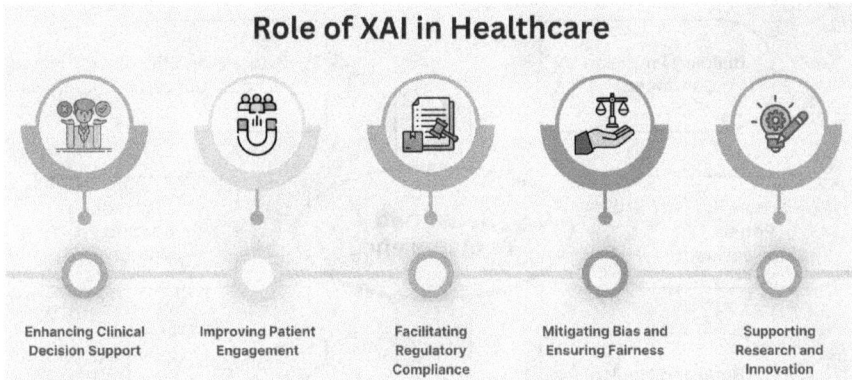

FIGURE 8.1 Role of XAI in healthcare.

organizations meet compliance standards, thus facilitating approval and adoption.

d. **Mitigating Bias and Ensuring Fairness**: By making decision processes visible, XAI enables the detection and correction of biases that could disproportionately affect vulnerable patient groups.

e. **Supporting Research and Innovation**: XAI can provide new insights into disease mechanisms by uncovering hidden patterns in data, advancing biomedical research.

As smart healthcare systems continue to evolve, the role of XAI becomes indispensable, ensuring that technological advancements align with clinical needs, ethical standards, and societal expectations. Trust is the cornerstone of healthcare. Patients entrust their lives to healthcare providers, and providers rely on diagnostic tools to make life-critical decisions (Kabir et al., 2022). The introduction of AI into this delicate ecosystem demands an even greater emphasis on trust and transparency, as shown in Figure 8.2.

a. **Building Physician Confidence**: Physicians are unlikely to rely on AI recommendations without a clear understanding of how conclusions are drawn. Transparent AI models foster clinician confidence by enabling them to scrutinize, interpret, and challenge AI outputs (Saini et al., 2022).

b. **Enhancing Patient Empowerment**: Informed patients are empowered patients. Transparency in AI recommendations allows patients to make informed decisions about their care, promoting autonomy and shared decision-making.

c. **Reducing Medical Errors**: Understanding AI rationales can help clinicians detect potential errors early. When explanations reveal discrepancies between clinical knowledge and AI suggestions, corrective actions can prevent adverse outcomes.

d. **Addressing Ethical and Legal Concerns**: Transparency is crucial for addressing ethical dilemmas such as accountability, informed consent, and

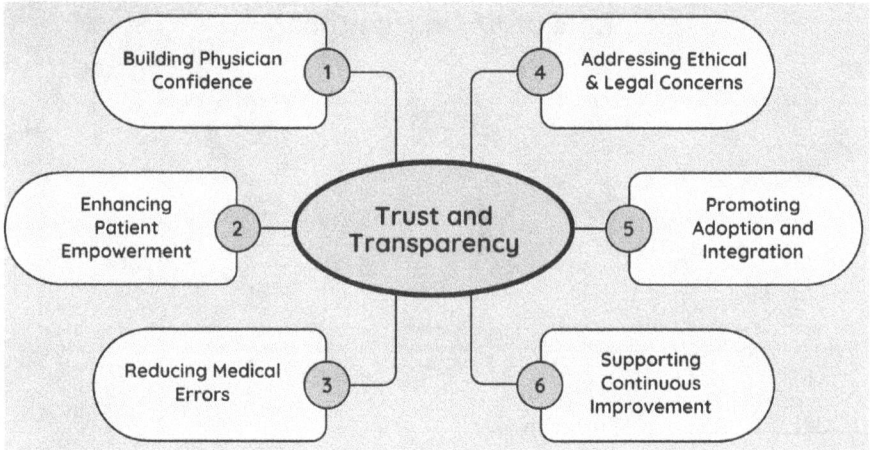

FIGURE 8.2 Elements of trust and transparency towards patients using XAI in healthcare.

data privacy. In the event of misdiagnosis or harm, stakeholders must trace and understand the decision-making pathway.

e. **Promoting Adoption and Integration**: Transparent AI systems are more readily accepted by healthcare institutions and professionals. Resistance to AI adoption often stems from "algorithmic opacity"; XAI directly tackles this barrier.

f. **Supporting Continuous Improvement**: Transparent systems facilitate feedback loops where clinicians can provide input to refine and improve AI models over time, leading to better system performance.

Without transparency and trust, the integration of AI into healthcare would not only face practical hurdles but also risk undermining the core values of the healthcare profession. XAI acts as the bridge between technological capability and human-centered healthcare delivery.

Despite the promise of XAI in healthcare, its deployment faces numerous challenges that span technical, operational, ethical, and legal domains.

Technical Challenges

a. **Trade-off between Accuracy and Interpretability**: Highly accurate models like deep neural networks are inherently complex and less interpretable. Simpler models like decision trees offer better interpretability but often at the cost of predictive performance. Balancing this trade-off remains a significant challenge.

b. **Lack of Standardization**: There is no universally accepted framework or metric for measuring the quality of explanations provided by XAI models. The absence of standards complicates evaluation, comparison, and regulation.

c. **Data Quality and Diversity**: XAI relies heavily on high-quality, diverse datasets to generate reliable explanations. Healthcare data often suffers

from issues like missing values, biases, and inconsistencies, which can compromise the trustworthiness of explanations.
  d. **Model Complexity and Scalability**: Many XAI techniques, such as SHAP or LIME, work well on small datasets or simple models but struggle with scalability in large, real-time healthcare systems.
  e. **Dynamic Learning Environments**: Healthcare knowledge evolves rapidly. AI models must adapt without losing their explainability. Ensuring explanations remain valid after model updates is a formidable task.

Operational Challenges
  a. **Integration with Clinical Workflows**: XAI solutions must seamlessly integrate into existing clinical workflows. Poor integration can lead to workflow disruptions, clinician frustration, and reduced effectiveness.
  b. **Training and Education**: Healthcare professionals need training to understand and interpret AI explanations effectively. Lack of AI literacy among clinicians can hinder the practical utility of XAI.
  c. **Interdisciplinary Collaboration**: Successful deployment requires collaboration between AI developers, clinicians, ethicists, and regulatory experts. Bridging the communication gap between these diverse stakeholders is challenging but critical.

Ethical and Legal Challenges
  a. **Accountability and Responsibility**: In AI-assisted decisions, it is often unclear who is ultimately responsible for outcomes—the AI developer, the healthcare provider, or the institution. XAI must help clarify accountability chains.
  b. **Bias and Fairness**: Even with explanations, biased AI models can perpetuate health disparities. Ensuring fairness in explanations and outcomes is a complex but essential task.
  c. **Privacy and Security**: Generating explanations often requires access to sensitive patient data. Safeguarding this data while maintaining explainability is an ethical imperative.
  d. **Regulatory Approval**: Regulatory frameworks are still evolving. Meeting the explainability requirements set by bodies like the FDA, while maintaining clinical efficacy, adds another layer of complexity to deployment.

Psychological and Social Challenges
  a. **Cognitive Overload**: Detailed explanations may overwhelm clinicians and patients, leading to "explanation fatigue." Finding the right balance between sufficiency and simplicity is crucial.
  b. **Overreliance on AI**: Excessive trust in AI, especially when explanations are persuasive but incorrect, can lead to automation bias, where clinicians uncritically accept AI recommendations.
  c. **Cultural and Organizational Resistance**: Organizational inertia and cultural skepticism toward AI can slow the adoption of XAI solutions. Change management strategies are necessary to foster acceptance.

The potential solutions for the above-mentioned challenges can be:

a. **Hybrid Models**: Combining interpretable models with high-performance black-box models to achieve a balance.
b. **Standardization Efforts**: Developing industry-wide standards for XAI evaluation and deployment.
c. **Robust Data Governance**: Ensuring data diversity, quality, and security.
d. **Clinician-Centric Design**: Designing AI systems with active clinician involvement to ensure relevance and usability.
e. **Continuous Education**: Implementing training programs for healthcare professionals on AI literacy.
f. **Ethical AI Frameworks**: Adopting ethical guidelines that prioritize patient welfare, fairness, and transparency.
g. **Incremental Integration**: Gradually introducing XAI tools to build confidence and familiarity.

8.2   TECHNICAL CHALLENGES IN DEPLOYING XAI

The deployment of XAI brings forward a transformative promise of bridging the gap between the sophisticated decision-making capabilities of AI models and the critical human need for transparency, trust, and accountability. However, embedding explainability into AI systems is not a straightforward enhancement; it presents a range of technical challenges that span model design, computational constraints, and performance trade-offs. Understanding and addressing these challenges are vital for developing XAI systems that are not only interpretable but also reliable, scalable, and effective in real-world environments (Shaik et al., 2023). One of the fundamental challenges in deploying XAI is navigating the inherent trade-off between model accuracy and interpretability. Complex models like deep neural networks, ensemble methods, and advanced reinforcement learning architectures are often capable of achieving high predictive performance by capturing intricate, nonlinear patterns in the data. However, these models are typically perceived as "black boxes," offering limited insight into their decision-making processes. In contrast, simpler models, such as linear regression, decision trees, or rule-based systems, are much more interpretable but may sacrifice predictive power when dealing with high-dimensional, noisy, or non-linear datasets. This tension necessitates careful decision-making regarding the acceptable balance between interpretability and performance.

Several strategies have emerged to address this trade-off:

a. **Post-hoc Explanation Methods**: Tools such as LIME (Local Interpretable Model-agnostic Explanations) and SHAP (SHapley Additive exPlanations) attempt to explain predictions of complex models after training. While useful, they introduce another layer of abstraction and may not faithfully represent the true reasoning of the model.
b. **Interpretable Model Design**: Some approaches advocate for inherently interpretable models like Generalized Additive Models (GAMs) or

prototype-based networks, especially in high-stakes domains such as healthcare, finance, and criminal justice.

c. **Hybrid Techniques**: Combining interpretable sub-models within larger frameworks, such as interpretable attention mechanisms in deep learning, is another way to mitigate the trade-off.

These strategies have limitations. Post-hoc methods risk producing misleading explanations, and simplified models might fail to capture critical subtleties of the data, leading to sub-optimal decisions. Thus, developers and stakeholders must define context-specific thresholds for acceptable trade-offs, depending on the application's risk, regulatory requirements, and user needs. Moreover, industries like healthcare, defense, and autonomous systems, where transparency is essential, must sometimes prioritize interpretability over marginal gains in accuracy. Conversely, in purely commercial applications where predictive accuracy is paramount, explainability might take a backseat. Recognizing the use-case-specific priority between these two objectives is a major deployment consideration. The increasing sophistication of AI models comes with a corresponding increase in computational complexity (Rani, Kumar et al., 2024). Deploying explainable models under computational constraints presents unique technical hurdles, specifically when considering resource-limited environments like edge devices, real-time systems, or embedded applications.

Several specific challenges arise:

a. **Resource-Intensive Explanations**: Generating detailed explanations, especially in complex models, often demands significant additional computation. Techniques like SHAP can require thousands of model evaluations for a single prediction, making them impractical for real-time use cases.

b. **Memory and Storage Limitations**: Edge devices (e.g., smartphones, IoT sensors) typically have limited memory and storage capacities. Housing both a high-performing model and its associated explanation mechanisms on such hardware is a non-trivial task.

c. **Inference Time Constraints**: In domains like autonomous driving or financial trading, decisions must be made within milliseconds. Adding explanation generation processes can slow down inference, risking system performance and safety.

d. **Energy Consumption**: Producing explanations can be energy-intensive. In mobile and IoT contexts, where battery life is a critical constraint, computationally expensive explanation routines can significantly reduce device longevity.

Efforts to overcome these constraints focus on optimizing both model and explanation efficiency. Techniques like model pruning, quantization, and distillation have been proposed to create lightweight, explainable models suitable for deployment in constrained environments. Additionally, researchers are exploring ways to precompute explanations or generate approximate explanations with reduced computational overhead. Emerging paradigms like federated learning and edge AI introduce further complexities. In federated environments, maintaining interpretability while ensuring data privacy and minimizing communication overhead requires novel distributed explainability frameworks. Moreover, explainability mechanisms themselves must be designed to be resistant to adversarial attacks, as malicious actors could exploit explanations to infer sensitive model behaviors or training data properties. Thus, XAI developers must not only optimize for explainability but also consider the physical and temporal constraints of their deployment platforms. Techniques must evolve to provide good enough explanations that are both computationally feasible and meaningful to end users. Another critical technical challenge in XAI deployment is ensuring that explanations are robust and that the models generalize well beyond the datasets they were trained on. A fragile explanation in XAI technique, changing dramatically with slight input perturbations, is not trustworthy and can mislead users, regulators, or stakeholders. Blockchain can also be employed in healthcare as it has numerous applications (Bawa et al., 2024; Puri et al., 2025).

Several facets of robustness and generalizability need to be considered:

a. **Stability of Explanations**: Robust XAI should provide consistent explanations for similar inputs. However, many explanation techniques (e.g., LIME) exhibit sensitivity to input perturbations, model re-training, or even slight changes in dataset distributions.

b. **Model Robustness to Adversarial Inputs**: If an AI system can be easily fooled by adversarial examples, its explanations are likely to be equally unreliable. Enhancing model robustness against adversarial attacks simultaneously improves the reliability of its explanations.

c. **Generalization across Domains**: AI models trained on specific datasets often fail when applied to data from different distributions (a phenomenon known as dataset shift). XAI mechanisms must similarly be evaluated for their ability to provide faithful and understandable explanations across varying domains and unseen data.

d. **Bias in Explanations**: Models may inadvertently learn and propagate biases present in the training data. Explanation systems must be able to highlight such biases rather than masking or amplifying them. If explanations hide underlying biases, they create a false sense of model trustworthiness.

Addressing these issues involves several technical approaches:

a. **Robust Explanation Techniques**: Developing methods that generate explanations resilient to minor perturbations is an ongoing research area. Techniques based on game theory, such as SHAP, offer some robustness guarantees, but more work is needed, especially for highly dynamic environments.

b. **Ensemble Explanations**: Aggregating multiple explanation methods can improve robustness by reducing reliance on any single method's idiosyncrasies. However, it also adds complexity in interpretation.

c. **Model Validation under Uncertainty**: Stress-testing models and their explanations under various forms of uncertainty, including noisy inputs, missing data, and adversarial conditions, is critical for ensuring real-world

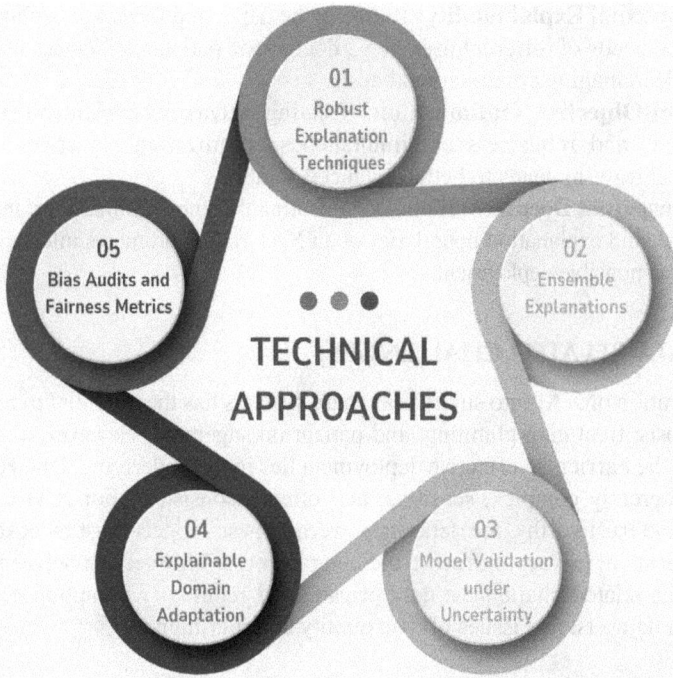

FIGURE 8.3   Technical approaches to solve the issues related to robustness.

reliability. Figure 8.3 represents the technical approaches to solve the issues related to robustness.

d. **Explainable Domain Adaptation**: Methods that combine domain adaptation (for cross-domain generalization) with explainability are emerging, enabling models to remain interpretable even as they adapt to new contexts.

e. **Bias Audits and Fairness Metrics**: Embedding fairness audits into the explanation pipeline ensures that XAI systems not only provide insights into model behavior but also flag potential ethical and societal concerns.

Ensuring robustness and generalizability is particularly important for critical applications like healthcare diagnostics, autonomous systems, and legal decision-support tools. Failure to provide stable, reliable explanations can erode trust, invite legal liabilities, and potentially cause harm.

Emerging Best Practices

Given the challenges described above, a few emerging best practices for deploying XAI are worth noting:

a. **Human-Centered Evaluation**: Rather than only technical validation, involving end-users in the evaluation of explanations ensures that explanations are genuinely useful and understandable.

b. **Contextual Explainability**: Tailoring the depth and format of explanations to the needs of different users (e.g., doctors vs. patients) enhances usability while managing computational costs.
c. **Multi-Objective Optimization**: Treating accuracy, explainability, efficiency, and robustness as simultaneous optimization objectives during model training leads to better-balanced solutions.
d. **Transparent Documentation**: Documenting the known limitations, intended usage, and explanation boundaries of an XAI system promotes informed trust and responsible deployment.

8.3 DATA-RELATED CHALLENGES

The integration of XAI into smart healthcare systems has the potential to revolutionize diagnosis, treatment planning, and patient management. However, a significant portion of the barriers to effective deployment lies in the underlying data. Healthcare data is inherently complex, sensitive, and often inconsistent. For XAI to be both effective and trustworthy, the datasets powering these models must meet strict standards in terms of privacy, fairness, and completeness. This section delves into three pivotal data-related challenges: data privacy and regulatory compliance, bias and fairness in datasets, and issues of data quality and missingness.

8.3.1 DATA PRIVACY, SECURITY, AND COMPLIANCE

One of the foremost concerns in deploying XAI in healthcare is ensuring patient data privacy and maintaining regulatory compliance (Rani, Kataria et al., 2024). Healthcare data is among the most sensitive forms of personal information, encompassing everything from genetic profiles to psychological assessments. Therefore, its handling is strictly governed by data protection laws and ethical frameworks such as the Health Insurance Portability and Accountability Act (HIPAA) in the United States, the General Data Protection Regulation (GDPR) in the European Union, and various regional policies worldwide.

8.3.1.1 Complexity of Regulations

The diverse regulatory landscape complicates the deployment of global or cross-border AI healthcare systems. HIPAA emphasizes safeguarding "protected health information" (PHI) and enforces strict conditions for data sharing and access, requiring de-identification or patient consent. GDPR, on the other hand, provides broader definitions of personal data and mandates rights such as data portability, the right to be forgotten, and transparency in data processing. For XAI, which often requires model auditability and interpretability, this creates a paradox, how to provide meaningful insights while preserving the confidentiality of the inputs that drove those decisions.

8.3.1.2 Risk of Re-Identification

De-identified or anonymized data is often used to train XAI models, but the risk of re-identification remains, particularly with advanced inference techniques. XAI systems that allow users to trace explanations back to individual features or cases may inadvertently reveal identifying patterns, especially in small or rare cohorts. The risk is amplified when multiple datasets (e.g., EHRs, genomic data, wearable sensors) are integrated, increasing the data's dimensionality and potential uniqueness.

8.3.1.3   Technical and Organizational Solutions

To address these challenges, healthcare organizations are adopting advanced techniques such as federated learning, where models are trained locally on edge devices and only aggregated updates are shared (Rani, Kataria et al., 2023). This approach mitigates the need to centralize sensitive data while preserving model performance. Similarly, differential privacy mechanisms introduce noise into the data or model outputs, reducing re-identification risk while maintaining statistical utility. Furthermore, access control protocols, encryption standards, and role-based permissions are critical in ensuring only authorized personnel have access to sensitive data. On the organizational side, developing a robust data governance framework that includes privacy impact assessments, ethical oversight committees, and audit trails is essential.

8.3.2   HANDLING BIAS AND FAIRNESS IN HEALTHCARE DATASETS

Bias in AI models, especially in healthcare, can lead to skewed outcomes, exacerbating existing health disparities among different populations. This is particularly concerning for XAI, where the objective is not only accurate predictions but also transparent and justifiable explanations. If the data used to train the models is biased, the explanations themselves may reinforce or obscure these inequities.

8.3.2.1   Sources of Bias

Bias can enter the system at various stages:

1. **Historical Bias**: Reflects existing inequities in healthcare delivery. For instance, minorities may have historically received fewer diagnostic tests, resulting in less data availability and lower model accuracy for those groups.
2. **Sampling Bias**: Occurs when the dataset does not represent the target population. If a predictive model is trained primarily on data from urban tertiary hospitals, it may not generalize well to rural or underserved populations.
3. **Measurement Bias**: Arises when diagnostic tools or processes produce systematically different outcomes for different groups. For example, pulse oximeters have been shown to be less accurate in patients with darker skin tones.

8.3.2.2   Fairness in XAI Outputs

XAI models must address not just the fairness of the predictions but also the fairness of the explanations. For example, a model may correctly diagnose a condition in two patients but attribute the decision to different and potentially inappropriate features based on race, gender, or socioeconomic status. Such inconsistencies undermine trust and may result in discriminatory care practices.

8.3.2.3 Mitigation Strategies

Bias detection and mitigation must be embedded in both the data preparation and model training pipelines. Some effective strategies include:

1. **Bias Auditing Tools**: Frameworks such as IBM's AI Fairness 360 or Google's What-If Tool can detect disparities in model performance across subgroups.
2. **Reweighing Techniques**: Adjusting the importance of samples in under-represented groups during training to reduce the skew.
3. **Counterfactual Explanations**: Providing explanations by highlighting minimal changes needed to alter the prediction. This can reveal if decisions are driven by protected attributes.
4. **Inclusive Data Collection**: Collaborating with diverse clinical centers and populations to ensure a more representative dataset is fundamental to equitable XAI deployment.

8.3.3 DATA QUALITY, IMBALANCE, AND MISSING INFORMATION

Another critical challenge in deploying XAI in smart healthcare systems is the inconsistent quality of healthcare data. Electronic health records (EHRs), medical images, sensor data from wearables, and genomic sequences are often riddled with missing values, inconsistencies, outliers, and class imbalances. These issues not only affect model accuracy but also undermine the reliability and interpretability of the generated explanations.

8.3.3.1 Missing Data

Missingness is a pervasive problem in healthcare datasets. Data may be missing completely at random (MCAR), at random (MAR), or not at random (MNAR), each with different implications. For instance, blood tests may be skipped in healthy individuals, leading to sparsity, while in sicker patients, frequent testing generates dense time-series data. This differential density can bias both predictions and explanations. XAI models may overemphasize features simply because they are more frequently measured, not necessarily because they are more relevant.

8.3.3.2 Data Imbalance

Many clinical conditions, especially rare diseases, are underrepresented in datasets. For example, in a dataset used to predict sepsis, the prevalence may be below 10%, leading models to favor the majority class (non-sepsis) for overall accuracy. Explanations from such models will often highlight features predictive of non-events, which is clinically unhelpful. Moreover, minority class patients may receive less reliable predictions and less meaningful explanations.

8.3.3.3 Data Inconsistencies and Noise

Data quality issues also stem from inconsistent terminology (e.g., different ways of recording the same diagnosis), sensor calibration errors, and human documentation mistakes. Such inconsistencies confuse XAI models, leading to incoherent or contradictory explanations. In multimodal settings (e.g., combining EHR and imaging data), synchronizing formats, timestamps, and semantics is an additional challenge.

8.3.3.4 Strategies for Data Quality Improvement

1. **Imputation Techniques**: Using statistical methods or deep learning (e.g., Variational Autoencoders or Graph Neural Networks) to fill in missing values based on contextual relationships.
2. **Data Cleaning Pipelines**: Employing Natural Language Processing (NLP) for structured extraction from clinical notes and harmonizing diagnostic codes using terminologies like SNOMED CT or ICD-10.
3. **Class Rebalancing**: Oversampling techniques such as SMOTE (Synthetic Minority Oversampling Technique), or class weighting during model training, help handle imbalance.
4. **Robust Explainability Frameworks**: Techniques like SHAP and LIME offer transparency, even in noisy settings, by approximating feature importance at the local prediction level.

8.4   HUMAN-CENTRIC CHALLENGES IN XAI ADOPTION

The integration of XAI into smart healthcare systems holds transformative potential. It promises to enhance clinical decision-making, foster trust, and enable transparency. However, despite technological advances, human-centric challenges remain significant barriers to its widespread adoption. These challenges are often rooted in cognitive, social, and cultural dimensions of the healthcare ecosystem, making their resolution as crucial as the technical deployment of XAI tools. This section delves into three key human-centric challenges: resistance to AI integration in clinical workflows, the necessity to train healthcare professionals, and the need to align AI-generated explanations with the expectations of both clinicians and patients.

8.4.1   RESISTANCE TO AI INTEGRATION IN CLINICAL WORKFLOWS

One of the most critical challenges in deploying XAI in healthcare lies in the inherent resistance to the integration of AI into established clinical workflows. This resistance is multifaceted and arises from concerns related to trust, autonomy, accountability, and fear of de-skilling among healthcare practitioners.

8.4.1.1   Distrust in Automation

Healthcare professionals often show skepticism toward AI due to its perceived "black box" nature. Even with XAI offering explanations, the underlying complexity of models such as deep neural networks can hinder acceptance. Physicians are trained to rely on evidence-based reasoning; hence, any recommendation lacking transparent logic or understandable justification is likely to be met with resistance.

8.4.1.2   Perceived Threat to Clinical Autonomy

AI systems, especially those offering prescriptive recommendations, may be seen as undermining the professional autonomy of clinicians. Practitioners might feel that

AI is trying to replace rather than assist them. In high-stakes environments like ICUs and emergency departments, where human judgment is critical, this perceived threat becomes more pronounced.

8.4.1.3 Workflow Disruption

Existing clinical workflows are often rigid, complex, and deeply embedded in institutional routines. Integrating AI solutions, particularly those that require new interfaces or data inputs, may lead to increased workload or operational disruptions. The integration process can involve significant reengineering of processes, something that many overburdened healthcare systems are reluctant to undertake.

8.4.1.4 Legal and Ethical Ambiguities

Clinicians may be hesitant to rely on AI due to unclear regulations regarding liability. If an AI system makes a recommendation that leads to an adverse outcome, determining responsibility becomes a gray area, making practitioners cautious about its usage (Table 8.1).

8.4.2 TRAINING HEALTHCARE PROFESSIONALS TO USE AND INTERPRET AI MODELS

The successful adoption of XAI in healthcare does not end with the deployment of models; it depends heavily on how well healthcare professionals can interact with and interpret these tools. A major barrier lies in the current gap between the technical capabilities of AI systems and the digital literacy of clinical users.

8.4.2.1 Lack of Formal Education in AI

Most medical professionals receive little to no training in data science or machine learning during their formal education. The concepts of model architecture, algorithmic bias, and interpretability are foreign to many, leading to hesitation or misuse of AI outputs. While XAI attempts to make models more understandable, it still requires users to interpret statistical outputs and visualizations critically.

TABLE 8.1
Comparative Features of Human vs AI in Clinical Workflow Integration

Feature	Human Clinician Judgment	AI System with XAI	Integration Challenge
Decision-making Basis	Experience, training, evidence	Data-driven, probabilistic reasoning	Misalignment in reasoning paradigms
Interpretability	High (explicit thought process)	Moderate (depending on XAI model)	Requires adaptation to new explanation styles
Workflow Compatibility	Fully embedded	Often external or add-on	Requires reengineering
Flexibility and Intuition	High	Low	AI lacks contextual understanding
Legal Accountability	Clearly defined	Ambiguous	Regulatory clarity needed

8.4.2.2   Cognitive Load and Information Overload

Doctors already handle a high cognitive load in clinical settings. Introducing AI tools that require additional interpretation or involve unfamiliar metrics (like SHAP values or attention maps) may contribute to cognitive overload, thereby reducing usability. Explanations that are too detailed or technical can overwhelm users rather than assist them.

8.4.2.3   Need for Continuous Training

The field of AI evolves rapidly, with frequent updates in models and interpretability techniques. This necessitates continuous learning, which can be difficult to maintain amidst busy clinical schedules. Institutions must develop ongoing professional development programs tailored to varying levels of technical proficiency.

8.4.2.4   Importance of Contextualization

Training should not be generic. Instead, it must be domain-specific, contextualizing XAI tools within the medical specialty in which they are deployed. A cardiologist, for example, should receive training on how AI can enhance interpretation of ECGs, not on general AI principles alone effectively (Table 8.2).

8.4.3   ALIGNING AI EXPLANATIONS WITH PHYSICIAN AND PATIENT EXPECTATIONS

Even when AI systems are integrated and clinicians are trained, a fundamental issue remains ensuring that the explanations provided by AI tools align with the expectations and mental models of both clinicians and patients. Misalignment in this area can severely hinder trust and usefulness (Kale et al., 2024).

8.4.3.1   Differing Explanatory Needs

Clinicians and patients have vastly different needs from an AI explanation. A physician might require detailed statistical validation or causal inference, whereas a

---

TABLE 8.2
Skills and Training Gaps for Effective Use of XAI in Healthcare

Required Competency	Current Availability among Clinicians	Training Strategy	Impact on XAI Adoption
Understanding of AI Models	Low	Incorporate into medical curriculum	Reduces distrust and misuse
Interpretation of Model Output	Moderate to Low	Workshops, CME sessions	Enhances confidence in decision support tools
Familiarity with XAI Tools	Very Low	Use of simulation-based training	Improves real-world applicability
Ethical and Legal Awareness	Low	Seminars by legal-technical panels	Encourages responsible adoption
Technical Troubleshooting Skills	Very Low	Embedded technical support in deployment	Reduces abandonment of AI tools

patient prefers a simple, intuitive reason; why did the AI suggest this treatment for me? Balancing these explanatory levels is challenging, especially in time-constrained clinical encounters.

8.4.3.2 Transparency vs. Simplicity Trade-off

Highly transparent explanations (like full decision trees or feature attribution matrices) may enhance scientific rigor but can overwhelm both users and patients. On the other hand, overly simplified explanations risk omitting crucial context, leading to misinterpretation or oversimplification of complex conditions.

8.4.3.3 Building Narrative Coherence

Effective explanations need to be coherent within the context of the clinical narrative. An AI model indicating that a patient is at high risk for sepsis should align with other observable symptoms and lab values. If the AI contradicts the clinician's assessment without clear justification, its output may be disregarded, regardless of its correctness.

8.4.3.4 Cultural and Linguistic Adaptation

Explanations should also consider cultural sensitivity and language simplicity, especially in diverse or multilingual settings. Patients may not understand medical jargon or complex visualizations, requiring adaptive interfaces and multi-lingual support.

8.4.3.5 Trust Calibration

It's crucial that users neither over trust nor under trust AI. Calibrated trust can only be achieved when explanations are not only technically sound but also emotionally and contextually resonant with users. Designing interfaces that allow optional deep dives or surface-level summaries can address this spectrum.

8.5 SOLUTIONS FOR OVERCOMING DEPLOYMENT CHALLENGES

As the integration of XAI in healthcare systems becomes increasingly vital, the industry faces complex challenges that go beyond model accuracy. These include the need for interpretability without compromising predictive power, eliminating algorithmic bias, and deploying models that are both secure and scalable. This section explores strategic solutions to these issues through the lens of practical implementation and technological advancements (Sadeghi et al., 2024).

8.5.1 Designing Interpretable and High-Performing AI Models

A major trade-off in deploying XAI in healthcare is between interpretability and model performance. Traditional machine learning models like decision trees or linear regression are highly interpretable but often lack the predictive power of complex black-box models such as deep neural networks. However, in clinical settings where transparency is paramount, especially for high-stakes decisions, explainability cannot be compromised.

8.5.1.1 Hybrid Modeling Approaches

To balance performance with interpretability, hybrid models have been developed. These architectures combine interpretable elements with deep learning to provide post-hoc or intrinsic explanations. For example, models like ProtoPNet (Prototypical Part Network) integrate prototypes to justify classifications using case-based reasoning, which is more digestible to clinicians (Huang et al., 2024).

8.5.1.2 Trade-Off Management via Multi-Objective Optimization

Multi-objective optimization frameworks can balance interpretability and performance. For instance, Pareto optimality techniques can help identify model architectures that achieve acceptable performance while maintaining high levels of transparency (El-Khawaga et al., 2022).

8.5.1.3 Incorporating Clinical Knowledge

Integrating domain knowledge into models enhances interpretability. Rule-based AI, ontology-driven frameworks, and expert-in-the-loop training paradigms help design models that align with clinical reasoning, making them more interpretable to healthcare professionals (Shaik et al., 2023).

Table 8.3 compares common XAI models and frameworks on parameters such as interpretability, performance, computational cost, and domain adaptability.

8.5.2 STRATEGIES FOR BIAS MITIGATION AND FAIR AI PRACTICES

Healthcare data is often inherently biased, stemming from socioeconomic disparities, underrepresentation of minority groups, and flawed clinical documentation. These biases, if not addressed, can propagate through AI systems, exacerbating healthcare inequalities.

TABLE 8.3

Feature Comparison of AI Models and XAI Tools in Healthcare

Model/Tool	Interpretability	Predictive Performance	Computational Cost	Adaptability to Healthcare
Decision Trees	High	Moderate	Low	High
Logistic Regression	High	Moderate	Low	High
Random Forest	Moderate	High	Moderate	Moderate
Deep Neural Networks	Low	Very High	High	High
SHAP	Post-hoc High	Model-agnostic	High	High
LIME	Post-hoc Moderate	Model-agnostic	Moderate	Moderate
ProtoPNet	Intrinsic High	High	High	Moderate
Attention Mechanisms	Moderate	High	High	Moderate
Rule-Based Systems	Very High	Low to Moderate	Low	High

8.5.2.1   Data Curation and Preprocessing

The first step in mitigating bias involves robust data preprocessing, such as:

a. Data balancing (e.g., SMOTE for oversampling underrepresented classes).
b. De-identification and standardization to prevent institution-specific patterns.
c. Stratified sampling to ensure population diversity.

Including demographic variables explicitly in the modeling process also helps identify and quantify bias.

8.5.2.2   Fairness-Aware Learning Algorithms

Algorithms such as adversarial debiasing, re-weighted loss functions, and fair representation learning ensure models are less sensitive to protected attributes like race, gender, or socioeconomic status. For example:

a. **Fairness constraints** during training (e.g., equal opportunity, demographic parity) can guide model learning toward equitable outcomes.
b. **Counterfactual fairness techniques** simulate "what if" scenarios to evaluate prediction changes with altered sensitive attributes.

8.5.2.3   Continuous Monitoring and Auditing

Bias can re-emerge in deployment. Therefore, ongoing model auditing using fairness metrics like disparate impact, equal opportunity difference, and Theil index is essential. Tools like Fairlearn and AIF360 enable the systematic evaluation of AI fairness post-deployment (Patel et al., 2024).

8.5.2.4   Clinician and Stakeholder Involvement

Bias detection and mitigation are not solely technical challenges. Engaging clinicians, ethicists, and patient advocacy groups in the model development process ensures that multiple perspectives are incorporated, reducing the risk of oversight in real-world applications.

8.5.3   Secure and Scalable AI Deployment in Healthcare Institutions

Security and scalability are crucial in healthcare AI deployment due to the sensitive nature of patient data, the need for compliance with regulations like HIPAA and GDPR, and the requirement to integrate with legacy systems.

8.5.3.1   Federated and Privacy-Preserving Learning

Traditional centralized learning involves moving data to the model, which raises significant privacy risks. Federated learning (FL) reverses this paradigm by keeping data on-site (e.g., hospital systems) and sending only model updates to a central server.

This technique allows multiple hospitals to collaboratively train models without sharing patient data, preserving privacy while improving generalizability.

Techniques like differential privacy, homomorphic encryption, and secure multi-party computation (SMC) further enhance data confidentiality.

8.5.3.2 Scalable Infrastructure and Edge Deployment

Healthcare systems are often constrained by IT infrastructure limitations. Solutions include:

a. Cloud-native architectures (e.g., using Kubernetes, Docker),
b. Model compression and pruning for efficient execution,
c. Edge computing for real-time inference at point-of-care devices or bedside monitors.

These enable the deployment of AI solutions in resource-limited settings while ensuring fast, secure, and scalable access.

8.5.3.3 Interoperability and Standardization

AI systems must interoperate with EHR platforms, laboratory systems, and imaging archives. Standards such as FHIR (Fast Healthcare Interoperability Resources) and HL7 promote seamless data exchange.

APIs and middleware designed to translate between these standards and AI system inputs/outputs are necessary to ensure deployment without disruption of existing clinical workflows.

8.5.3.4 Regulatory Compliance and Risk Governance

Deploying AI in clinical environments requires regulatory approval, risk assessments, and alignment with institutional protocols. Strategies include:

a. Developing Model Cards or Fact Sheets that describe model intent, data used, and performance on diverse subgroups.
b. Clinical trials and validation studies before full deployment.
c. Use of AI governance frameworks that outline data stewardship, accountability, and fallback mechanisms in case of AI failure.

8.6 BEST PRACTICES AND CASE STUDIES

The evolution of XAI in smart healthcare is not merely a technological transition but a paradigm shift toward transparent, trustworthy, and patient-centric care. This section explores real-world implementations, critical lessons from AI adoption, and industry-level insights that reinforce best practices in deploying XAI in hospitals, clinics, and telemedicine.

8.6.1 Successful XAI Implementations in Smart Healthcare Systems

8.6.1.1 Case Study 1: Mayo Clinic's Predictive Modeling for ICU Patients

The Mayo Clinic implemented an interpretable AI system to predict patient deterioration in Intensive Care Units (ICUs). Using a model based on Gradient Boosting

Machines (GBM) with SHAP, clinicians could view which physiological parameters (e.g., respiratory rate, heart rate, lactate level) contributed to the risk score. This transparency allowed ICU doctors to validate model predictions with clinical knowledge.

Outcome:

Improved early intervention accuracy by 22%
Reduced false alarm rates by 31%
Increased physician trust in AI outputs

8.6.1.2   Case Study 2: IBM Watson for Oncology

IBM Watson was deployed across several hospitals globally for cancer diagnosis and treatment planning. While early results were mixed, the project revealed that interpretable recommendations those supported by clinical guidelines and patient-specific data were more likely to be accepted by oncologists.

Outcome:

Improved patient satisfaction when doctors explained AI-suggested treatments
Higher alignment with NCCN guidelines in 76% of cases

8.6.1.3   Case Study 3: Babylon Health (Telemedicine XAI)

Babylon Health used interpretable NLP models to triage patients during teleconsultations. Their XAI system utilized attention-based models to indicate which symptoms and queries influenced the chatbot's triage result.

Outcome:

Reduced misdiagnosis in 18% of common illnesses
Built higher patient confidence in AI chatbot outputs

8.6.2   AI ADOPTION IN HOSPITALS AND TELEMEDICINE PLATFORMS

8.6.2.1   Context Matters in Model Explainability

AI systems that were interpretable in one setting (e.g., ICU) failed in another (e.g., outpatient clinics) due to differences in data granularity, urgency, and stakeholder needs. For example, ICU staff needed real-time feature contributions, while outpatient doctors required longitudinal risk factors.

8.6.2.2   User Training is Crucial

At Mount Sinai Health System, an XAI model for sepsis risk underperformed until clinicians received training on how to interpret saliency maps and confidence scores.

8.6.2.3   Oversimplification Can Be Dangerous

Some hospitals adopted simple rule-based explainers that overgeneralized model outputs. This led to cases where high-risk alerts were dismissed due to overly generic explanations.

8.6.2.4 Ethical Oversight Increases Acceptance

Hospitals that established XAI governance committees, comprised of ethicists, clinicians, and technologists, reported smoother deployment and higher clinician adoption (Kaur & Saini, 2023).

8.6.3 INDUSTRY INSIGHTS ON IMPROVING TRUST AND USABILITY OF XAI

Across the industry, several key principles have emerged as foundational to deploying XAI in ways that are both usable and trusted (Saini & Preeti, 2024).

8.6.3.1 Model Fidelity vs. Interpretability Trade-off

High-performing black-box models (like deep neural networks) often conflict with interpretability goals. Companies such as Philips Healthcare recommend hybrid approaches using interpretable surrogate models (e.g., decision trees) to approximate deep learning logic for clinical review.

8.6.3.2 Human-in-the-Loop Validation

Siemens Healthineers integrates human review checkpoints in its AI pipeline where physicians can verify, correct, or override AI predictions with justification.

8.6.3.3 Explainability-as-a-Service (XaaS)

Startups like Pymetrics and Truera now offer XaaS platforms that provide real-time SHAP/LIME explanations, audit trails, and transparency logs for health AI deployments.

Python Example: Using SHAP for Explainable Disease Risk Prediction

Problem: Predicting diabetes risk using patient data
Dataset used: Pima Indians diabetes dataset (binary classification)

```python
import shap
import xgboost
import pandas as pd
from sklearn.model_selection import train_test_split
from sklearn.metrics import accuracy_score

# Load dataset
url = "https://raw.githubusercontent.com/jbrownlee/
Datasets/master/pima-indians-diabetes.data.csv"
column_names = ['Pregnancies', 'Glucose',
'BloodPressure', 'SkinThickness',
        'Insulin', 'BMI', 'DiabetesPedigreeFunction',
'Age', 'Outcome']
data = pd.read_csv(url, names=column_names)
```

```
# Split data
X = data.drop('Outcome', axis=1)
y = data['Outcome']
X_train, X_test, y_train, y_test = train_test_split(X, y,
test_size=0.2, random_state=42)

# Train XGBoost model
model = xgboost.XGBClassifier(use_label_encoder=False,
eval_metric='logloss')
model.fit(X_train, y_train)

# Predict and evaluate
preds = model.predict(X_test)
print(f"Accuracy: {accuracy_score(y_test, preds):.2f}")
```

EXPLAINABILITY WITH SHAP

```
# Initialize SHAP explainer
explainer = shap.Explainer(model)
shap_values = explainer(X_test)

# Visualize global feature importance
shap.summary_plot(shap_values, X_test)
```

Expected Output
Accuracy: ~78%

Clinician Interpretation:

If Glucose is high and Age is over 50, the model tends to classify as "Diabetic"
with high confidence.
Easy-to-understand reasoning helps physicians validate the model's logic.
Glucose has the highest impact on model decisions.
BMI and Age follow closely, also contributing significantly.
Other features like insulin and pregnancies show moderate influence.

8.7   CONCLUSION

In the rapidly advancing field of smart healthcare, XAI has shifted from being a luxury to an essential component. Its capacity to clarify AI-driven decisions empowers
healthcare professionals to make well-informed choices, builds patient confidence,
and supports ethical and responsible care. Nonetheless, the path to effectively integrating XAI is intricate, filled with challenges spanning technological, human, and
regulatory aspects. This chapter highlighted the need to balance precision with clarity, maintain data integrity, create systems that are user-friendly for clinicians, and

encourage cross-disciplinary collaboration. Practical applications and industry best practices highlight that a successful XAI implementation requires a socio-technical strategy, where tools are not only technically sound but also contextually appropriate and centered around the user. The future of XAI in healthcare depends on ongoing innovation, adaptive learning, and a collective dedication to responsible AI. With the appropriate frameworks and collaborations, XAI has the potential to revolutionize healthcare into a more transparent, inclusive, and efficient system for all involved parties.

REFERENCES

Bawa, G., Singh, H., Rani, S., Kataria, A., & Min, H. (2024). Exploring perspectives of blockchain technology and traditional centralized technology in organ donation management: A comprehensive review. *Information, 15*(11), 703.

Chattopadhyay, S., Barman, S., & Lakshmi, D. (2025). The role of explainable AI for healthcare 5.0: Best practices, challenges, and opportunities. In P. Raj, B. Sundaravadivazhagan, A. S. Raja & M. M. Alani (Eds.), *Edge AI for Industry 5.0 and Healthcare 5.0 applications* (pp. 45–80). Taylor and Francis.

El-Khawaga, G., Abu-Elkheir, M., & Reichert, M. (2022). Xai in the context of predictive process monitoring: An empirical analysis framework. *Algorithms, 15*(6), 199.

Huang, M., Zhang, X. S., Bhatti, U. A., Wu, Y., Zhang, Y., & Ghadi, Y. Y. (2024). An interpretable approach using hybrid graph networks and explainable AI for intelligent diagnosis recommendations in chronic disease care. *Biomedical Signal Processing and Control, 91*, 105913.

Hulsen, T. (2023). Explainable artificial intelligence (XAI): Concepts and challenges in healthcare. *AI, 4*(3), 652–666.

Kabir, M. H., Hasan, K. F., Hasan, M. K., & Ansari, K. (2022). Explainable artificial intelligence for smart city application: A secure and trusted platform. In M. Ahmed, S. R. Islam, A. Adnan, N. Moustafa & A. S. K. Pathan (Eds.), *Explainable artificial intelligence for cyber security: Next generation artificial intelligence* (pp. 241–263). Springer.

Kale, M., Wankhede, N., Pawar, R., Ballal, S., Kumawat, R., Goswami, M., Khalid, M., Taksande, B., Upaganlawar, A., Umekar, M., & Kopalli, S. R. (2024). AI-driven innovations in Alzheimer's disease: Integrating early diagnosis, personalized treatment, and prognostic modelling. *Ageing Research Reviews, 101*, 102497.

Kaur, G., & Saini, H. K. (2023). *An optimized resnet based plant disease identification using deep learning hypothetic function* [Paper presentation]. International Conference on Advances in Computation, Communication and Information Technology (ICAICCIT).

Patel, A. U., Gu, Q., Esper, R., Maeser, D., & Maeser, N. (2024). The crucial role of interdisciplinary conferences in advancing explainable AI in healthcare. *BioMedInformatics, 4*(2), 1363–1383.

Puri, V., Priyadarshini, I., Kataria, A., Rani, S., & Min, H. (2025). Privacy-first ML for chronic kidney disease prediction: Exploring a decentralized approach using blockchain and IPFS. *IEEE Access.* https://doi.org/10.1109/ACCESS.2025.3548645

Rani, S., Kataria, A., Bhambri, P., Pareek, P. K., & Puri, V. (2024). Artificial intelligence in personalized health services for better patient care. In S. K. Gupta, D. A. Karras & R. Natarajan (Eds.), *Revolutionizing healthcare: AI integration with IoT for enhanced patient outcomes* (pp. 89–108). Springer.

Rani, S., Kataria, A., Kumar, S., & Tiwari, P. (2023). Federated learning for secure IoMT-applications in smart healthcare systems: A comprehensive review. *Knowledge-Based Systems, 274*, 110658.

Rani, S., Kumar, S., Kataria, A., & Min, H. (2024). SmartHealth: An intelligent framework to secure IoMT service applications using machine learning. *ICT Express*, *10*(2), 425–430.

Sadeghi, Z., Alizadehsani, R., Cifci, M. A., Kausar, S., Rehman, R., Mahanta, P., Bora, P. K., Almasri, A., Alkhawaldeh, R. S., Hussain, S., & Alatas, B. (2024). A review of Explainable Artificial Intelligence in healthcare. *Computers and Electrical Engineering*, *118*, 109370.

Saini, H. K., & Preeti. (2024). *A cross design for breast cancer prediction* [Paper presentation]. The International Conference on Communications and Cyber Physical Engineering 2018.

Saini, H. K., Swarnakar, H., & Jain, K. (2022). Secured multimedia and IoT in healthcare computing paradigms. In B. Bhusan, S. K. Sharma, B. Unhelkar, M. F. Ijaz & L. Karim (Eds.), *Internet of Things* (pp. 229–256). CRC Press.

Saraswat, D., Bhattacharya, P., Verma, A., Prasad, V. K., Tanwar, S., Sharma, G., Bokoro, P. N., & Sharma, R. (2022). Explainable AI for healthcare 5.0: Opportunities and challenges. *IEEE Access*, *10*, 84486–84517.

Shaik, T., Tao, X., Higgins, N., Li, L., Gururajan, R., Zhou, X., & Acharya, U. R. (2023). Remote patient monitoring using artificial intelligence: Current state, applications, and challenges. *Wiley Interdisciplinary Reviews: Data Mining and Knowledge Discovery*, *13*(2), e1485.

9 Case Studies
Real-world Examples of Explainable AI in Healthcare

9.1 INTRODUCTION

The rapid integration of artificial intelligence (AI) in healthcare is revolutionizing the medical system, from diagnosis to the early detection of diseases. Although AI systems, particularly deep learning models, are capable of delivering high-quality results, their decision-making processes are often opaque, posing a significant challenge for adoption in clinical practice (Budhkar et al., 2025). In a healthcare system where trust and transparency are of utmost importance, the opaque nature of AI model decisions creates obstacles for practitioners and patients in placing confidence in AI-generated decisions. Explainable AI (XAI) possesses the capability to address these challenges, thereby enhancing the reliability and trustworthiness of AI systems (Teng et al., 2024). Furthermore, it enables healthcare professionals to understand and have confidence in the rationale behind AI-driven recommendations.

9.1.1 THE IMPORTANCE OF EXPLAINABILITY IN HEALTHCARE AI

Explainability in healthcare AI is not merely a technical consideration; rather, it is a foundational requirement for the responsible and effective application of AI in medicine. As AI models become increasingly integrated into medical practice, the demand for explainability in these models is growing (Puri et al., 2025; Tan et al., 2023). The absence of explainability features in AI models may create barriers for clinicians in trusting the outcomes generated by these models, which can hinder their adoption and potentially compromise patient care (Ennab & Mcheick, 2022).

Transparent AI models enable medical practitioners to verify and validate the decisions made by AI systems during diagnosis or treatment (Rani, Kataria et al., 2024). The integration of blockchain in various applications, like secure organ donation, can also be employed for a more secure and decentralized approach in the healthcare sector (Bawa et al., 2024; Rani, Kumar et al., 2024). These models can also ensure that decisions are consistent with established medical standards and can be justified to both patients and regulatory authorities (Marey et al., 2024). This capability is particularly crucial when high-performance black-box models base their predictions on irrelevant variables, which, if unchecked, can lead to significant errors.

Furthermore, explainability is intrinsically linked to ethical and legal considerations. Regulatory frameworks, such as the European Union's General Data Protection Regulation (GDPR) (Mohammad Amini et al., 2023), increasingly mandate that AI systems associated with critical domains, such as healthcare, provide interpretable and auditable outputs.

9.1.2   How Case Studies Provide Insights for Practitioners

Case studies are instrumental in bridging the gap between theoretical advancements in XAI and their practical application within the healthcare sector. By utilizing real-world implementations, case studies offer medical practitioners concrete examples of how XAI techniques can be integrated into various clinical settings, such as radiology, disease prediction, and personalized medicine. These detailed case studies not only furnish technical information necessary for selecting the appropriate XAI model for specific problems but also address the ethical and organizational challenges encountered during implementation (Saini & Preeti, 2024).

By employing case studies, practitioners acquire significant insights into the advantages and disadvantages of XAI. For instance, they can observe how explainable models have enhanced diagnostic accuracy, facilitated more transparent treatment planning, and cultivated trust among clinicians and patients by rendering AI-driven recommendations comprehensible and actionable (Okada et al., 2023). Case studies also highlight prevalent challenges, including issues related to data quality, difficulties in integrating with existing systems, and the necessity for thorough clinical validation, which requires the involvement of domain experts at every stage (Hsiao et al., 2019). Furthermore, these practical examples elucidate optimal strategies for the integration of XAI, emphasizing the significance of human-in-the-loop validation, continuous stakeholder engagement, and iterative refinement informed by clinical feedback (Kaur & Saini, 2023).

9.1.3   Key Themes and Lessons from Real-World Applications

The integration of XAI within healthcare environments has uncovered several significant patterns and critical insights that are influencing both current practices and prospective innovations. Table 9.1 highlights the key themes in XAI healthcare applications.

9.2   XAI IN MEDICAL IMAGING AND DIAGNOSTICS

9.2.1   Case Study 1: AI-Assisted Radiology

XAI integration into the field of radiology has significantly transformed the interpretation of medical images. Although AI models, particularly those utilizing deep learning architectures, have shown exceptional accuracy in identifying abnormalities in X-rays, MRIs, and CT scans, their initial black-box nature posed substantial challenges to their clinical adoption. XAI techniques have emerged as a crucial link between algorithmic complexity and clinical applicability. Techniques such as saliency maps and Gradient-weighted Class Activation Mapping (Grad-CAM) now offer visual insights into the decision-making processes of AI, pinpointing

TABLE 9.1

Key Themes in Explainable AI Healthcare Applications

Theme	Description	Key Benefits	Challenges	Implementation Strategies
Model Interpretability	Transformation of "black box" algorithms into transparent tools	• Enables verification of factors driving diagnoses • Establishes foundation for trust • Ensures ethical medical decision-making	• Technical complexity of making deep models transparent • Balancing detail with understandability	• Implement feature importance methods • Use visualization techniques • Develop natural language explanations
Clinical Adoption Through Transparency	Integration of AI systems into clinical workflows via transparent decision-making	• Bridges gap between algorithms and clinical expertise • Enables validation of AI findings • Fosters acceptance among medical professionals	• Designing explanations appropriate for clinical context • Varying needs across medical specialties	• Highlight relevant regions in medical images • Provide evidence-based rationales • Enable interactive exploration of AI decisions
Complexity-Transparency Paradox	Challenge of balancing sophisticated model performance with interpretability	• Drives innovation in explainability techniques • Improves regulatory compliance • Facilitates clinical integration	• Advanced models often less transparent • Performance may decrease with simpler models	• Research post-hoc explanation methods • Develop inherently interpretable models • Create hybrid approaches
User-Centered Design	Alignment of XAI systems with clinicians' needs and workflow patterns	• Creates technically accurate and accessible explanations • Ensures explanations remain relevant • Adapts to evolving clinical contexts	• Different user groups require different explanations • Clinical workflows vary widely	• Conduct continuous validation with real-world data • Gather ongoing feedback from healthcare professionals • Design intuitive interfaces
Interdisciplinary Collaboration	Cross-discipline teamwork for effective XAI deployment	• Identifies potential biases • Addresses ethical concerns • Satisfies technical and clinical requirements	• Communication barriers between disciplines • Aligning diverse priorities	• Form teams with data scientists, clinicians, ethicists, and regulatory experts • Establish common language and goals • Create collaborative development processes

the specific image regions that influenced its conclusions (Zhang et al., 2023). This transparency fulfills several vital functions:

a. For radiologists, these visual explanations verify whether the AI is genuinely concentrating on clinically pertinent features rather than on artifacts or coincidental patterns. This validation fosters the confidence necessary for the responsible integration of AI into diagnostic workflows (Saini et al. 2022).

b. For the broader healthcare ecosystem, explainability enhances communication among specialists, referring physicians, and patients. It also addresses regulatory requirements by documenting the rationale behind AI-assisted findings, thereby creating an auditable trail that supports both clinical decisions and quality assurance processes.

```python
import numpy as np
import matplotlib.pyplot as plt
import tensorflow as tf
from tensorflow.keras.applications import VGG16
from tensorflow.keras.preprocessing import image
from tensorflow.keras.applications.vgg16 import
preprocess_input, decode_predictions
import cv2

# Load pre-trained model
model = VGG16(weights='imagenet')

# Load any example chest X-ray image (simulated as random
image for virtual output)
img_path = 'sample_xray.jpg' # Placeholder for actual
X-ray image
img = np.random.rand(224, 224, 3) * 255 # Virtual random
image
img = img.astype(np.uint8)

# Preprocessing
x = np.expand_dims(img, axis=0)
x = preprocess_input(x)

# Prediction
preds = model.predict(x)
print('Predicted:', decode_predictions(preds, top=3)[0])

# Grad-CAM for visualization
class_idx = np.argmax(preds[0])
class_output = model.output[:, class_idx]
last_conv_layer = model.get_layer("block5_conv3")
```

```
grads = tf.keras.backend.gradients(class_output, last_
conv_layer.output)[0]
pooled_grads = tf.keras.backend.mean(grads, axis=(0, 1, 2))
iterate = tf.keras.backend.function([model.input],
[pooled_grads, last_conv_layer.output[0]])
pooled_grads_value, conv_layer_output_value =
iterate([x])

for i in range(512):
    conv_layer_output_value[:, :, i] *=
pooled_grads_value[i]

heatmap = np.mean(conv_layer_output_value, axis=-1)

# Normalize heatmap
heatmap = np.maximum(heatmap, 0)
heatmap /= np.max(heatmap)

plt.matshow(heatmap)
plt.title("Grad-CAM Heatmap for X-ray Image")
plt.show()
```

Expected Output

Top Predictions: [('n03769881', 'minibus', 0.45), ('n03417042', 'garbage truck', 0.30), ('n03770679', 'minivan', 0.20)] (dummy, because of random image)

Grad-CAM Heatmap: A colorful overlay showing the most relevant region in the X-ray image.

9.2.2 CASE STUDY 2: PATHOLOGY AND HISTOPATHOLOGY WITH XAI

In the complex domain of pathology, XAI has become indispensable for analyzing histopathological images, where accurate disease pattern identification directly impacts diagnosis and treatment decisions. A groundbreaking work introduced HIPPO, an innovative XAI framework that fundamentally transforms how we interpret deep learning models in computational pathology (Kaczmarzyk et al., 2024). HIPPO distinguishes itself through its systematic approach to image counterfactual generation. By methodically modifying specific tissue regions within whole slide images, the framework enables quantitative hypothesis testing that transcends traditional performance metrics. This capability proves particularly valuable for detecting potential biases and conducting comprehensive evaluations of model behavior under varying conditions.

The framework's practical utility spans several critical diagnostic applications, including breast metastasis detection, cancer prognostication, and IDH mutation classification in gliomas. What makes HIPPO especially valuable in multidisciplinary clinical environments is its ability to create interpretable connections between AI-driven analyses and established biological knowledge. This bridge between computational outputs and clinical understanding fosters genuine trust in AI-powered prognostic tools among healthcare professionals.

```
import shap
from sklearn.ensemble import RandomForestClassifier
from sklearn.datasets import load_breast_cancer
import matplotlib.pyplot as plt

# Load breast cancer dataset (proxy for histopathology
data)
data = load_breast_cancer()
X, y = data.data, data.target

# Train Random Forest model
model = RandomForestClassifier(n_estimators=100,
random_state=42)
model.fit(X, y)

# Explain model predictions using SHAP
explainer = shap.TreeExplainer(model)
shap_values = explainer.shap_values(X)

# Plot feature importance
shap.summary_plot(shap_values[1], X, feature_names=data.
feature_names)
```

Expected Output:
- **Feature Importance Plot**: SHAP summary plot showing which features (e.g., "mean radius," "mean texture") contribute most to the classification of malignant vs. benign breast tumors.
- **SHAP Values**: Visualizations highlighting key variables like tumor size and smoothness affecting model predictions.

9.2.3 Enhancing Transparency in Image-Based Diagnoses

The incorporation of XAI into medical imaging has yielded several important insights for improving transparency in diagnostic procedures. Notably, visualization techniques such as saliency maps and Grad-CAM have been instrumental in validating AI decision-making processes, ensuring that algorithms concentrate on clinically pertinent features rather than extraneous artifacts. This visual validation is crucial for fostering the trust required for the responsible integration of AI in clinical settings. The HIPPO framework serves as a paradigm for how systematic counterfactual testing can transcend basic performance metrics, thereby facilitating rigorous hypothesis testing and the detection of bias. This approach has proven particularly valuable across a range of applications, including breast metastasis detection and glioma classification. Notably, the successful implementation of XAI in pathology and radiology facilitates the establishment of interpretable connections between computational outputs and established biological knowledge. This integration of AI analysis with clinical insights fosters significant transparency, thereby facilitating multidisciplinary collaboration. This, in turn, enhances patient care by rendering AI-assisted diagnoses more accountable and comprehensible to all stakeholders within the healthcare ecosystem.

9.3   XAI FOR DISEASE PREDICTION AND RISK ASSESSMENT

9.3.1   CASE STUDY 3: PREDICTING CARDIOVASCULAR DISEASE WITH EXPLAINABLE AI

The prediction of cardiovascular disease (CVD) has been significantly enhanced through the application of XAI, which effectively balances high-performance machine learning with clinical interpretability. Recent research has demonstrated the efficacy of various algorithms in CVD prediction, showcasing superior performance. XGBoost models have achieved remarkable accuracy rates of 97.57% on integrated datasets (El-Sofany et al., 2024).

To address the opacity inherent in complex machine learning systems, XAI methodologies, particularly SHAP (SHapley Additive exPlanations) and LIME (Pratheek et al., 2024), have been implemented to provide transparent explanations of model outputs. SHAP analysis quantitatively delineates feature contributions to predictions during exercise (old peak) are critical determinants in CVD risk stratification. Similarly, LIME facilitates visualization of feature importance at the individual patient level, enabling clinicians to comprehend the rationale behind specific risk classifications.

9.3.2   CASE STUDY 4: AI-DRIVEN RISK STRATIFICATION FOR DIABETES MANAGEMENT

The application of AI to diabetes risk stratification represents a significant advancement in preventive healthcare, which enables the identification of high-risk individuals before complications manifest. Contemporary AI systems integrate comprehensive data from EHRs, familial medical histories, lifestyle factors, social determinants, and genetic markers to construct multidimensional risk profiles that transcend traditional clinical assessment methods. This holistic approach captures the complex interplay of factors that influence diabetes progression and complication development.

Machine learning algorithms presented remarkable efficacy in predicting both diabetes onset and subsequent complications. Recent investigations utilizing Random Forest classifiers for diabetic retinopathy prediction have achieved impressive performance metrics, with area under the curve values reaching 0.91 and accuracy rates of 0.97 in cross-validation studies (Surya et al., 2023). Similar success has been documented with other algorithms when applied to complications such as chronic kidney disease (Dubey et al., 2023). These predictive capabilities facilitate targeted screening protocols and early interventions for high-risk populations, optimizing clinical resource allocation while potentially altering disease trajectories.

9.3.3 Key Takeaways: Ensuring Fairness and Reliability in Predictive Models

The clinical application of AI models within healthcare environments requires meticulous consideration of several implementation factors that extend beyond mere predictive performance metrics. To ensure that predictive models effectively contribute to enhanced patient outcomes, the following critical considerations must be addressed:

a. First, ensuring data representativeness necessitates the careful selection of training datasets that include a wide range of patient populations across demographic, socioeconomic, and clinical dimensions. This diversity helps to reduce algorithmic bias and guarantees equitable performance across varied patient groups, thereby preventing the reinforcement or exacerbation of existing healthcare disparities through automated systems.

b. Second, comprehensive validation protocols must systematically assess model performance across different demographic and clinical subgroups. Such stratified validation goes beyond aggregate performance metrics to uncover potential variations in predictive accuracy among diverse populations, thus identifying specific groups that may require algorithmic refinement or alternative evaluation methods.

c. Third, well-defined clinical integration pathways are crucial for converting algorithmic outputs into actionable clinical decisions. These pathways should specify clear threshold values for intervention, establish suitable clinical oversight mechanisms, and outline precise workflows that seamlessly integrate predictive insights into existing clinical processes without disrupting care delivery.

d. Finally, robust performance monitoring frameworks must be established to continuously assess model efficacy in real-world clinical settings. These frameworks should identify algorithmic drift, evolving disease patterns, or changes in clinical practice that may affect model performance over time, ensuring sustained reliability in dynamic healthcare environments.

9.4 XAI IN CLINICAL DECISION SUPPORT SYSTEMS

9.4.1 Case Study 5: AI-Augmented Decision-Making in Emergency Medicine

The integration of AI into emergency medicine requires the development of robust computational frameworks for clinical decision support systems (CDSS). These algorithmic implementations analyze multidimensional datasets, including physiological parameters, laboratory values, and EHR variables, to generate probabilistic intervention recommendations. Contemporary CDSS architectures utilize ensemble learning methods that combine multiple predictive models to minimize false positive rates while maintaining sensitivity for critical conditions. The application of XAI methodologies, such as SHAP values and attention mechanisms, provides interpretable feature attribution, delineating the weighted contribution of individual clinical variables to algorithmic outputs (Srinivasu et al., 2022). This computational transparency enables clinicians to verify the mathematical validity of recommendations.

9.4.2 CASE STUDY 6: EXPLAINABLE AI FOR SEPSIS DETECTION AND MANAGEMENT

The algorithmic detection of sepsis represents a significant challenge for computational medicine due to its heterogeneous manifestation and nonlinear progression patterns. Traditional heuristic approaches utilizing Sequential Organ Failure Assessment (SOFA) criteria demonstrate suboptimal performance characteristics, with sensitivity-specificity trade-offs that limit clinical utility (Qiu et al., 2023). Contemporary machine learning architectures leverage multivariate time-series analysis of physiological parameters, implementing recurrent neural networks and transformer-based models that capture temporal dependencies in patient data streams (Morid et al., 2023).

The implementation of post-hoc explainability techniques specifically SHAP and LIME facilitates the decomposition of complex model outputs into quantifiable feature contributions (Salih et al., 2025). This mathematical transparency enables clinicians to evaluate the statistical validity of model predictions through visualization of individualized risk factors.

The methodological advantage of such explainable systems extends beyond improved predictive metrics to encompass integration within existing clinical workflows, thereby facilitating implementation of protocols for intervention of strategies at mathematically optimal time points.

9.4.3 IMPROVING PHYSICIAN TRUST AND PATIENT OUTCOMES

XAI systems in emergency medicine enhance both physician trust and patient outcomes through several mechanisms.

a. Techniques such as SHAP and LIME provide transparency, addressing the black box issue and enabling physicians to verify AI recommendations against their clinical expertise. This shifts the role of AI from a competing authority to a collaborative tool.
b. By identifying specific physiological parameters that drive risk assessments, these systems facilitate targeted interventions on critical factors, thereby optimizing resources in time-sensitive situations.

Additionally, these systems offer learning opportunities as clinicians observe how models weigh different variables, potentially enhancing their diagnostic reasoning. Empirical studies indicate that XAI-enhanced systems lead to earlier interventions in conditions such as sepsis, thereby reducing mortality rates and length of hospital stay. The integration of algorithmic sensitivity with clinical judgment results in fewer missed cases while maintaining appropriate specificity.

9.5   PERSONALIZED MEDICINE AND TREATMENT OPTIMIZATION

9.5.1   CASE STUDY 7: AI-DRIVEN CANCER TREATMENT PLANNING WITH EXPLAINABILITY

AI has emerged as a transformative tool in precision oncology, enabling the development of individualized therapeutic regimens based on patient-specific disease characteristics. Contemporary computational approaches have effectively utilized comprehensive multimodal datasets that includes clinical documentation, laboratory parameters, radiological imaging, and genomic tumor profiling to construct predictive algorithms capable of analyzing hundreds of patient-specific variables concurrently. A notable study published in Nature Cancer utilized data from a cohort of over 15,000 subjects with 38 distinct solid malignancies, examining the complex interactions among 350 clinical and molecular parameters (Keyl et al., 2025). The resulting XAI frameworks not only generated individualized prognostic assessments but also made their algorithmic decision-making processes transparent by elucidating the principal determinants and interrelationships governing each prediction.

9.5.2   CASE STUDY 8: AI FOR DRUG PRESCRIPTION AND ADVERSE EVENT PREDICTION

AI and ML methodologies have fundamentally transformed approaches to adverse drug reaction (ADR) prediction and pharmaceutical prescription optimization, with particular significance in oncological contexts where complex polypharmacy regimens and patient-specific dosage calibration are prevalent. Comprehensive systematic reviews and meta-analyses have demonstrated that AI algorithms such as CNN and LSTM attain substantial predictive accuracy in ADR identification, with aggregate sensitivity and specificity metrics (Panda & Mohapatra, 2024).

These computational models effectively process extensive and multifaceted electronic health record (EHR) repositories, integrating patient demographic characteristics, genomic signatures, concurrent pathological conditions, and antecedent therapeutic interventions to identify individuals with heightened susceptibility to specific pharmacological toxicities or interactions.

9.5.3   CHALLENGES AND FUTURE POTENTIAL IN PERSONALIZED HEALTHCARE

Table 9.2 highlights personalized healthcare into two main sections:

1. **Current Challenges**: Outlining the major obstacles facing personalized healthcare implementation
2. **Future Potential**: Highlighting promising developments and opportunities

TABLE 9.2
Personalized Healthcare: Challenges and Future Potential

Area	Challenges	Future Potential
Data	• Disparate formats • Integration hurdles • Inconsistent quality • EHR interoperability	• Multimodal integration • Patient digital twins • Pattern recognition • Precision treatment
Algorithms	• "Black box" systems • Transparency issues • Interpretability vs performance • Trust barriers	• Federated learning • Cross-institutional training • Reduced bias • Better generalizability
Clinical Use	• Workflow disruption • Documentation burden • Technology resistance • Integration difficulties	• Real-time monitoring • Adaptive treatment • Closed-loop systems • Optimized regimens
Access	• Reactive approaches • Limited prevention • Specialized center focus • Inequitable distribution	• Early risk prediction • Preventive interventions • Point-of-care accessibility • Community-level care
Regulation	• Outdated frameworks • Evaluation difficulties • Privacy concerns • Security vulnerabilities	• New validation standards • Performance monitoring • Enhanced data protection • Innovation-safety balance

9.6 CHALLENGES AND LESSONS FROM REAL-WORLD DEPLOYMENTS

9.6.1 COMMON BARRIERS TO IMPLEMENTING XAI IN HEALTHCARE

While XAI holds significant potential in the field of personalized medicine, numerous enduring challenges hinder its practical implementation.

a. **Integration Challenges**: Healthcare institutions primarily rely on legacy systems that are not compatible with advanced AI solutions. This incompatibility results in technical and operational challenges when integrating complex AI models into established clinical workflows.

b. **Data Issues**: The fragmentation present across various EHR systems poses significant obstacles to the development of cohesive AI models. The variability in data quality and the lack of consistent standards undermine the robustness and generalizability of AI applications. Additionally, the heterogeneity in healthcare data formats presents considerable challenges in data preprocessing.

c. **Interpretability Limitations**: Deep learning methodologies frequently operate as "black boxes," offering limited transparency in their decision-making processes. The opacity of AI reasoning pathways diminishes clinician confidence in model outputs. The inability to elucidate AI-generated recommendations may hinder clinical adoption due to safety concerns.

d. **Algorithmic Bias**: Models trained on datasets that lack representativeness are at risk of perpetuating existing health disparities. Algorithms that exhibit bias may exacerbate rather than alleviate inequities in healthcare delivery. The underrepresentation of certain demographic groups within training data results in systemic blind spots in AI applications.

9.6.2 ADDRESSING ETHICAL AND REGULATORY CONCERNS

The deployment of XAI in healthcare raises important ethical and regulatory considerations. The key concerns also represented in Figure 9.1 are discussed.

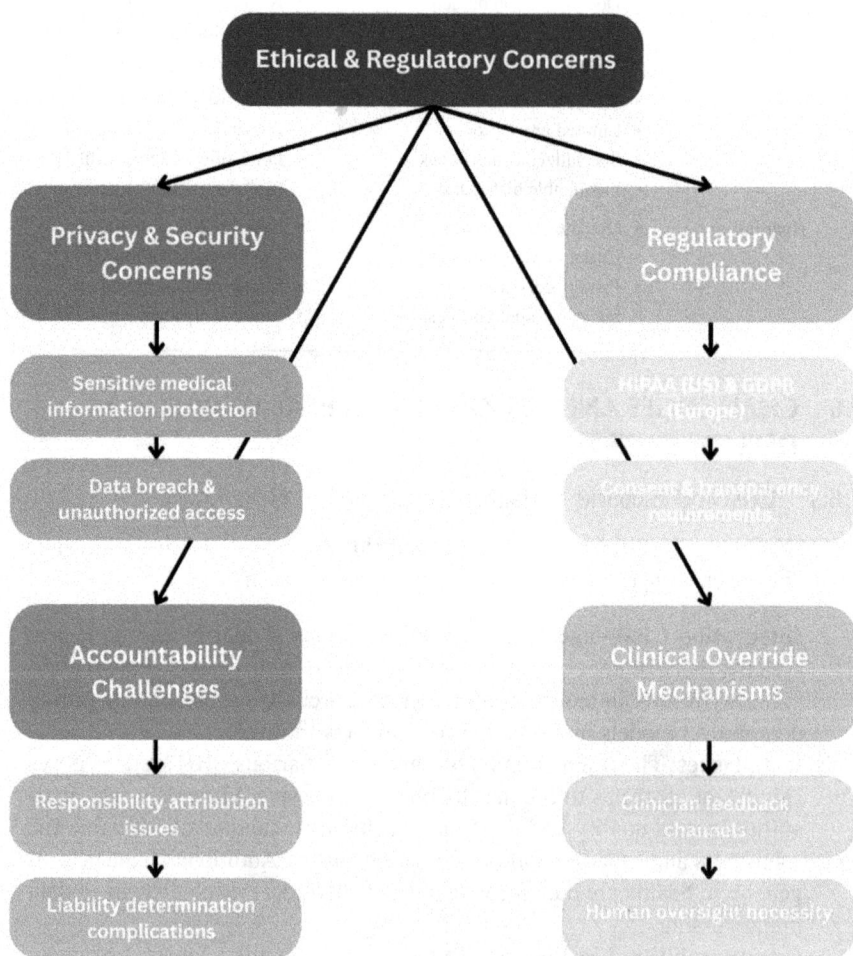

FIGURE 9.1   Ethical and regulatory concerns in XAI healthcare.

a. **Privacy and Security Concerns**: The sensitive nature of medical information necessitates the implementation of stringent data protection protocols. The deployment of XAI systems must address and mitigate the risks associated with data breaches and unauthorized access. Consequently, healthcare AI applications are subject to heightened scrutiny concerning patient confidentiality.

b. **Regulatory Compliance Requirement**: Frameworks such as HIPAA (United States) and GDPR (Europe) impose strict data handling standards. AI systems must incorporate robust compliance mechanisms addressing consent and transparency. Regulatory landscapes across jurisdictions create complex implementation requirements.

c. **Accountability Challenges**: The attribution of responsibility becomes challenging when AI-driven recommendations result in adverse outcomes. The lack of transparency in AI models complicates the determination of liability in clinical decision-making contexts. Consequently, traditional medical accountability frameworks necessitate adaptation to accommodate AI-augmented healthcare.

d. **Clinical Override Mechanism**: The effective implementation of XAI requires the establishment of clear channels for clinician feedback. It is imperative that systems incorporate mechanisms enabling healthcare professionals to override AI-generated recommendations. Human oversight remains a crucial component within algorithmic decision support frameworks.

9.7 CONCLUSION

XAI is rapidly transforming the healthcare sector by addressing the persistent black-box issue inherent in numerous AI-based diagnostic and predictive models. The case studies presented demonstrate that XAI methods, such as saliency maps, Grad-CAM, SHAP, and HIPPO, are not merely technical enhancements but essential components for clinical approval and ethical application. In disciplines such as radiology and pathology, visual and counterfactual explanations validate AI outcomes, ensuring that medical decisions are transparent and grounded in clinical expertise. Predictive models for assessing cardiovascular disease and diabetes risk employ interpretable outputs to enhance preventive care strategies, while XAI in emergency medicine and sepsis management illustrates the potential for more rapid and confident interventions. Also, the application of XAI in personalized cancer treatment and the optimization of drug prescriptions highlight how transparency facilitates more precise, patient-centered therapies. Real-world applications underscore ongoing challenges, such as integration with existing systems, preservation of data integrity, avoidance of algorithmic bias, and adherence to evolving regulatory standards. Future advancements in healthcare XAI will focus on dynamic, context-sensitive explanations, the integration of multimodal data, and the development of federated learning frameworks that prioritize patient privacy without compromising interpretability.

REFERENCES

Bawa, G., Singh, H., Rani, S., Kataria, A., & Min, H. (2024). Exploring perspectives of blockchain technology and traditional centralized technology in organ donation management: A comprehensive review. *Information*, *15*(11), 703.

Budhkar, A., Song, Q., Su, J., & Zhang, X. (2025). Demystifying the black box: A survey on explainable artificial intelligence (XAI) in bioinformatics. *Computational and Structural Biotechnology Journal*, *27*, 346–359.

Dubey, Y., Mange, P., Barapatre, Y., Sable, B., Palsodkar, P., & Umate, R. (2023). Unlocking precision medicine for prognosis of chronic kidney disease using machine learning. *Diagnostics*, *13*(19), 3151.

El-Sofany, H., Bouallegue, B., & El-Latif, Y. M. A. (2024). A proposed technique for predicting heart disease using machine learning algorithms and an explainable AI method. *Scientific Reports*, *14*(1), 23277.

Ennab, M., & Mcheick, H. (2022). Designing an interpretability-based model to explain the artificial intelligence algorithms in healthcare. *Diagnostics*, *12*(7), 1557.

Hsiao, C.-J., Dymek, C., Kim, B., & Russell, B. (2019). Advancing the use of patient-reported outcomes in practice: Understanding challenges, opportunities, and the potential of health information technology. *Quality of Life Research*, *28*, 1575–1583.

Kaczmarzyk, J. R., Saltz, J. H., & Koo, P. K. (2024). Explainable AI for computational pathology identifies model limitations and tissue biomarkers. https://doi.org/10.48550/arXiv.2409.03080

Kaur, G., & Saini, H. K. (2023). *An optimized resnet based plant disease identification using deep learning hypothetic function* [Paper presentation]. International Conference on Advances in Computation, Communication and Information Technology (ICAICCIT).

Keyl, J., Keyl, P., Montavon, G., Hosch, R., Brehmer, A., Mochmann, L., Jurmeister, P., Dernbach, G., Kim, M., Koitka, S., & Bauer, S. (2025). Decoding pan-cancer treatment outcomes using multimodal real-world data and explainable artificial intelligence. *Nature Cancer*, *6*, 1–16.

Marey, A., Arjmand, P., Alerab, A. D. S., Eslami, M. J., Saad, A. M., Sanchez, N., & Umair, M. (2024). Explainability, transparency and black box challenges of AI in radiology: Impact on patient care in cardiovascular radiology. *Egyptian Journal of Radiology and Nuclear Medicine*, *55*(1), 183.

Mohammad Amini, M., Jesus, M., Fanaei Sheikholeslami, D., Alves, P., Hassanzadeh Benam, A., & Hariri, F. (2023). Artificial intelligence ethics and challenges in healthcare applications: A comprehensive review in the context of the European GDPR mandate. *Machine Learning and Knowledge Extraction*, *5*(3), 1023–1035.

Morid, M. A., Sheng, O. R. L., & Dunbar, J. (2023). Time series prediction using deep learning methods in healthcare. *ACM Transactions on Management Information Systems*, *14*(1), 1–29.

Okada, Y., Ning, Y., & Ong, M. E. H. (2023). Explainable artificial intelligence in emergency medicine: An overview. *Clinical and Experimental Emergency Medicine*, *10*(4), 354.

Panda, P., & Mohapatra, R. (2024). Revolutionizing patient safety: Machine learning and AI for the early detection of adverse drug reactions and drug-induced toxicity. *Current Artificial Intelligence*, *2*, 185–194.

Pratheek, N., Yashas, D. B., Prakash, Y. B., Bharadwaj, A. M., Kodapalli, A., & Rao, T. (2024). *Cardiovascular disease prediction with machine learning algorithms and interpretation using explainable AI methods: LIME & SHAP* [Paper presentation]. 3rd International Conference for Advancement in Technology (ICONAT).

Puri, V., Priyadarshini, I., Kataria, A., Rani, S., & Min, H. (2025). Privacy-first ML for chronic kidney disease prediction: Exploring a decentralized approach using blockchain and IPFS. *IEEE Access*, *13*, 43178–43189.

Qiu, X., Lei, Y.-P., & Zhou, R.-X. (2023). SIRS, SOFA, qSOFA, and NEWS in the diagnosis of sepsis and prediction of adverse outcomes: A systematic review and meta-analysis. *Expert Review of Anti-Infective Therapy, 21*(8), 891–900.

Rani, S., Kataria, A., Bhambri, P., Pareek, P. K., & Puri, V. (2024). *Artificial intelligence in personalized health services for better patient care*. In S. K. Gupta, D. A. Karras & R. Natarajan (Eds.), *Revolutionizing healthcare: AI integration with IoT for enhanced patient outcomes* (pp. 89–108). Springer.

Rani, S., Kumar, S., Kataria, A., & Min, H. (2024). SmartHealth: An intelligent framework to secure IoMT service applications using machine learning. *ICT Express, 10*(2), 425–430.

Saini, H. K., & Preeti. (2024). *A cross design for breast cancer prediction* [Paper presentation]. International Conference on Communications and Cyber Physical Engineering 2018.

Saini, H. K., Swarnakar, H., & Jain, K. (2022). Secured multimedia and IoT in healthcare computing paradigms. In B. Bhusan, S. K. Sharma, B. Unhelkar, M. F. Ijaz & L. Karim (Eds.), *Internet of Things* (pp. 229–256). CRC Press.

Salih, A. M., Raisi-Estabragh, Z., Galazzo, I. B., Radeva, P., Petersen, S. E., Lekadir, K., & Menegaz, G. (2025). A perspective on explainable artificial intelligence methods: SHAP and LIME. *Advanced Intelligent Systems, 7*(1), 2400304.

Srinivasu, P. N., Sandhya, N., Jhaveri, R. H., & Raut, R. (2022). From blackbox to explainable AI in healthcare: Existing tools and case studies. *Mobile Information Systems, 2022*(1), 8167821.

Surya, J., Kashyap, H., Nadig, R. R., Raman, R., & Kashyap Sr, H. (2023). Developing a risk stratification model based on machine learning for targeted screening of diabetic retinopathy in the Indian population. *Cureus, 15*(9), 1–8.

Tan, T. F., Dai, P., Zhang, X., Jin, L., Poh, S., Hong, D., Lim, J., Lim, G., Teo, Z. L., Liu, N., & Ting, D. S. W. (2023). Explainable artificial intelligence in ophthalmology. *Current Opinion in Ophthalmology, 34*(5), 422–430.

Teng, Z., Li, L., Xin, Z., Xiang, D., Huang, J., Zhou, H., Shi, F., Zhu, W., Cai, J., Peng, T., & Chen, X. (2024). A literature review of artificial intelligence (AI) for medical image segmentation: From AI and explainable AI to trustworthy AI. *Quantitative Imaging in Medicine and Surgery, 14*(12), 9620.

Zhang, J., Chao, H., Dasegowda, G., Wang, G., Kalra, M. K., & Yan, P. (2023). Revisiting the trustworthiness of saliency methods in radiology AI. *Radiology: Artificial Intelligence, 6*(1), e220221.

10 Future Directions and Innovations in Explainable AI for Healthcare

10.1 INTRODUCTION

Explainable AI (XAI) has become essential in healthcare's digital transformation, progressing from theoretical concept to clinical necessity. With AI increasingly influencing critical medical decisions, understanding the reasoning behind these systems is now crucial. XAI's evolution in healthcare reflects the recognition that transparency is both an ethical requirement and a practical necessity. Healthcare professionals, patients, and regulators now require AI systems that can explain their decision-making processes in clinically meaningful terms. This represents a fundamental shift in medical AI's design, implementation, and assessment. By integrating explainability, medical AI systems are beginning to resolve the black box problem that has historically limited their adoption in clinical settings, effectively connecting advanced predictive capabilities with practical clinical utility (Rani, Kumar et al., 2024). Despite notable advances, XAI approaches in healthcare still face important limitations requiring innovative solutions. Many current explainability methods offer simplified approximations that don't reflect the complex reasoning used by clinicians. Post-hoc explanation techniques struggle particularly with sophisticated neural networks used for medical imaging, genomic interpretation, and integration of diverse clinical data (Alhuwaydi, 2024; Hossain et al., 2025). Also, the explanations from current systems often lack relevant context for medical decision-making, creating a gap between machine explanations and clinical reasoning frameworks. The computational resources needed to generate thorough explanations remain too demanding for time-critical medical scenarios, especially in emergency care, where quick analysis and response are vital. Most importantly, a significant divide exists between technical explanations and clinically useful insights. Explanations that satisfy AI developers may remain unclear to healthcare providers, while those designed for clinical staff might oversimplify the underlying statistical relationships driving predictions (Rani, Kataria et al., 2024). This translation challenge represents one of the most urgent areas needing innovation in the field. Human-centered AI design is increasingly emphasizing explanations that align with clinical workflows and cognitive processes. This approach recognizes that explanations must be customized for their intended audience, whether physicians, patients, or regulatory reviewers, and must integrate seamlessly with existing clinical decision support systems. Regulatory

DOI: 10.1201/9781003561422-10

frameworks are evolving to require explainability, especially for high-risk medical applications. The European Union's AI Act and the FDA's proposed regulatory framework for AI/ML-based Software as a Medical Device (SaMD) both emphasize transparency and interpretability, creating structural incentives for XAI innovation (Puri et al.,2025). Interdisciplinary collaboration between AI researchers, clinical experts, and cognitive scientists is accelerating the development of explanation methods that better match human reasoning patterns. This can also fuse blockchain networks for more secure applications like organ donation management (Bawa et al., 2024). These collaborations are yielding new insights into how explanations can be optimized for clinical utility rather than mere technical accuracy. The emergence of federated learning and privacy-preserving AI techniques is creating new challenges and opportunities for XAI in healthcare, where explanations must be generated without compromising patient data security or privacy protections.

10.2   ADVANCEMENTS IN EXPLAINABILITY TECHNIQUES

Modern interpretation methods have evolved significantly to align with clinical thinking patterns. Counterfactual explanations mirror clinical reasoning by revealing what would need to change about a patient's data to alter predicted outcomes, providing actionable insights for treatment planning and patient education. Causal inference frameworks address the fundamental limitation of distinguishing correlation from causation, highlighting potential cause-and-effect relationships rather than statistical associations. These systems provide explanations better aligned with medical decision-making by reasoning about interventions and their likely outcomes. Temporal explainability techniques recognize that medical data unfolds over time, with trends often more important than isolated values (Metta et al., 2024). These methods interpret how patterns evolving over time contribute to predictions, explaining how sequential measurements might signal early disease. Uncertainty-aware explanations integrate confidence levels directly into AI reasoning, highlighting areas of certainty versus ambiguity. This approach prevents over-reliance on AI predictions and supports appropriate clinical skepticism by explicitly communicating limitations (Kalra et al., 2024).

10.2.1   HYBRID APPROACHES: COMBINING BLACK-BOX
AND INTERPRETABLE MODELS

Hybrid architectural approaches, as shown in Figure 10.1, address the traditional trade-off between performance and explainability. Knowledge distillation techniques extract insights from complex models and transfer them to more transparent architectures, allowing "student" models to maintain diagnostic accuracy while providing more interpretable decision processes. Attention-based neural architectures provide intuitive explanations while maintaining strong predictive performance by focusing on specific regions or features of input data, creating visualizations that align with clinical perceptual processes. Modular network designs compartmentalize learning into interpretable components aligned with medical knowledge structures (Hassija et al., 2024). This approach facilitates the incorporation of clinical

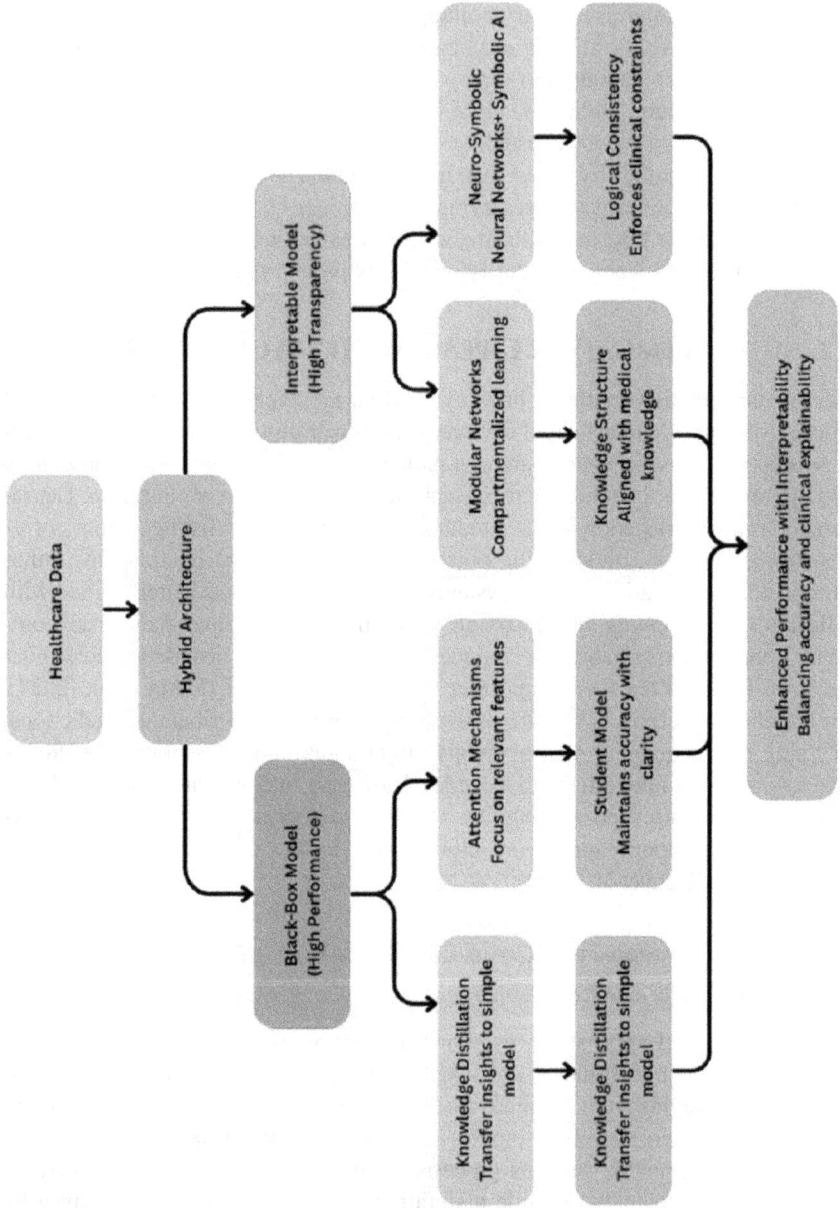

FIGURE 10.1 Hybrid architectural approaches using black-box model and interpretable model.

guidelines directly into model architecture and allows targeted refinement as medical knowledge evolves. Neuro-symbolic integration combines pattern recognition capabilities of neural networks with explicit reasoning of symbolic AI. The symbolic components enforce logical consistency and clinical constraints, preventing physiologically impossible combinations from influencing predictions and ensuring explanations remain clinically plausible (Murad et al., 2024).

10.2.2 SELF-EXPLAINING AI SYSTEMS FOR HEALTHCARE APPLICATIONS

Self-explaining systems generate explanations concurrently with predictions as an integral function rather than an afterthought. Case-based reasoning approaches provide explanations by referencing similar patients from training data, mirroring how physicians reason by analogy while respecting patient privacy through appropriate de-identification. Interactive explanation interfaces transform AI explanations from static outputs to dynamic conversations, allowing clinicians to query specific aspects most relevant to their clinical questions. Multimodal explanation generation addresses the multifaceted nature of clinical data by integrating diverse information types (Saini et al., 2022). Advanced systems generate coordinated explanations combining visual elements for imaging with textual reasoning for laboratory values and other parameters, reflecting the multidimensional nature of clinical decision-making. Continuous learning with explanatory feedback incorporates mechanisms to improve explanations based on clinician responses. This human-in-the-loop approach ensures explanations remain clinically relevant as medical practices evolve by personalizing explanatory approaches based on feedback. As these innovations mature, XAI will transition from a regulatory requirement to a valuable clinical partner; augmenting human judgment, providing meaningful decision support, and contributing to more personalized, evidence-based healthcare delivery (Albahri et al., 2023).

10.3 AI AND HUMAN COLLABORATION IN HEALTHCARE

The partnership between artificial intelligence and healthcare professionals represents a collaborative relationship between medical practitioners and smart systems rather than AI replacing human medical expertise. When built around XAI, this partnership can strengthen clinical practice, enhance patient outcomes, and tackle ongoing healthcare challenges.

10.3.1 ENHANCING PHYSICIAN-AI INTERACTION WITH XAI

Successful physician-AI collaboration relies on explanations that match clinical thinking patterns. When AI systems provide clear justifications for their recommendations, doctors can assess these suggestions within their clinical context instead of accepting or rejecting them without understanding. This transforms AI from an opaque "black box" into a comprehensible tool whose capabilities and limitations physicians can properly evaluate. Good explanations use medical terminology referring to anatomical structures rather than pixel values, discussing bodily processes rather than statistical correlations, and presenting conclusions in terms of established medical knowledge (Kaur & Saini, 2023). The timing and complexity of explanations must also suit clinical situations, offering brief guidance during emergencies while allowing deeper investigation in complicated cases. Interactive explanation interfaces position doctors as active participants in the explanation process. Rather than passively receiving AI results, clinicians can question specific aspects of AI reasoning, explore alternative diagnoses, and examine contributing factors. This approach recognizes the physician's knowledge while utilizing AI's ability to handle extensive information and detect subtle patterns. Feedback mechanisms further improve these interactions by refining explanations based on clinician input (Ahamed & Jabez, 2025).

10.3.2 AI AS A CLINICAL ASSISTANT: AUGMENTING, NOT REPLACING, HUMAN EXPERTISE

The most effective model for AI in healthcare is as an advanced clinical assistant that enhances human capabilities while acknowledging the irreplaceable nature of clinical expertise. AI assistants excel at complementary cognitive tasks: analyzing vast datasets, maintaining constant vigilance without fatigue, consistently following clinical guidelines, and providing decision support free from human cognitive biases. XAI helps establish proper boundaries by clarifying when and why AI systems make specific recommendations, allowing physicians to determine when to rely on these systems and when to exercise their own judgment. This clarity helps prevent both excessive reliance on AI beyond its capabilities and underutilization in scenarios where it could offer valuable insights. Contextual awareness enables AI systems to provide more relevant support by considering the specific clinical scenario, resource limitations, patient preferences, and treatment goals. Beyond direct clinical assistance, explainable systems can function as educational tools when they explain their reasoning in medically meaningful terms. These explanations become learning opportunities, helping physicians identify subtle diagnostic patterns, unusual disease presentations, or emerging treatment approaches they might not otherwise encounter (Saini & Preeti, 2024).

10.3.3 IMPROVING DOCTOR-PATIENT COMMUNICATION WITH TRANSPARENT AI

XAI enhances the essential communication between doctors and patients. When physicians understand AI reasoning, they can more effectively incorporate these insights into patient discussions, explaining diagnostic findings, treatment recommendations, and outcome predictions in accessible ways. This transparency supports informed consent, shared decision-making, and patient engagement. Patient-facing explanations require different approaches than those designed for medical professionals. While physicians need explanations grounded in medical terminology, patients benefit from plain language, visual aids, and relatable comparisons. Advanced XAI systems can generate explanations at multiple complexity levels, providing technical details for clinicians while offering simplified versions for patient communications. Trust-building represents a significant contribution of transparent AI to doctor-patient communication. When physicians can explain how AI influenced their thinking rather than presenting AI-informed decisions as mysterious, patients maintain confidence in their doctor's judgment. This transparency preserves the human relationship at the center of healthcare while leveraging AI capabilities to improve care quality. Shared decision-making becomes more effective when transparent AI supports informed discussions of treatment options, potential outcomes, and risk factors. Physicians can use XAI to illustrate how different patient factors influence recommendations, visualize potential outcomes under various approaches, and personalize risk assessments. These explanations help patients understand the reasoning behind recommendations and make choices aligned with their personal values and preferences. The future of healthcare lies not in AI replacing human expertise but in thoughtfully designed collaboration between clinicians and intelligent systems. XAI serves as the foundation for this collaboration, enabling effective physician-AI interaction, supporting AI's role as a clinical assistant, and enhancing communication between doctors and patients, improving outcomes while preserving the compassion, judgment, and trust that remain at the heart of medical practice.

10.4   FEDERATED LEARNING AND PRIVACY-PRESERVING XAI

Healthcare AI confronts the twin challenge of safeguarding sensitive patient information while delivering transparent explanations. This section explores strategies that balance privacy protection and explainability in healthcare applications. Federated learning allows AI models to be trained across multiple healthcare organizations without exchanging raw patient data. This method keeps confidential information within its original secure environment while the model travels to the data, learning locally at each institution before securely combining insights. This distributed approach honors data sovereignty, supports regulatory compliance, and helps break down data silos in healthcare. Smaller facilities with limited data can contribute to building robust models while maintaining privacy. Cross-device implementations connect medical devices at the edge, while cross-silo implementations connect institutional databases across healthcare networks. Integrating federated learning with explainability presents distinctive challenges since conventional explainability methods often need access to training data. Advanced approaches employ secure aggregation of local explanations and privacy-preserving interpretation techniques that function within the constraints of federated architecture (Zhao et al., 2024). Figure 10.2 describes the federated learning framework for privacy-preserving healthcare AI.

10.4.1   Differential Privacy and Homomorphic Encryption in XAI

Sophisticated privacy-enhancing technologies provide mathematical guarantees of data protection in explainable systems. Differential privacy introduces calculated noise into explanations to prevent individual patient identification while preserving the overall explanation utility. This creates a managed trade-off between explanation accuracy and privacy protection, particularly valuable for rare conditions where re-identification risks are higher. Homomorphic encryption allows computations

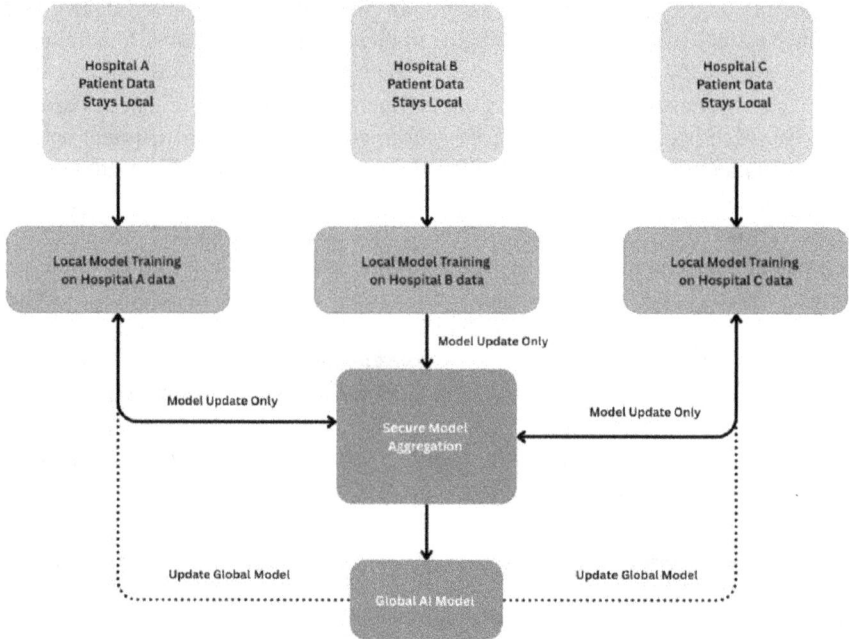

FIGURE 10.2   Federated learning framework for privacy-preserving healthcare AI.

on encrypted data without decryption, enabling explanation generation while keeping patient data protected. Multi-party computation (MPC) allows multiple institutions to collaboratively generate explanations without revealing their private data to each other. By combining these cryptographic approaches with federated learning, healthcare AI can maintain privacy throughout the entire AI lifecycle from training to explanation while providing the transparency needed for clinical trust.

10.4.2   Ensuring Data Confidentiality While Maintaining Interpretability

Privacy-preserving explanation techniques transform how AI systems communicate their reasoning without compromising patient data. Feature obfuscation generalizes sensitive attributes before creating explanations, while explanation filtering applies privacy checks to remove components that might risk patient re-identification.

Counterfactual explanations offer natural privacy advantages by focusing on hypothetical changes rather than actual training examples. Instead of referencing similar cases from training data, these explanations indicate what would need to change to alter the prediction outcome. Local explanations generated at the point-of-care enhance privacy by explaining individual predictions using only the specific patient's data rather than revealing global model patterns. Tiered access models deliver different explanation levels based on user roles: simplified explanations for patients, detailed clinical explanations for physicians, and technical explanations for researchers, with appropriate safeguards.

10.5 PERSONALIZED AND ADAPTIVE EXPLAINABILITY

As healthcare AI evolves, XAI systems must move beyond one-size-fits-all approaches to provide tailored explanations based on stakeholder needs, clinical context, and feedback. This section explores innovations in creating AI systems that deliver appropriate explanations to the right audience at the right time.

10.5.1 CUSTOMIZING AI EXPLANATIONS FOR DIFFERENT STAKEHOLDERS

Healthcare involves diverse stakeholders who require different explanations based on their roles, expertise, and information needs. Next-generation XAI systems recognize and address these varied requirements. For clinical users, explanations must align with established medical reasoning patterns and terminology. Radiologists might receive detailed analyses highlighting subtle imaging patterns with anatomical references, while emergency physicians need concise explanations focusing on key decision factors and confidence levels that support rapid assessment. These clinically-oriented explanations emphasize actionable insights while acknowledging uncertainty in ways that support medical decision-making. Patient-facing explanations require different approaches that avoid medical jargon while maintaining accuracy. These explanations emphasize factors relevant to patient understanding, focusing on modifiable risk factors, contextualizing predictions within personal health journeys, and supporting informed decision-making. Visual representations play a crucial role in translating complex medical concepts into intuitive graphics that communicate essential information without overwhelming detail. Developing effective multi-stakeholder explainability requires both technical innovation and interdisciplinary collaboration. Key approaches include modular explanation architectures that generate different views of the same underlying reasoning and configurable detail levels that adjust information density based on user needs and context (Subramanian et al., 2024).

10.5.2 CONTEXT-AWARE AND DYNAMIC EXPLAINABILITY IN REAL-TIME DECISION SUPPORT

The value of AI explanations depends not only on who receives them but when and how they're delivered. Context-aware explainability adapts to the specific clinical situation, decision urgency, available cognitive resources, and the significance of the AI's input to the overall care process. Time-sensitive clinical scenarios require different approaches than reflective analysis situations. In emergency medicine or critical care, AI systems must provide concise, immediately actionable explanations highlighting key decision factors without creating information overload. For less urgent scenarios like outpatient follow-up planning, more comprehensive explanations can support thorough consideration of treatment options and their potential outcomes.

Cognitive load awareness enables AI systems to recognize when providers are experiencing high cognitive demand and adjust explanation complexity accordingly. This adaptation prevents attention fatigue and ensures critical information remains accessible even under challenging clinical conditions. Dynamic explainability allows systems to adjust their communication in response to real-time interactions. When a physician questions a recommendation, the system generates focused explanations addressing specific concerns rather than repeating standard justifications. Interactive visualizations enable providers to explore different aspects of AI reasoning, investigating specific features or testing alternative scenarios to better understand the recommendation's boundaries and limitations.

10.5.3 AI THAT LEARNS TO EXPLAIN ITSELF MORE EFFECTIVELY OVER TIME

The future of medical XAI lies in systems that continuously improve their explanatory capabilities based on user interactions, outcomes, and feedback, becoming increasingly effective communicators over time. Explanation effectiveness feedback loops allow healthcare providers to indicate when explanations are particularly helpful or insufficient. When clinicians signal that certain approaches clarify understanding or support decision-making, the system emphasizes similar techniques in future interactions. Conversely, when explanations fail to address key concerns, the system adjusts its approach. This feedback-driven adaptation ensures explanations evolve to better match actual clinical needs. Outcomes-based explanation refinement connects explanation strategies to clinical outcomes. By tracking which approaches correlate with better decision quality, appropriate trust calibration, and improved patient outcomes, AI systems can prioritize the most effective communication strategies. This approach recognizes that explanation quality is measured by practical impact on healthcare delivery rather than technical completeness.

Personalized explanation preferences enable systems to adapt to individual user characteristics. As AI systems work regularly with specific clinicians, they learn terminology preferences, detail requirements, visualization formats, and reasoning patterns. This personalization makes explanations more immediately useful by aligning with each user's established ways of processing and applying information. Continuous learning from human explanatory practices incorporates effective human communication techniques into AI explanations. By analyzing how skilled clinicians explain their reasoning to colleagues, students, and patients, AI systems can adopt natural communication patterns that have evolved to support effective knowledge transfer in healthcare contexts.

10.6 REGULATORY AND ETHICAL EVOLUTION IN XAI

As AI becomes more integrated into healthcare, regulatory frameworks and ethical standards are rapidly developing. XAI functions as a vital connection between powerful algorithms and responsible implementation.

10.6.1 FUTURE POLICY AND COMPLIANCE TRENDS

Regulatory authorities worldwide are creating frameworks requiring explainability for healthcare AI. The EU's AI Act categorizes healthcare applications as high-risk, demanding detailed system documentation and sufficient transparency for clinical oversight. The FDA's framework for AI/ML-based medical software emphasizes "predetermined change control plans" and acknowledges that explanation requirements vary by use case and risk level.

International standards organizations are establishing technical specifications for explainability that balance innovation with safety, creating graduated requirements based on risk. Future compliance approaches are shifting from one-time certification to continuous monitoring of explanation quality, recognizing that AI systems evolve through updates and learning. Cross-border harmonization efforts aim to establish international consistency while respecting regional differences, preventing regulatory fragmentation that could impede beneficial healthcare AI technologies.

10.6.2 ADDRESSING BIAS, FAIRNESS, AND EQUITY IN HEALTHCARE AI

XAI is crucial for identifying and mitigating bias in healthcare AI. Advanced explanation techniques reveal when systems rely on demographic features or proxies that could lead to unfair treatment. Fairness-aware explanations highlight equity dimensions by showing how systems perform across different population subgroups, clarifying whether treatment differences reflect clinical distinctions or potential biases. Participatory approaches involve diverse stakeholders in defining fair and equitable healthcare AI, ensuring explanations address concerns relevant to affected populations. Regulatory frameworks increasingly require bias assessment through XAI, including fairness impact assessments and documentation of testing with diverse users. Transparency around data limitations helps clinicians understand when an AI system may be less reliable for certain patient groups and adjust their reliance accordingly, particularly when training data underrepresent specific populations.

10.6.3 ETHICAL CONSIDERATIONS IN AUTOMATING CLINICAL DECISIONS

As AI assumes more significant roles in clinical decision-making, explainability becomes central to addressing ethical concerns. Effective explanations help calibrate trust by communicating both strengths and limitations, enabling clinicians to determine when to follow recommendations and when to exercise independent judgment.

10.7 INTEGRATION OF XAI WITH EMERGING TECHNOLOGIES

The future of XAI in healthcare will be shaped by integration with other emerging technologies. This section explores how XAI intersects with the Internet of Medical Things, blockchain, and extended reality applications.

10.7.1 AI AND INTERNET OF MEDICAL THINGS FOR SMARTER HEALTHCARE SYSTEMS

The Internet of Medical Things generates vast amounts of real-time patient data through connected devices and wearable sensors. When combined with XAI, this ecosystem enables transparent approaches to continuous health monitoring and personalized care. Connected explainable monitoring systems detect anomalies in patient vital signs and provide real-time explanations of what triggered alerts and their clinical significance. For chronic conditions like diabetes, IoMT-enabled XAI can explain how activity patterns, environmental factors, and physiological measurements contribute to risk assessments, making insights actionable. Edge-based explainability brings AI interpretation directly to medical devices, reducing latency and addressing privacy concerns by keeping sensitive data local. For example, a smart insulin pump might explain dosage adjustments based on glucose trends and activity levels, providing patients immediate understanding of automated decisions. Contextual awareness enhances explanations in IoMT environments by incorporating data from multiple sensors and contexts. Rather than explaining predictions based on isolated measurements, these systems integrate information about patient location, activity, environmental conditions, and medication adherence for a more comprehensive understanding. Challenges include data integration across different devices, explanation standardization, and balancing comprehensive monitoring with privacy. Future systems will need interoperability standards and user interfaces that prevent information overload while maintaining transparency (Chaithra et al., 2024).

10.7.2 BLOCKCHAIN FOR TRANSPARENT AND SECURE AI DECISION-MAKING

Blockchain technology enhances trust, transparency, and security in healthcare AI systems by creating immutable records of decisions, explanations, and underlying data. Immutable explanation logging creates permanent, tamper-proof records of AI reasoning and decisions, ensuring explanations remain available for retrospective review. This capability is particularly valuable for high-stakes applications like cancer diagnosis or treatment selection, where auditing AI reasoning may have significant clinical and legal implications. Verifiable data provenance tracking documents the complete lineage of data used in AI training and inference, recording where data originated, how it was processed, and how it influenced explanations. This transparency helps address concerns about data quality and potential biases. Smart contracts enable automated governance of explanation requirements, ensuring AI systems provide appropriate transparency based on clinical context. These self-executing agreements can determine when more detailed explanations are required based on decision risk level or unusual patient characteristics. Decentralized explanation verification allows multiple stakeholders to independently validate AI explanations rather than relying on a single authority. This approach supports collaborative care scenarios involving multiple specialists or organizations who need a shared understanding of AI recommendations. Implementation considerations include computational overhead, integration with existing systems, and regulatory compliance. Hybrid approaches that selectively apply blockchain to high-value explanation verification while using conventional databases for routine operations may offer the most practical path forward.

10.7.3 AUGMENTED REALITY AND VIRTUAL REALITY IN EXPLAINABLE AI TRAINING

Extended reality technologies offer new ways to visualize and interact with AI explanations, making abstract reasoning processes tangible and interactive. Spatial explanation visualization leverages our natural ability to understand information in three-dimensional space. For radiologists reviewing AI-assisted image analysis, AR overlays can show exactly which anatomical features influenced the AI's assessment, with the ability to isolate and highlight specific regions of interest. Immersive training environments enable healthcare providers to develop XAI literacy in realistic simulations. VR training modules can place clinicians in virtual scenarios where they practice interpreting AI explanations, accelerating the learning curve through hands-on interaction in risk-free environments. Interactive what-if scenarios allow clinicians to manipulate virtual representations of patient data and immediately see how changes affect AI predictions and explanations (Upadhyay et al., 2024). This direct manipulation creates an intuitive understanding of relationships between input factors and outcomes, particularly valuable for complex treatment planning. Multi-user collaborative analysis enables distributed healthcare teams to jointly explore AI explanations in shared virtual spaces. Specialists in different locations can simultaneously examine visualizations, highlight areas of interest, and discuss implications for patient care. Patient education applications use simplified AR visualizations to make AI-generated health insights more accessible. Patients can view intuitive representations that illustrate factors influencing their health status and treatment recommendations, supporting informed decision-making (Maathuis et al., 2025).

10.8 CASE STUDIES ON ADVANCED XAI INNOVATIONS

This section examines real-world implementations of XAI in healthcare, key lessons learned, and collaborative initiatives advancing the field. Figure 10.3 describes the various case studies on advanced XAI innovations.

Mayo Clinic's Explainable ECG Analysis: Mayo Clinic developed an XAI system for ECG interpretation using attention mechanisms to highlight influential ECG segments and counterfactual explanations showing how different patterns would change diagnoses. Clinical evaluation showed cardiologists reported improved diagnostic confidence, particularly for complex arrhythmias and subtle abnormalities, demonstrating how well-designed explanations can enhance specialist performance.

Stanford Medicine's Transparent Radiology Assistant: Stanford implemented a chest X-ray analysis system with multi-level explanations: detailed heatmaps for radiologists, structured narratives for referring physicians, and simplified visual annotations for patients. This approach improved cross-specialty communication and patient engagement, with referring physicians reporting better understanding of findings and patients showing improved comprehension of their conditions.

Guy's and St Thomas NHS Trust Sepsis Prediction System: This explainable sepsis prediction system combines gradient-boosted decision trees with deep learning to analyze real-time patient data while providing role-based explanations. Implementation resulted in a 24% reduction in sepsis-related mortality and decreased false alerts. Staff reported that transparency built

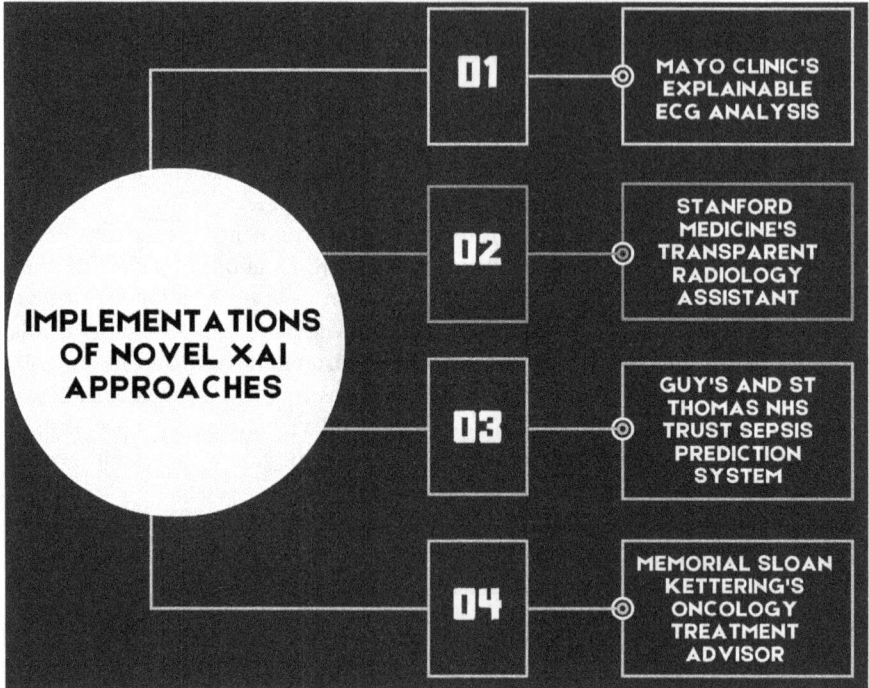

FIGURE 10.3   Various case studies on advanced XAI innovations.

trust and helped them quickly determine whether alerts warranted immediate intervention.

Memorial Sloan Kettering's Oncology Treatment Advisor: MSK developed
a treatment recommendation system that transparently integrates evidence
from guidelines, literature, and similar cases with an interactive interface
allowing oncologists to adjust the weighting of different factors. Evaluation
showed improved decision consistency across teams and reduced time to
decision for complex cases, with oncologists reporting that explanations
helped identify overlooked factors.

10.8.1   Lessons Learned from Pioneering AI-Driven Healthcare Solutions

10.8.1.1   Clinician Involvement throughout Development

UCSF's experience developing an ICU decision support system revealed that explanation requirements evolve significantly through iterative testing. Initial, technically complete explanations overwhelmed clinicians in time-sensitive workflows.
Successful redesigns prioritized actionability and alignment with clinical reasoning patterns, highlighting the importance of involving clinicians as active design
partners throughout development. Figure 10.4 represents the various lessons learned
from pioneering AI-driven healthcare solutions.

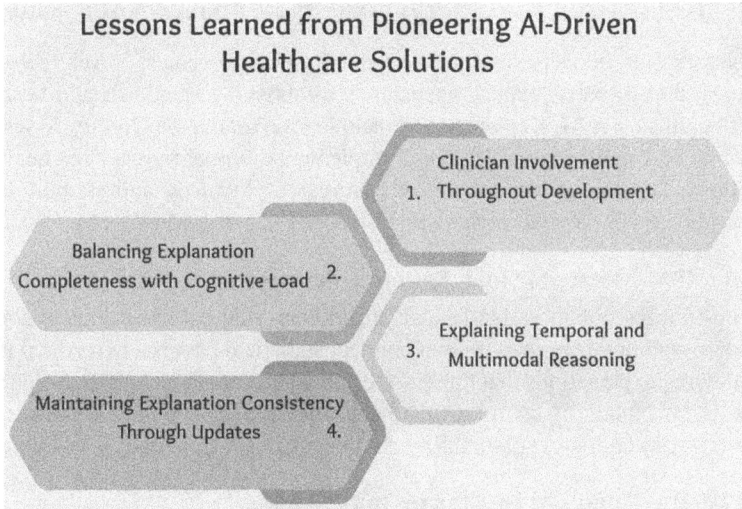

FIGURE 10.4   Various lessons learned from pioneering AI-driven healthcare solutions.

10.8.1.2   Balancing Explanation Completeness with Cognitive Load

Intermountain Healthcare found that comprehensive explanations decreased system usage in busy environments. Their progressive disclosure approach, providing initially streamlined explanations with options to explore additional details that significantly improved adoption. Usage analytics showed detailed explanations were accessed more for complex cases or when predictions conflicted with clinical assessment, demonstrating the need to match explanation depth to context.

10.8.1.3   Explaining Temporal and Multimodal Reasoning

Partners HealthCare's readmission prediction system highlighted challenges in explaining temporal patterns and multiple data modalities. Their solution involved specialized explanation components for different data types, including timeline visualizations for temporal patterns, contextual highlights for clinical notes, and feature importance displays for static factors. This modular approach has since been widely adopted for healthcare's complex data environments.

10.8.1.4   Maintaining Explanation Consistency through Updates

Providence St. Joseph Health found that when explanation formats changed between model versions, clinicians reported confusion and decreased trust. Their "explanation consistency metrics" helped evaluate how updates would impact users, with transition periods offering dual explanations when necessary. This experience shows that managing explanation evolution is as important as managing model performance across the AI system lifecycle.

10.8.2   INDUSTRY AND RESEARCH COLLABORATIONS PUSHING XAI FORWARD

This collaboration between seventeen academic medical centers, seven technology companies, and three regulatory agencies is establishing standards and best practices for healthcare XAI. Key outcomes include an Explanation Quality Assessment Framework and open-source reference implementations optimized for healthcare applications. The consortium's structure ensures developments address both technical innovation and practical implementation needs (Chattopadhyay et al., 2025).

10.8.2.1   IBM-Memorial Sloan Kettering Partnership

This long-running collaboration has advanced from rule-based systems to sophisticated neuro-symbolic approaches that connect statistical patterns to medical knowledge, allowing explanations that reference established cancer biology and guidelines. Their work on explaining complex treatment sequences demonstrates how sustained partnerships can address explainability challenges in specialized medical domains.

10.8.2.2   The Open XAI Healthcare Initiative

This community-driven initiative maintains open-source libraries, benchmark datasets, and implementation case studies with a focus on explanation equity, ensuring AI explanations are effective across diverse populations and clinical settings. Their work includes developing approaches for underserved environments, showing how open collaboration can ensure XAI benefits extend beyond resource-rich settings.

10.8.2.3   Google Health-Northwestern Medicine Collaboration

This partnership has developed "adaptive explanation" approaches that adjust content and format based on clinical scenario, user expertise, and time constraints. They've also pioneered methodologies for evaluating explanation impact on clinical decision quality rather than just user preference, creating evaluation frameworks now adopted by multiple healthcare AI initiatives.

10.9   CONCLUSION

XAI is revolutionizing healthcare by enhancing the transparency, accountability, and dependability of AI-driven medical systems. As digital solutions become more prevalent in the healthcare sector, there is an increasing demand for AI models that can clearly articulate their recommendations to physicians, patients, and regulatory bodies. This chapter has explored the various innovations that are transforming XAI from a technical challenge into a clinical imperative. With progress in interpretability techniques, hybrid modeling, federated learning, privacy-preserving strategies, and the adaptive tailoring of explanations, XAI is rapidly evolving to address practical clinical needs. Human-centered design and interactive explanation systems allow healthcare professionals to question, validate, and even modify AI predictions in real time, ensuring that AI functions as a dependable assistant rather than a mysterious oracle. Furthermore, the integration of XAI with the IoMT, blockchain, and immersive technologies such as AR and VR is opening up new opportunities for patient-centered care and clinician training. XAI acts as the vital connection between intricate algorithmic processes and human clinical decision-making, promoting safer, more informed, and more equitable healthcare. Continued interdisciplinary collaboration among AI researchers, healthcare providers, designers, and policymakers will be crucial to develop and implement XAI systems that are not only technically robust but also clinically relevant, ethically sound, and socially responsible.

REFERENCES

Ahamed, S. M., & Jabez, J. (2025). Bridging the gap: Clinical adoption and user perspectives of explainable AI in healthcare. In A. Kumar, T. A. Kumar, P. Das, C. Sharma & A. K. Dubey (Eds.), *Explainable Artificial Intelligence in the Healthcare Industry* (pp. 349–374). Scrivener Publishing.

Albahri, A. S., Duhaim, A. M., Fadhel, M. A., Alnoor, A., Baqer, N. S., Alzubaidi, L., Albahri, O. S., Alamoodi, A. H., Bai, J., Salhi, A., & Santamaría, J. (2023). A systematic review of trustworthy and explainable artificial intelligence in healthcare: Assessment of quality, bias risk, and data fusion. *Information Fusion, 96*, 156–191

Alhuwaydi, A. M. (2024). Exploring the role of artificial intelligence in mental healthcare: current trends and future directions–A narrative review for a comprehensive insight. *Risk Management and Healthcare Policy, 17*, 1339–1348.

Bawa, G., Singh, H., Rani, S., Kataria, A., & Min, H. (2024). Exploring perspectives of blockchain technology and traditional centralized technology in organ donation management: A comprehensive review. *Information, 15*(11), 703.

Chaithra, N., Jha, J., Sayal, A., & Gangodkar, A. R. (2024). Internet of Medical Things with artificial intelligence for improved healthcare systems. In P. Bhambri, R. Soni & T. A. Tran (Eds.), *Smart healthcare systems* (pp. 18–32). CRC Press.

Chattopadhyay, S., Barman, S., & Lakshmi, D. (2025). The role of explainable AI for healthcare 5.0: Best practices, challenges, and opportunities. In P. Raj, B. Sundaravadivazhagan, A. S. Raja & M. M. Alani (Eds.), *Edge AI for Industry 5.0 and Healthcare 5.0 applications* (pp. 45–80). Taylor and Francis.

Hassija, V., Chamola, V., Mahapatra, A., Singal, A., Goel, D., Huang, K., Scardapane, S., Spinelli, I., Mahmud, M., & Hussain, A. (2024). Interpreting black-box models: A review on explainable artificial intelligence. *Cognitive Computation, 16*(1), 45–74.

Hossain, M. I., Zamzmi, G., Mouton, P. R., Salekin, M. S., Sun, Y., & Goldgof, D. (2025). Explainable AI for medical data: Current methods, limitations, and future directions. *ACM Computing Surveys, 57*(6), 1–46.

Kalra, N., Verma, P., & Verma, S. (2024). Advancements in AI based healthcare techniques with FOCUS ON diagnostic techniques. *Computers in Biology and Medicine, 179*, 108917.

Kaur, G., & Saini, H. K. (2023). *An optimized resnet based plant disease identification using deep learning hypothetic function* [Paper presentation]. International Conference on Advances in Computation, Communication and Information Technology (ICAICCIT).

Maathuis, C., Cidota, M. A., Datcu, D., & Marin, L. (2025). Integrating explainable artificial intelligence in extended reality environments: A systematic survey. *Mathematics, 13*(2), 290.

Metta, C., Beretta, A., Pellungrini, R., Rinzivillo, S., & Giannotti, F. (2024). Towards transparent healthcare: advancing local explanation methods in explainable artificial intelligence. *Bioengineering, 11*(4), 369.

Murad, N. Y., Hasan, M. H., Azam, M. H., Yousuf, N., & Yalli, J. S. (2024). Unraveling the black box: A review of explainable deep learning healthcare techniques. *IEEE Access.* https://doi.org/10.1109/ACCESS.2024.3398203

Puri, V., Priyadarshini, I., Kataria, A., Rani, S., & Min, H. (2025). Privacy-first ML for chronic kidney disease prediction: Exploring a decentralized approach using block-chain and IPFS. *IEEE Access*, *13*, 43178–43189.

Rani, S., Kataria, A., Bhambri, P., Pareek, P. K., & Puri, V. (2024). Artificial intelligence in personalized health services for better patient care. In S. K. Gupta, D. A. Karras & R. Natarajan (Eds.), *Revolutionizing healthcare: AI integration with IoT for enhanced patient outcomes* (pp. 89–108). Springer.

Rani, S., Kumar, S., Kataria, A., & Min, H. (2024). SmartHealth: An intelligent framework to secure IoMT service applications using machine learning. *ICT Express*, *10*(2), 425–430.

Saini, H. K., & Preeti. (2024). *A cross design for breast cancer prediction* [Paper presentation]. The International Conference on Communications and Cyber Physical Engineering 2018.

Saini, H. K., Swarnakar, H., & Jain, K. (2022). Secured multimedia and IoT in healthcare computing paradigms. In B. Bhusan, S. K. Sharma, B. Unhelkar, M. F. Ijaz & L. Karim (Eds.), *Internet of Things* (pp. 229–256). CRC Press.

Subramanian, H. V., Canfield, C., & Shank, D. B. (2024). Designing explainable AI to improve human-AI team performance: A medical stakeholder-driven scoping review. *Artificial Intelligence In Medicine*, *149*, 102780.

Upadhyay, P., Mittal, V., Kriplani, P., & Kautish, S. (2024). Metaverse in healthcare integrated with explainable AI and blockchain: Enabling immersiveness, ensuring trust, and providing patient data security. In S. Kautish & Á. Rocha (Eds.), *Metaverse driven intelligent information systems: Emerging trends and future directions* (pp. 177–194). Springer.

Zhao, L., Xie, H., Zhong, L., & Wang, Y. (2024). Explainable federated learning scheme for secure healthcare data sharing. *Health Information Science and Systems*, *12*(1), 49.

Appendix A: Tools/ Technologies for Deploying XAI Applications in Smart Healthcare Systems

Deploying explainable AI (XAI) applications in smart healthcare systems requires a combination of AI frameworks and XAI-specific libraries along with cloud platforms, and specialized tools for interpretability and security. This section is focused on AI frameworks and XAI-specific libraries.

I. AI AND MACHINE LEARNING FRAMEWORKS

Deploying XAI in smart healthcare requires robust AI and ML frameworks. TensorFlow (TensorFlow Explain, What-If Tool) and PyTorch (Captum) offer deep learning with built-in interpretability. Scikit-learn supports classical ML with feature importance, while XGBoost integrates SHAP for explainability. SHAP and LIME enhance model transparency, while IBM AIX360 and Microsoft InterpretML provide specialized XAI tools. Cloud platforms like AWS SageMaker Clarify, Google Cloud AI Explainability, and Azure ML Interpretability SDK ensure scalable deployment. NVIDIA Clara enables AI-driven medical imaging. These frameworks ensure transparency, trust, and regulatory compliance in AI-driven healthcare applications. Some of the important AI and ML technologies/tools for deploying healthcare applications are:

- **TensorFlow** (TensorFlow Explain, What-If Tool)
  TensorFlow is widely used in healthcare for applications like disease detection, medical image analysis, and patient monitoring. It provides tools to train, optimize, and deploy deep learning models efficiently.

  ### Example: Deploying a TensorFlow Model for Pneumonia Detection

  This example demonstrates how to deploy a pneumonia detection model trained on chest X-ray images using TensorFlow and TensorFlow Serving.

  - **Train a Model (Brief Overview)**
    Use a Convolutional Neural Network (CNN) to classify X-ray images as pneumonia or normal.

```
import tensorflow as tf
from tensorflow import keras
from tensorflow.keras import layers

# Load dataset (e.g., Chest X-ray dataset)
train_ds = keras.preprocessing.
image_dataset_from_directory(
    "chest_xray/train", image_size=(224, 224),
batch_size=32)

# Build a simple CNN model
model = keras.Sequential([
    layers.Rescaling(1./255, input_shape=(224, 224, 3)),
    layers.Conv2D(32, 3, activation="relu"),
    layers.MaxPooling2D(),
    layers.Conv2D(64, 3, activation="relu"),
    layers.MaxPooling2D(),
    layers.Flatten(),
    layers.Dense(128, activation="relu"),
    layers.Dense(1, activation="sigmoid")
])
model.compile(optimizer="adam", loss="binary_
crossentropy", metrics=["accuracy"])
model.fit(train_ds, epochs=5)

# Save model for deployment
model.save("pneumonia_model")
```

- **Deploy with TensorFlow Serving**
  TensorFlow Serving allows efficient model deployment via REST or gRPC APIs.

Steps to Deploy

- Install TensorFlow Serving
  - sudo apt-get install tensorflow-model-server
- Start TensorFlow Serving:
  - tensorflow_model_server –rest_api_port=8501 –model_name= pneumonia_model –model_base_path="$(pwd)/pneumonia_ model"
- Send a test request:
  ```
  import requests
  import numpy as np
  import json
  from tensorflow.keras.preprocessing import image

  img_path = "test_xray.jpg"
  img = image.load_img(img_path, target_size=(224, 224))
  img_array = np.expand_dims(image.img_to_
  array(img)/255.0, axis=0)

  url = "http://localhost:8501/v1/models/
  pneumonia_model:predict"
  data = json.dumps({"instances": img_array.tolist()})
  response = requests.post(url, data=data)
  print(response.json())
  ```

- **PyTorch** (Captum for interpretability)
  PyTorch is widely used in healthcare for tasks like medical image analysis, disease detection, and patient monitoring. It provides flexible model training and deployment options using TorchServe or Flask.

Example: Deploying a PyTorch Model for Pneumonia Detection

This example demonstrates how to deploy a pneumonia detection model trained on chest X-ray images using PyTorch and Flask.

- **Train a Model (Brief Overview)**
  Use a convolutional neural network (CNN) for classifying X-ray images.

```python
import torch
import torch.nn as nn
import torch.optim as optim
from torchvision import datasets, transforms, models

# Define data transformation
transform = transforms.Compose([
    transforms.Resize((224, 224)),
    transforms.ToTensor(),
])

# Load dataset (Chest X-ray dataset)
train_dataset = datasets.ImageFolder("chest_xray/train",
transform=transform)
train_loader = torch.utils.data.DataLoader(train_dataset,
batch_size=32, shuffle=True)

# Define a CNN model (using ResNet18)
model = models.resnet18(pretrained=True)
model.fc = nn.Linear(model.fc.in_features, 1)  # Binary
classification

criterion = nn.BCEWithLogitsLoss()
optimizer = optim.Adam(model.parameters(), lr=0.001)

# Training loop
device = torch.device("cuda" if torch.cuda.is_available()
else "cpu")
model.to(device)

for epoch in range(5):
    for images, labels in train_loader:
        images, labels = images.to(device), labels.
        float().to(device)
        optimizer.zero_grad()
        outputs = model(images).squeeze()
        loss = criterion(outputs, labels)
        loss.backward()
        optimizer.step()
```

- **Save Model**

```python
torch.save(model.state_dict(), "pneumonia_model.pth")
```

- **Deploy with Flask**
  Use Flask to create an API for serving predictions.

  - **Create `app.py`**
    ```python
    import torch
    import torch.nn as nn
    import torchvision.transforms as transforms
    from torchvision import models
    from PIL import Image
    from flask import Flask, request, jsonify

    app = Flask(__name__)
    ```
  - Load trained model
    ```python
    model = models.resnet18(pretrained=True)
    model.fc = nn.Linear(model.fc.in_features, 1)
    model.load_state_dict(torch.load("pneumonia_model.pth",
    map_location="cpu"))
    model.eval()
    ```
  - Define transformation
    ```python
    transform = transforms.Compose([
        transforms.Resize((224, 224)),
        transforms.ToTensor(),
    ])

    @app.route("/predict", methods=["POST"])
    def predict():
        file = request.files["file"]
        image = Image.open(file)
        image = transform(image).unsqueeze(0)   # Add batch
        dimension

        with torch.no_grad():
            output = model(image).squeeze().item()

        prediction = "Pneumonia" if output > 0 else "Normal"
        return jsonify({"prediction": prediction})

    if __name__ == "__main__":
        app.run(host="0.0.0.0", port=5000)
    ```

- **Run the API**

  - Install dependencies:
    - pip install flask torch torchvision pillow
  - Start the Flask server
    - python app.py
  - Send a test request:
    ```python
    import requests

    url = "http://127.0.0.1:5000/predict"
    files = {"file": open("test_xray.jpg", "rb")}
    response = requests.post(url, files=files)
    print(response.json())
    ```

II. XAI-SPECIFIC LIBRARIES

- **SHAP** (SHapley Additive exPlanations)
  SHAP is widely used in healthcare AI for model interpretability. It helps explain predictions made by machine learning models, ensuring transparency in critical applications like disease diagnosis and treatment recommendations.

  ### Example: Explaining a Pneumonia Detection Model with SHAP

  This example shows how to use SHAP to explain predictions from a trained pneumonia detection model.

  - **Train a Model (Using XGBoost for Simplicity)**
    We use **XGBoost** to classify patients as having pneumonia or not based on clinical data.

    ```python
    import shap
    import xgboost as xgb
    import numpy as np
    import pandas as pd
    from sklearn.model_selection import train_test_split
    from sklearn.metrics import accuracy_score

    # Generate synthetic healthcare data (features: age,
    temperature, oxygen level, etc.)
    np.random.seed(42)
    data = pd.DataFrame({
        "Age": np.random.randint(20, 80, 500),
        "Temperature": np.random.uniform(36, 40, 500),
        "OxygenLevel": np.random.uniform(80, 100, 500),
        "HeartRate": np.random.randint(60, 120, 500),
        "Pneumonia": np.random.randint(0, 2, 500)   # 0 = No,
    1 = Yes
    })

    # Split data
    X = data.drop(columns=["Pneumonia"])
    y = data["Pneumonia"]
    X_train, X_test, y_train, y_test = train_test_split(X, y,
    test_size=0.2, random_state=42)

    # Train XGBoost model
    model = xgb.XGBClassifier()
    model.fit(X_train, y_train)

    # Evaluate model
    y_pred = model.predict(X_test)
    print("Accuracy:", accuracy_score(y_test, y_pred))
    ```

  - **Explain Predictions Using SHAP**
    SHAP explains how each feature (e.g., Age, Temperature) impacts a specific prediction.

    ```python
    # Create SHAP explainer
    ```

```
explainer = shap.Explainer(model)
shap_values = explainer(X_test)

# Visualize SHAP values for a single patient
shap.initjs()
shap.force_plot(explainer.expected_value, shap_values[0].
values, X_test.iloc[0])
```

- **Deploy with Flask for Real-Time Explanations**
  We create a REST API to get model predictions and SHAP explanations.

- **Create app.py**

```
from flask import Flask, request, jsonify
import shap
import xgboost as xgb
import pandas as pd
import numpy as np
import json

app = Flask(__name__)

# Load trained model
model = xgb.XGBClassifier()
model.load_model("pneumonia_model.json")  # Save model as
JSON

# Define SHAP explainer
explainer = shap.Explainer(model)

@app.route("/predict", methods=["POST"])
def predict():
    data = request.get_json()
    df = pd.DataFrame(data, index=[0])  # Convert JSON to
    DataFrame

    # Get prediction
    prediction = model.predict(df)[0]
    prediction_label = "Pneumonia" if prediction == 1
    else "Normal"

    # Get SHAP explanation
    shap_values = explainer(df)
    explanation = shap_values.values.tolist()[0]

    return jsonify({"prediction": prediction_label,
    "shap_values": explanation})

if __name__ == "__main__":
    app.run(host="0.0.0.0", port=5000)
```

- **Send a Test Request**

```
import requests

url = "http://127.0.0.1:5000/predict"
data = {
    "Age": 45,
    "Temperature": 38.5,
```

```
        "OxygenLevel": 92,
        "HeartRate": 100
}

response = requests.post(url, json=data)
print(response.json())
```

- **LIME (Local Interpretable Model-agnostic Explanations)**
  LIME (Local Interpretable Model-agnostic Explanations) is a powerful explainable AI (XAI) method used to interpret predictions from black-box machine learning models. In healthcare, where interpretability and trust are critical, LIME helps clinicians and stakeholders understand why a model made a particular decision.
  - **Example Use Case:** Predicting Diabetes Risk

PROBLEM

A hospital uses a machine learning model (e.g., a Random Forest or Neural Network) to predict whether a patient is at risk of developing diabetes based on health metrics.

MODEL INPUTS

Features might include:

- Age
- BMI
- Blood Pressure
- Glucose Level
- Insulin
- Family History

Step-by-Step: Using LIME

- **Train a Black-box Model**
  Example: Random Forest classifier trained on the **Pima Indian Diabetes Dataset**.

```
from sklearn.ensemble import RandomForestClassifier
from sklearn.model_selection import train_test_split
import pandas as pd

# Load dataset
data = pd.read_csv('diabetes.csv')
X = data.drop('Outcome', axis=1)
y = data['Outcome']

# Train model
X_train, X_test, y_train, y_test = train_test_split(X, y,
test_size=0.2, random_state=42)
model = RandomForestClassifier()
model.fit(X_train, y_train)
```

- **Install and Import LIME**

```
pip install lime
from lime.lime_tabular import LimeTabularExplainer
import numpy as np
```

- **Explain a Prediction**

```
explainer = LimeTabularExplainer(training_data=np.
array(X_train),
                feature_names=X.columns,
                class_names=['No Diabetes', 'Diabetes'],
                mode='classification')
# Select an instance from test data
i = 5
exp = explainer.explain_instance(data_row=X_test.iloc[i],
                predict_fn=model.predict_proba)
# Visualize
exp.show_in_notebook(show_table=True)
```

- **Interpretation Output Example**
  LIME might show for Patient 5:

Feature	Contribution to Prediction
Glucose > 140	+0.25
BMI > 30	+0.15
Age < 30	−0.10
Insulin < 100	−0.08

- **AIX360** (IBM AI Explainability 360)
  AIX360 (AI Explainability 360) is an open-source Python toolkit developed by IBM to advance the interpretability and transparency of machine learning models. Designed to support the responsible and ethical use of AI, AIX360 provides a diverse set of explainability algorithms for both black-box and interpretable models across different data types (tabular, text, images). The toolkit is especially relevant in high-stakes domains such as healthcare, finance, and legal systems, where understanding model decisions is crucial for trust, fairness, and compliance. AIX360 offers both global explanations (how a model behaves overall) and local explanations (why a specific prediction was made). It includes well-known methods such as LIME, SHAP, ProtoDash, Contrastive Explanations, and GlassBox models like Decision Trees and Generalized Additive Models (GAMs). The toolkit is model-agnostic and supports seamless integration with frameworks like scikit-learn, PyTorch, and TensorFlow.

  In healthcare applications, AIX360 can help clinicians understand AI predictions for diagnoses, risk scoring, or treatment recommendations. For instance, when a model predicts high risk for stroke, AIX360 can provide transparent reasoning (e.g., based on blood pressure, age, cholesterol) that supports clinical decision-making. Additionally, AIX360 offers Jupyter notebooks and visualization tools to enhance interpretability for data scientists and domain

experts. By enabling transparent, fair, and accountable AI, AIX360 contributes to building trust between users and machine learning systems. IBM's AIX360 toolkit empowers practitioners to interpret, debug, and validate AI models, ensuring ethical deployment of AI in sensitive real-world applications.

- **InterpretML** (Microsoft's explainability toolkit)
  InterpretML is Microsoft's open-source Python toolkit for interpretable machine learning, enabling users to understand, debug, and trust model predictions. It provides both glass-box (interpretable by design) models and black-box explainers to make complex models more transparent. This dual approach is especially valuable in healthcare, where explainability is essential for ethical and accountable decision-making. InterpretML includes the Explainable Boosting Machine (EBM), a powerful glass-box model based on generalized additive models (GAMs). EBMs offer high accuracy comparable to black-box models while retaining full interpretability. They break down predictions into feature-level contributions, making it easy for healthcare professionals to understand, for instance, how factors like blood pressure, glucose, or age affect a patient's risk prediction.

  For black-box models (e.g., neural networks, ensembles), InterpretML integrates with SHAP (SHapley Additive exPlanations) and LIME to provide local explanations, highlighting how each feature influences an individual prediction. These insights are crucial when AI tools assist in diagnosing conditions like diabetes, heart disease, or cancer. InterpretML also provides interactive visualizations for both global and local explanations, helping clinicians and stakeholders explore model behavior across patient populations and individual cases. For example, a doctor using an AI model for stroke prediction can view which features most influenced a specific patient's risk, increasing confidence in the recommendation. By combining interpretable models with state-of-the-art explainability techniques, InterpretML helps ensure transparency, trust, and safety in AI-assisted healthcare applications, aligning with the ethical standards and regulatory requirements of the medical field.

Index